THE
Expositor's Bible Commentary

with The New International Version

PHILIPPIANS • COLOSSIANS • PHILEMON

Homer A. Kent Jr., Curtis Vaughan & Arthur A. Rupprecht

ZondervanPublishingHouse

Grand Rapids, Michigan

A Division of HarperCollinsPublishers

General Editor:

FRANK E. GAEBELEIN

Former Headmaster, Stony Brook School
Former Coeditor, *Christianity Today*

Associate Editors:

J. D. DOUGLAS

Editor, *The New International
Dictionary of the Christian Church*

RICHARD P. POLCYN

Philippians, Colossians, Philemon
Copyright © 1996 by Homer A. Kent Jr., Curtis Vaughan, Arthur A. Rupprecht

Requests for information should be addressed to:
Zondervan Publishing House
Grand Rapids, Michigan 49530

Library of Congress Cataloging-in-Publication Data

The expositor's Bible commentary : with the New International Version of the Holy Bible /
Frank E. Gaebelein, general editor of series.
p. cm.
Includes bibliographical references and index.
Contents: v. 1–2. Matthew / D. A. Carson — Mark / Walter W. Wessel — Luke / Walter
L. Liefeld — John / Merrill C. Tenney — Acts / Richard N. Longenecker — Romans /
Everett F. Harrison — 1 and 2 Corinthians / W. Harold Mare and Murray J. Harris —
Galatians and Ephesians / James Montgomery Boice and A. Skevington Wood—Philippians,
Colossians, Philemon / Homer A. Kent Jr., Curtis Vaughan, and Arthur A. Rupprecht—
1, 2 Thessalonians; 1, 2 Timothy; Titus / Robert L. Thomas, Ralph Earle, and D. Edmond
Hiebert—Hebrews, James / Leon Morris and Donald W. Burdick—1, 2 Peter;
1, 2, 3 John; Jude / Edwin A. Blum and Glenn W. Barker—Revelation / Alan F. Johnson
ISBN: 0-310-20385-6 (softcover)
1. Bible N.T.—Commentaries. I. Gaebelein, Frank Ely, 1899–1983.
BS2341.2.E96 1995
220.7-dc 00   94-47450
                                                                                 CIP

Printed in the United States of America

96 97 98 99 00 01 / ❖ DH / 10 9 8 7 6 5 4 3 2 1

CONTENTS

PREFACE

The title of this work defines its purpose. Written primarily by expositors for expositors, it aims to provide preachers, teachers, and students of the Bible with a new and comprehensive commentary on the books of the Old and New Testaments. Its stance is that of a scholarly evangelicalism committed to the divine inspiration, complete trustworthiness, and full authority of the Bible. Its seventy-eight contributors come from the United States, Canada, England, Scotland, Australia, New Zealand, and Switzerland, and from various religious groups, including Anglican, Baptist, Brethren, Free, Independent, Methodist, Nazarene, Presbyterian, and Reformed churches. Most of them teach at colleges, universities, or theological seminaries.

No book has been more closely studied over a longer period of time than the Bible. From the Midrashic commentaries going back to the period of Ezra, through parts of the Dead Sea Scrolls and the Patristic literature, and on to the present, the Scriptures have been expounded. Indeed, there have been times when, as in the Reformation and on occasions since then, exposition has been at the cutting edge of Christian advance. Luther was a powerful exegete, and Calvin is still called "the prince of expositors."

Their successors have been many. And now, when the outburst of new translations and their unparalleled circulation have expanded the readership of the Bible, the need for exposition takes on fresh urgency.

Not that God's Word can ever become captive to its expositors. Among all other books, it stands first in its combination of perspicuity and profundity. Though a child can be made "wise for salvation" by believing its witness to Christ, the greatest mind cannot plumb the depths of its truth (2 Tim. 3:15; Rom. 11:33). As Gregory the Great said, "Holy Scripture is a stream of running water, where alike the elephant may swim, and the lamb walk." So, because of the inexhaustible nature of Scripture, the task of opening up its meaning is still a perennial obligation of biblical scholarship.

How that task is done inevitably reflects the outlook of those engaged in it. Every biblical scholar has presuppositions. To this neither the editors of these volumes nor the contributors to them are exceptions. They share a common commitment to the supernatural Christianity set forth in the inspired Word. Their purpose is not to supplant the many valuable commentaries that have preceded this work and from which both the editors and contributors have learned. It is rather to draw on the resources of contemporary evangelical scholarship in producing a new reference work for understanding the Scriptures.

A commentary that will continue to be useful through the years should handle contemporary trends in biblical studies in such a way as to avoid becoming outdated when critical fashions change. Biblical criticism is not in itself inadmissible, as some have mistakenly thought. When scholars investigate the authorship, date, literary characteristics, and purpose of a biblical document, they are practicing biblical criticism. So also when, in order to ascertain as nearly as possible the original form of the text, they deal with variant readings, scribal errors, emendations, and other phenomena in the manuscripts. To do these things is essential to responsible exegesis and exposition. And always there is the need to distinguish hypothesis from fact, conjecture from truth.

iv

The chief principle of interpretation followed in this commentary is the grammatico-historical one—namely, that the primary aim of the exegete is to make clear the meaning of the text at the time and in the circumstances of its writing. This endeavor to understand what in the first instance the inspired writers actually said must not be confused with an inflexible literalism. Scripture makes lavish use of symbols and figures of speech; great portions of it are poetical. Yet when it speaks in this way, it speaks no less truly than it does in its historical and doctrinal portions. To understand its message requires attention to matters of grammar and syntax, word meanings, idioms, and literary forms—all in relation to the historical and cultural setting of the text.

The contributors to this work necessarily reflect varying convictions. In certain controversial matters the policy is that of clear statement of the contributors' own views followed by fair presentation of other ones. The treatment of eschatology, though it reflects differences of interpretation, is consistent with a general premillennial position. (Not all contributors, however, are premillennial.) But prophecy is more than prediction, and so this commentary gives due recognition to the major lode of godly social concern in the prophetic writings.

THE EXPOSITOR'S BIBLE COMMENTARY is presented as a scholarly work, though not primarily one of technical criticism. In its main portion, the Exposition, and in Volume 1 (General and Special Articles), all Semitic and Greek words are transliterated and the English equivalents given. As for the Notes, here Semitic and Greek characters are used but always with transliterations and English meanings, so that this portion of the commentary will be as accessible as possible to readers unacquainted with the original languages.

It is the conviction of the general editor, shared by his colleagues in the Zondervan editorial department, that in writing about the Bible, lucidity is not incompatible with scholarship. They are therefore endeavoring to make this a clear and understandable work.

The translation used in it is the New International Version (North American Edition). To the International Bible Society thanks are due for permission to use this most recent of the major Bible translations. The editors and publisher have chosen it because of the clarity and beauty of its style and its faithfulness to the original texts.

To the associate editor, Dr. J. D. Douglas, and to the contributing editors—Dr. Walter C. Kaiser, Jr. and Dr. Bruce K. Waltke for the Old Testament, and Dr. James Montgomery Boice and Dr. Merrill C. Tenney for the New Testament—the general editor expresses his gratitude for their unfailing cooperation and their generosity in advising him out of their expert scholarship. And to the many other contributors he is indebted for their invaluable part in this work. Finally, he owes a special debt of gratitude to Dr. Robert K. DeVries, executive vice-president of the Zondervan Publishing House; Rev. Gerard Terpstra, manuscript editor; and Miss Elizabeth Brown, secretary to Dr. DeVries, for their continual assistance and encouragement.

Whatever else it is—the greatest and most beautiful of books, the primary source of law and morality, the fountain of wisdom, and the infallible guide to life—the Bible is above all the inspired witness to Jesus Christ. May this work fulfill its function of expounding the Scriptures with grace and clarity, so that its users may find that both Old and New Testaments do indeed lead to our Lord Jesus Christ, who alone could say, "I have come that they may have life, and have it to the full" (John 10:10).

FRANK E. GAEBELEIN

ABBREVIATIONS

A. General Abbreviations

A	Codex Alexandrinus	MT	Masoretic text
Akkad.	Akkadian	n.	note
ℵ	Codex Sinaiticus	n.d.	no date
Ap. Lit.	Apocalyptic Literature	Nestle	Nestle (ed.) *Novum*
Apoc.	Apocrypha		*Testamentum Graece*
Aq.	Aquila's Greek Translation	no.	number
	of the Old Testament	NT	New Testament
Arab.	Arabic	obs.	obsolete
Aram.	Aramaic	OL	Old Latin
b	Babylonian Gemara	OS	Old Syriac
B	Codex Vaticanus	OT	Old Testament
C	Codex Ephraemi Syri	p., pp.	page, pages
c.	*circa*, about	par.	paragraph
cf.	*confer*, compare	‖	parallel passage(s)
ch., chs.	chapter, chapters	Pers.	Persian
cod., codd.	codex, codices	Pesh.	Peshitta
contra	in contrast to	Phoen.	Phoenician
D	Codex Bezae	pl.	plural
DSS	Dead Sea Scrolls (see E.)	Pseudep.	Pseudepigrapha
ed., edd.	edited, edition, editor; editions	Q	Quelle ("Sayings" source
e.g.	*exempli gratia*, for example		in the Gospels)
Egyp.	Egyptian	qt.	quoted by
et al.	*et alii*, and others	q.v.	*quod vide*, which see
EV	English Versions of the Bible	R	Rabbah
fem.	feminine	rev.	revised, reviser, revision
ff.	following (verses, pages, etc.)	Rom.	Roman
fl.	flourished	RVm	Revised Version margin
ft.	foot, feet	Samar.	Samaritan recension
gen.	genitive	SCM	Student Christian Movement Press
Gr.	Greek	Sem.	Semitic
Heb.	Hebrew	sing.	singular
Hitt.	Hittite	SPCK	Society for the Promotion
ibid.	*ibidem*, in the same place		of Christian Knowledge
id.	*idem*, the same	Sumer.	Sumerian
i.e.	*id est*, that is	s.v.	*sub verbo*, under the word
impf.	imperfect	Syr.	Syriac
infra.	below	Symm.	Symmachus
in loc.	*in loco*, in the place cited	T	Talmud
j	Jerusalem or	Targ.	Targum
	Palestinian Gemara	Theod.	Theodotion
Lat.	Latin	TR	Textus Receptus
LL.	Late Latin	tr.	translation, translator,
LXX	Septuagint		translated
M	Mishnah	UBS	The United Bible Societies'
masc.	masculine		Greek Text
mg.	margin	Ugar.	Ugaritic
Mid	Midrash	u.s.	*ut supra*, as above
MS(S)	Manuscript(s)	viz.	*videlicet*, namely

	volume	Vul.	Vulgate
vv.	verse, verses	WH	Westcott and Hort, *The*
	versus		*New Testament in Greek*

Abbreviations for Modern Translations and Paraphrases

T	Smith and Goodspeed,	LB	The Living Bible
	The Complete Bible,	Mof	J. Moffatt, *A New Trans-*
	An American Translation		*lation of the Bible*
/	American Standard Version,	NAB	The New American Bible
	American Revised Version	NASB	New American Standard Bible
	(1901)	NEB	The New English Bible
k	Beck, *The New Testament in*	NIV	The New International Version
	the Language of Today	Ph	J. B. Phillips *The New Testa-*
	Berkeley Version (The		*ment in Modern English*
	Modern Language Bible)	RSV	Revised Standard Version
	The Jerusalem Bible	RV	Revised Version — 1881–1885
	Jewish Publication Society	TCNT	Twentieth Century
	Version of the Old Testament		New Testament
J	King James Version	TEV	Today's English Version
ox	R.G. Knox, *The Holy Bible:*	Wey	*Weymouth's New Testament*
	A Translation from the Latin		*in Modern Speech*
	Vulgate in the Light of the	Wms	C. B. Williams, *The New*
	Hebrew and Greek Original		*Testament: A Translation in*
			the Language of the People

Abbreviations for Periodicals and Reference Works

SOR	*Annual of the American Schools*	BAG	Bauer, Arndt, and Gingrich:
	of Oriental Research		*Greek-English Lexicon*
	Anchor Bible		*of the New Testament*
	de Vaux: *Ancient Israel*	BC	Foakes-Jackson and Lake: *The*
	American Journal of		*Beginnings of Christianity*
	Archaeology	BDB	Brown, Driver, and Briggs:
L	*American Journal of Semitic*		*Hebrew-English Lexicon*
	Languages and Literatures		*of the Old Testament*
	American Journal of	BDF	Blass, Debrunner, and Funk:
	Theology		*A Greek Grammar of the*
	Alford: *Greek Testament*		*New Testament and Other*
	Commentary		*Early Christian Literature*
EA	*Ancient Near Eastern*	BDT	Harrison: *Baker's Dictionary*
	Archaeology		*of Theology*
ET	Pritchard: *Ancient Near*	Beng.	Bengel's *Gnomon*
	Eastern Texts	BETS	*Bulletin of the Evangelical*
F	Roberts and Donaldson:		*Theological Society*
	The Ante-Nicene Fathers	BJRL	*Bulletin of the John*
T	M. R. James: *The Apocryphal*		*Rylands Library*
	New Testament	BS	*Bibliotheca Sacra*
	Abbot-Smith: *Manual Greek*	BT	*Babylonian Talmud*
	Lexicon of the New Testament	BTh	*Biblical Theology*
ıR	*Anglican Theological Review*	BW	*Biblical World*
	Biblical Archaeologist	CAH	*Cambridge Ancient History*
SOR	*Bulletin of the American*	CanJTh	*Canadian Journal of Theology*
	Schools of Oriental Research	CBQ	*Catholic Biblical Quarterly*

CBSC	*Cambridge Bible for Schools and Colleges*	HUCA	*Hebrew Union College Annual*
CE	*Catholic Encyclopedia*	IB	*The Interpreter's Bible*
CGT	*Cambridge Greek Testament*	ICC	*International Critical Commentary*
CHS	Lange: *Commentary on the Holy Scriptures*	IDB	*The Interpreter's Dictionary of the Bible*
ChT	*Christianity Today*	IEJ	*Israel Exploration Journal*
Crem	Cremer: *Biblico-Theological Lexicon of the New Testament Greek*	Int	*Interpretation*
		INT	E. Harrison: *Introduction to the New Testament*
DDB	*Davis' Dictionary of the Bible*	IOT	R. K. Harrison: *Introduction to the Old Testament*
Deiss BS	Deissmann: *Bible Studies*		
Deiss LAE	Deissmann: *Light From the Ancient East*	ISBE	*The International Standard Bible Encyclopedia*
DNTT	*Dictionary of New Testament Theology*	ITQ	*Irish Theological Quarterly*
EBC	*The Expositor's Bible Commentary*	JAAR	*Journal of American Academy of Religion*
EBi	*Encyclopaedia Biblica*	JAOS	*Journal of American Oriental Society*
EBr	*Encyclopaedia Britannica*		
EDB	*Encyclopedic Dictionary of the Bible*	JBL	*Journal of Biblical Literature*
EGT	Nicoll: *Expositor's Greek Testament*	JE	*Jewish Encyclopedia*
		JETS	*Journal of Evangelical Theological Society*
EQ	*Evangelical Quarterly*		
ET	*Evangelische Theologie*	JFB	Jamieson, Fausset, and Brown: *Commentary on the Old and New Testament*
ExB	*The Expositor's Bible*		
Exp	*The Expositor*		
ExpT	*The Expository Times*	JNES	*Journal of Near Eastern Studies*
FLAP	Finegan: *Light From the Ancient Past*		
		Jos. Antiq.	Josephus: *The Antiquities of the Jews*
GR	*Gordon Review*		
HBD	*Harper's Bible Dictionary*	Jos. War	Josephus: *The Jewish War*
HDAC	Hastings: *Dictionary of the Apostolic Church*	JQR	*Jewish Quarterly Review*
		JR	*Journal of Religion*
HDB	Hastings: *Dictionary of the Bible*	JSJ	*Journal for the Study of Judaism in the Persian, Hellenistic and Roman Periods*
HDBrev.	Hastings: *Dictionary of the Bible*, one-vol. rev. by Grant and Rowley		
		JSOR	*Journal of the Society of Oriental Research*
HDCG	Hastings: *Dictionary of Christ and the Gospels*	JSS	*Journal of Semitic Studies*
		JT	*Jerusalem Talmud*
HERE	Hastings: *Encyclopedia of Religion and Ethics*	JTS	*Journal of Theological Studies*
HGEOTP	Heidel: *The Gilgamesh Epic and Old Testament Parallels*	KAHL	Kenyon: *Archaeology in the Holy Land*
		KB	Koehler-Baumgartner: *Lexicon in Veteris Testament Libros*
HJP	Schurer: *A History of the Jewish People in the Time of Christ*		
		KD	Keil and Delitzsch: *Commentary on the Old Testament*
HR	Hatch and Redpath: *Concordance to the Septuagint*	LSJ	Liddell, Scott, Jones: *Greek-English Lexicon*
		LTJM	Edersheim: *The Life and Times of Jesus the Messiah*
HTR	*Harvard Theological Review*		

MM   Moulton and Milligan: *The Vocabulary of the Greek Testament*

MNT   Moffatt: *New Testament Commentary*

MST   McClintock and Strong: *Cyclopedia of Biblical, Theological, and Ecclesiastical Literature*

NBC   Davidson, Kevan, and Stibbs: *The New Bible Commentary*, 1st ed.

NBCrev.   Guthrie and Motyer: *The New Bible Commentary*, rev. ed.

NBD   J. D. Douglas: *The New Bible Dictionary*

NCB   *New Century Bible*

NCE   *New Catholic Encyclopedia*

NIC   *New International Commentary*

NIDCC   Douglas: *The New International Dictionary of the Christian Church*

NovTest   *Novum Testamentum*

NSI   Cooke: *Handbook of North Semitic Inscriptions*

NTS   *New Testament Studies*

ODCC   *The Oxford Dictionary of the Christian Church*, rev. ed.

Peake   Black and Rowley: *Peake's Commentary on the Bible*

PEQ   *Palestine Exploration Quarterly*

PNFl   P. Schaff: *The Nicene and Post-Nicene Fathers* (1st series)

PNF2   P. Schaff and H. Wace: *The Nicene and Post-Nicene Fathers* (2nd series)

PTR   *Princeton Theological Review*

RB   *Revue Biblique*

RHG   Robertson's *Grammar of the Greek New Testament in the Light of Historical Research*

RTWB   Richardson: *A Theological Wordbook of the Bible*

SBK   Strack and Billerbeck: *Kommentar zum Neuen Testament aus Talmud und Midrash*

SHERK   *The New Schaff-Herzog Encyclopedia of Religious Knowledge*

SJT   *Scottish Journal of Theology*

SOT   Girdlestone: *Synonyms of Old Testament*

SOTI   Archer: *A Survey of Old Testament Introduction*

ST   *Studia Theologica*

TCERK   Loetscher: *The Twentieth Century Encyclopedia of Religious Knowledge*

TDNT   Kittel: *Theological Dictionary of the New Testament*

TDOT   *Theological Dictionary of the Old Testament*

Theol   *Theology*

ThT   *Theology Today*

TNTC   *Tyndale New Testament Commentaries*

Trench   Trench: *Synonyms of the New Testament*

UBD   *Unger's Bible Dictionary*

UT   Gordon: *Ugaritic Textbook*

VB   Allmen: *Vocabulary of the Bible*

VetTest   *Vetus Testamentum*

Vincent   Vincent: *Word-Pictures in the New Testament*

WBC   *Wycliffe Bible Commentary*

WBE   *Wycliffe Bible Encyclopedia*

WC   *Westminster Commentaries*

WesBC   *Wesleyan Bible Commentaries*

WTJ   *Westminster Theological Journal*

ZAW   *Zeitschrift für die alttestamentliche Wissenschaft*

ZNW   *Zeitschrift für die neutestamentliche Wissenschaft*

ZPBD   *The Zondervan Pictorial Bible Dictionary*

ZPEB   *The Zondervan Pictorial Encyclopedia of the Bible*

ZWT   *Zeitschrift für wissenschaftliche Theologie*

D. Abbreviations for Books of the Bible, the Apocrypha, and the Pseudepigrapha

OLD TESTAMENT

Gen	2 Chron	Dan
Exod	Ezra	Hos
Lev	Neh	Joel
Num	Esth	Amos
Deut	Job	Obad
Josh	Ps(Pss)	Jonah
Judg	Prov	Mic
Ruth	Eccl	Nah
1 Sam	S of Songs	Hab
2 Sam	Isa	Zeph
1 Kings	Jer	Hag
2 Kings	Lam	Zech
1 Chron	Ezek	Mal

NEW TESTAMENT

Matt	1 Tim
Mark	2 Tim
Luke	Titus
John	Philem
Acts	Heb
Rom	James
1 Cor	1 Peter
2 Cor	2 Peter
Gal	1 John
Eph	2 John
Phil	3 John
Col	Jude
1 Thess	Rev
2 Thess	

APOCRYPHA

1 Esd	1 Esdras	Ep Jer	Epistle of Jeremy
2 Esd	2 Esdras	S Th Ch	Song of the Three Children
Tobit	Tobit		(or Young Men)
Jud	Judith	Sus	Susanna
Add Esth	Additions to Esther	Bel	Bel and the Dragon
Wisd Sol	Wisdom of Solomon	Pr Man	Prayer of Manasseh
Ecclus	Ecclesiasticus (Wisdom of	1 Macc	1 Maccabees
	Jesus the Son of Sirach)	2 Macc	2 Maccabees
Baruch	Baruch		

PSEUDEPIGRAPHA

As Moses	Assumption of Moses	Pirke Aboth	Pirke Aboth
2 Baruch	Syriac Apocalypse of Baruch	Ps 151	Psalm 151
3 Baruch	Greek Apocalypse of Baruch	Pss Sol	Psalms of Solomon
1 Enoch	Ethiopic Book of Enoch	Sib Oracles	Sibylline Oracles
2 Enoch	Slavonic Book of Enoch	Story Ah	Story of Ahikar
3 Enoch	Hebrew Book of Enoch	T Abram	Testament of Abraham
4 Ezra	4 Ezra	T Adam	Testament of Adam
JA	Joseph and Asenath	T Benjamin	Testament of Benjamin
Jub	Book of Jubilees	T Dan	Testament of Dan
L Aristeas	Letter of Aristeas	T Gad	Testament of Gad
Life AE	Life of Adam and Eve	T Job	Testament of Job
Liv Proph	Lives of the Prophets	T Jos	Testament of Joseph
MA Isa	Martyrdom and Ascension	T Levi	Testament of Levi
	of Isaiah	T Naph	Testament of Naphtali
3 Macc	3 Maccabees	T 12 Pat	Testaments of the Twelve
4 Macc	4 Maccabees		Patriarchs
Odes Sol	Odes of Solomon	Zad Frag	Zadokite Fragments
P Jer	Paralipomena of Jeremiah		

E. Abbreviations of Names of Dead Sea Scrolls and Related Texts

CD — Cairo (Genizah text of the) Damascus (Document)

DSS — Dead Sea Scrolls

Hev — Nahal Hever texts

Mas — Masada Texts

Mird — Khirbet mird texts

Mur — Wadi Murabba'at texts

P — Pesher (commentary)

Q — Qumran

1Q,2Q,etc. — Numbered caves of Qumran, yielding written material; followed by abbreviation of biblical or apocryphal book.

QL — Qumran Literature

1QapGen — Genesis Apocryphon of Qumran Cave 1

1QH — *Hodayot* (Thanksgiving Hymns) from Qumran Cave 1

1QIsa^{a, b} — First or second copy of Isaiah from Qumran Cave 1

1QpHab — Pesher on Habakkuk from Qumran Cave 1

1QM — *Milhamah* (War Scroll)

1QS — *Serek Hayyahad* (Rule of the Community, Manual of Discipline)

1QSa — Appendix A (Rule of the Congregation) to 1QS

1QSb — Appendix B (Blessings) to 1QS

3Q15 — Copper Scroll from Qumran Cave 3

4QFlor — Florilegium (or Eschatological Midrashim) from Qumran Cave 4

4Qmess ar — Aramaic "Messianic" text from Qumran Cave 4

4QPrNab — Prayer of Nabonidus from Qumran Cave 4

4QTest — Testimonia text from Qumran Cave 4

4QTLevi — Testament of Levi from Qumran Cave 4

4QPhyl — Phylacteries from Qumran Cave 4

11QMelch — Melchizedek text from Qumran Cave 11

11QtgJob — Targum of Job from Qumran Cave 11

TRANSLITERATIONS

Greek

α	—	a	π	—	p	αι	—	ai
β	—	b	ρ	—	r	αὐ	—	au
γ	—	g	σ,ς	—	s	ει	—	ei
δ	—	d	τ	—	t	εὐ	—	eu
ε	—	e	υ	—	y	ηὐ	—	ēu
ζ	—	z	φ	—	ph	οι	—	oi
η	—	ē	χ	—	ch	οὐ	—	ou
θ	—	th	ψ	—	ps	υι	—	hui
ι	—	i	ω	—	ō			
κ	—	k				ῥ	—	rh
λ	—	l	γγ	—	ng	‘	—	h
μ	—	m	γκ	—	nk			
ν	—	n	γξ	—	nx	ᾳ	—	ā
ξ	—	x	γχ	—	nch	ῃ	—	ē
ο	—	o				ῳ	—	ō

PHILIPPIANS

Homer A. Kent, Jr.

PHILIPPIANS

Introduction

1. Background

Philippi was located in Macedonia about ten miles inland from the Aegean Sea. The original settlement was called Krenides (presumably because of the presence of a good water supply, inasmuch as the name means "springs"), but in 356 B.C. the name was changed by Philip II, king of Macedonia (359–336 B.C.), when he enlarged the city with many new inhabitants and considerable construction.

In 42 B.C. the Battle of Philippi was fought west of the city between the Second Triumvirate (Octavian, Antony, Lepidus) and the Republicans of Rome (Brutus, Cassius). The victory of Octavian resulted in Philippi's being made a military colony. Following the Battle of Actium in 31 B.C., in which Octavian defeated Antony, the status of Philippi was raised; the city was first given the title "Colonia Julia Philippensis," and later, in 27 B.C., "Colonia Augusta Julia Philippensis" (Jack Finegan, IDB, K–Q, p. 786). The change in status provided the inhabitants with numerous advantages, including autonomous government, immunity from tribute, and treatment as if they actually lived in Italy.[1] Luke calls Philippi *prōtē* ("first, chief ") of the district of Macedonia (Acts 16:12). This cannot mean that Philippi was the capital of the province, for Thessalonica held that distinction; nor does it mean that Philippi was the capital of its district, for Amphipolis served that function. Evidence from a later period shows that *prōtē* was an honorary title given certain cities, and perhaps this explains Luke's use of the term.[2] Some have adopted the conjectural *prōtēs* in place of *prōtē*, and so arrive at this meaning: "a city of the first district of Macedonia" (so UBS). But this can claim no Greek manuscript support. More likely, absence of the article with *prōtē* simply implies "a leading city" in that part of Macedonia. In fact, Philippi was the only "colony" in the area. Reflections of the Philippians' pride in their city may appear in Acts 16:20, 21, as well as in some of Paul's terminology (Phil 1:27; 3:20).

---

[1]F.J. Foakes-Jackson and Kirsopp Lake, *The Acts of the Apostles* (Grand Rapids: Baker, reprint 1965), 4:187–190).

[2]Ibid., pp. 187–189.

The Via Egnatia, the main highway from Asia to the west, passed through Philippi and ran alongside the forum of the city. Near the city was the river Gangites (modern Angitis).

The church at Philippi was founded in A.D. 50 in the course of Paul's second missionary journey (Acts 16). While the apostle was in Troas, he was instructed in a vision to proceed into Macedonia, and Philippi became the first European city in which he preached. Apparently the Jewish population in Philippi was small, at least there was no synagogue. The missionary party, consisting of Paul, Silas, Timothy, and Luke, met first with some women at a Jewish place of prayer by the river bank outside the city. The first convert was Lydia, a "God-fearer" (a term denoting a Gentile who had become a partial adherent to Judaism) who responded to Paul by receiving Christian baptism and opening her home to the missionary party. Other significant incidents were the exorcism of the demon from a slave girl and the conversion of the jailer and his family. These early converts were a most diverse and unlikely group with which to found a local church, but the grace of God overcame their differences.

When the apostolic party moved on, Luke may have been left behind to guide the new work (the use of "we" in the narrative of Acts is dropped until 20:5–6 when Paul returns to Philippi). Luke himself is thought by some to have been a Philippian, and was perhaps the "man from Macedonia" Paul saw in his vision.[3] The new church did not forget its founder, however, for gifts were sent to Paul on several occasions (Phil 4:15, 16).

Paul made a second visit to Philippi in A.D. 55–56 on his third missionary journey (Acts 20:1–6). Actually, he must have passed through the city twice: on his outward trip toward Corinth and again on his return at the time when he was on the way to Jerusalem with the collection for the poor there. Luke apparently rejoined the party at this latter visit. This visit to Jerusalem culminated in Paul's arrest and eventual imprisonment in Rome (Acts 21f.), which in turn brought about the occasion for this Epistle.

2. Authorship and Unity

That the apostle Paul wrote the Epistle to the Philippians is virtually unquestioned. Not until the nineteenth century, beginning with F.C. Baur (1792–1860) and the Tübingen school of Germany, were serious questions raised, and these negative views have not been widely accepted. The straightforward claim of the Epistle (1:1) is supported by the reference to Paul's acquaintances, the reflection of known circumstances in his life, and the many indications of Pauline thought. Even those who have questioned the unity of Philippians have usually concluded that Paul was the author of the various parts.

The unity of Philippians has been questioned on several grounds: (1) the use of "finally" at 3:1, (2) the change in subject matter and tone at 3:1 or 3:2, and (3) Polycarp's use of the plural "epistles" in referring to Paul's communications with the Philippians (*To the Philippians*, 3.2). These observations have led to various reconstructions, some suggesting a combining of two letters and others of three. Beare has proposed a combination of three units: an interpolated fragment (3:2–4:1), the letter of thanks (4:10–20), and the final letter (1:1–3:1; 4:2–9, 21–23). He concludes that all were written by Paul, but on different occasions, and perhaps one of them to a different group of readers (pp.

---

[3]Ramsay, pp. 200–205; E.M. Blaiklock, *The Acts of the Apostles* (Grand Rapids: Eerdmans, 1959), pp. 123–125.

24–29). A slightly different alignment was proposed by Rahtjen (pp. 167–173), a critique of which was given by Mackay (pp. 161–170).

Although the case for a composite document has been skillfully presented, it has not commended itself to the majority of scholars for the reason that the objections to the unity of Philippians can be answered. There is no manuscript evidence that Philippians ever existed as two or three separate letters. The evidence from Polycarp can be understood either as including other canonical letters from Paul to Macedonia (e.g., the Thessalonian Epistles) or other letters to the Philippians not now extant. The use of "finally" (3:1) can be understood in the sense of "in addition" (BAG, p. 481), and is paralleled by Paul's usage elsewhere (1 Thess 4:1). The change in subject matter and tone could have been due to the receiving of new information from Philippi as Paul was writing the letter or to an interval of several hours or even days between the several parts. Such changes in mood in the light of the problems being discussed should not be surprising.

3. Date and Place of Origin

Inasmuch as Paul was a prisoner at the time Philippians was written (1:7, 13, 16), identification of this imprisonment would make possible the fixing of the date and place of origin of the Epistle. Three possibilities must be considered: Caesarea, Rome, and Ephesus.

1. *Caesarea.* Paul was a prisoner in Caesarea for two years (A.D. 57–59) and his friends had access to him (Acts 24:23, 27). The fugitive slave Onesimus could have fled there (this assumes that the Epistles to the Colossians and Philemon came out of the same imprisonment as Philippians). The "praetorium" (1:13; NIV, "palace guard") could be understood of Herod's palace at Caesarea (Acts 23:35). Furthermore, the polemic against Jewish teachers (3:1–16) fits well the period of Jewish-Gentile controversy.

This theory has not been widely adopted, because there is no positive evidence favoring it. Paul expected prompt release (2:24), but there was little reason for optimism while he was at Caesarea, and this prospect was no longer possible after he had appealed to Caesar. Lack of any mention of the prominent Philip, who lived at Caesarea and had been Paul's host (Acts 21:8–10), also makes this view doubtful.

2. *Rome.* The traditional view places the writing of Philippians during Paul's first imprisonment in Rome during A.D. 59–61 (Acts 28:30). This is the most natural understanding of "palace guard" (1:13) and "Caesar's household" (4:22). Paul's trial was evidently going on during the writing, and its outcome could bring either life or death. Apparently there could be no appeal from its verdict (1:19–24). This was not the situation at Caesarea, for there he could appeal to Caesar (Acts 25:10–12). His circumstances reflected in the letter fit the Roman imprisonment better than the one at Caesarea, since he had freedom to arrange itineration for his associates and opportunity to carry on considerable correspondence. He hoped to visit Philippi soon (2:24); at Caesarea, however, his aim was to go to Rome, and his appeal to Caesar made a trip to Philippi out of the question. The Marcionite Prologue (c. A.D. 170) states that Philippians was sent from Rome. This view is the one most widely held. It will be assumed in this commentary.

3. *Ephesus.* The case for the origination of this Epistle at Ephesus has received increasing attention in recent years (Guthrie, pp. 146–154). This view places the writing in A.D. 53–55 during Paul's three-year stay in Ephesus (Acts 19). The problem that Acts mentions no imprisonment of Paul in Ephesus is met by explaining Romans 16:4, 7; 1 Corinthians 15:32; 2 Corinthians 1:8–10; 11:23 as pointing to such an imprisonment.

But this is by no means established, for it demands treating these passages in Corinthians with wooden literalness rather than as the dramatic figures they are. Furthermore, this view requires taking Romans 16 as written to Ephesus rather than to Rome, a conclusion not warranted by the documentary evidence.

Philippians presupposes several time-consuming journeys between Philippi and Paul's location. Consequently, some scholars hold that an Ephesus origin is more likely than one at Rome. As many as six trips may' have occurred (requiring at least one month each between Philippi and Rome, but only one week between Philippi and Ephesus): (1) News of Paul's plight reaches Philippi, (2) Epaphroditus travels to Rome with a gift to Paul, (3) news of Epaphroditus's illness reaches Philippi, (4) the report of the Philippians' concern reaches Epaphroditus, (5) a trip was made by Timothy to Philippi, and (6) a return trip by Timothy to Paul was contemplated. Nevertheless, several factors weaken the force of this argument. Not all of these trips necessarily originated after Paul's arrival in Rome. It is conceivable that the gift to Paul had been timed to reach him shortly after his arrival. Furthermore, Epaphroditus may have become sick while en route to Rome, and someone could have immediately returned to Philippi with the report. So the time span may not have been so long as some have thought. In any event, Paul's two years in Rome provided sufficient time for these trips, even if they all must be included within that period.

Supporters of the case for Ephesus remind us that reference to the palace guard (1:13) and Caesar's household (4:22) are not proof of the letter's having been written at Rome and that Paul's desire to visit Philippi after his release is easier to fit into an Ephesian imprisonment than a Roman one, inasmuch as Paul had expressed his wish to visit Spain after going to Rome (Rom 15:24). They also assert that the Philippians' not giving to Paul before sending a contribution by Epaphroditus (4:10) is easier to explain by the Ephesus theory, since Paul had been in Ephesus only a short time before leaving for Palestine. Yet it is hardly fair to insist that Paul's desire to visit Spain, expressed before nearly five years of continuous imprisonment, did not undergo some modification. As to the lack of opportunity for a gift, Paul was raising money for the collection when he passed through Philippi and Ephesus earlier and may have avoided taking anything for himself at that time lest suspicion be attached to his motives and the collection project be undermined.

In addition to the above factors, the Ephesus theory is weakened by the fact that at Ephesus Paul could have appealed to Caesar as he did at Caesarea (contra 1:20, 23, 24). Philippians also says nothing about the collection—a project Paul was engaged in while at Ephesus. On the whole, therefore, the Ephesus theory does not seem to have sufficient foundation to dislodge the traditional view that Philippians came out of Paul's first imprisonment at Rome. It seems, however, to be separated from the other prison Epistles (Ephesians, Colossians, Philemon), because it was carried by a different messenger and reflects circumstances apparently somewhat later than those relating to the other three Epistles (his case was actually in court). A date of A.D. 61 is suggested.

4. Occasion and Purpose

The Philippian church sent Epaphroditus to Paul with a gift from the congregation (4:18) and with instructions to minister to his needs through personal service (2:25). He also must have brought news of the progress and problems of the church. In the performance of his responsibilities, Epaphroditus became gravely ill, and the Philippians heard about it. For some reason, this latter circumstance greatly distressed Epaphroditus. Was he embarrassed because he felt he had disappointed the church? Or was he aware that his condition had been misinterpreted and criticized? Paul's request that the church receive Epaphroditus with all joy and that they hold him in high regard (2:29) implies that some misunderstanding had occurred.

But Epaphroditus recovered and was ready to return home. This furnished the occasion for writing the Epistle. Paul wanted the church at Philippi to understand clearly that Epaphroditus had been a real fellow soldier in the Lord's work (2:25), that his illness had been extremely serious (2:27-30), and that he was worthy of a hero's welcome (2:29).

The mention of the Philippians' gift (4:10-20) should not be regarded as Paul's first acknowledgment of their help. Too much time had elapsed since Epaphroditus's arrival for this to be a reasonable inference, nor would this mention have been delayed to the end if it had been the occasion for Paul's writing the Epistle. Because of the several contacts between Philippi and Rome before this time, Paul had undoubtedly sent his initial thanks promptly. We may adequately account for the additional mention of the gift in this Epistle as the apostle's grateful recollection of a very generous contribution.

Other factors of a secondary nature may also have prompted the Epistle, such as Timothy's approaching visit (2:19), Paul's own hope of visiting the church (2:24), and the problem of the two women at Philippi (4:2).

Of all the letters Paul wrote to churches, this one to the Philippians stands out as being the most personal. No sharp rebukes of the congregation mar its joyful spirit: no disturbing problems threaten the progress of the church. The warnings are of a cautionary and preventive nature that are always in order. The frequent emphasis on Christ explains the underlying relationship of Paul to his readers. The names Jesus Christ, Christ Jesus, Lord Jesus Christ, Lord Jesus, Jesus, Christ, Lord, and Savior, occur 51 times in the 104 verses of the Epistle.

5. Literary Form

Philippians exhibits all the characteristics of contemporary letters. Its initial mention of the author and addressees is followed by the greeting. After this comes the body of the letter. Concluding words of greeting round it out.

Except for the question of unity (see 2 above), the only problem of literary form in Philippians concerns the nature of 2:5-11. The rhythmical nature of this portion has caused some to describe it as a christological hymn, either borrowed by Paul from an even earlier Christian source[4] or composed by a Christian contemporary of Paul using language borrowed from pagan songs to "divine Heroes" (Beare, pp. 1, 2), or as composed by Paul himself (Scott, IB, 11:46, 47). An excellent review of the arguments for and against Pauline authorship of the hymn is given by Martin in *Carmen Christi* (pp. 42-62). Textual evidence does not support the view that the passage is a later addition.

There is no problem in seeing the passage as the incorporating of an earlier Christian hymn (1 Tim 3:16 may be another Pauline instance of such quotation). However, Paul himself could write highly poetic passages (as Rom 8:35-39 and 1 Cor 13 show), and the exposition will demonstrate that the content is harmonious with Pauline thought, without any need for resorting to pagan concepts. What is clear is that Paul has provided in

---

[4]Ernst Lohmeyer, *Der Brief an die Philipper* ... , 13th ed. (Gottingen: Vandenhoeck & Ruprecht, 1964), pp. 8, 90, 91.

this concise statement a sublime summary of Christology, from preexistence to exaltation.

6. Canonicity

Evidence for the early acceptance of this Epistle by the leaders of the church is plentiful and raises no questions. Allusions to its contents appear in Clement of Rome (first century) and Ignatius (early second century). More explicit testimony is found in Polycarp (early second century), who refers directly to Paul's communication with the Philippians by letter and utilizes the terminology of the canonical Epistle (*To the Philippians*, chs. 3, 9, 12).

Philippians appears in the extant second-century lists of canonical books. The Muratorian fragment (c. A.D. 170) includes it among Paul's Epistles, as does the list of the heretic Marcion. It is quoted and attributed to Paul by Irenaeus, Tertullian, and Clement of Alexandria (late second and early third centuries). It was included in the "acknowledged books" of Eusebius (fourth century) and in the list of Athanasius (A.D. 367). No suspicion regarding the canonicity of Philippians is to be found in early external testimony.

7. Bibliography

Books:

Alford, Henry. *The Greek Testament.* London: Rivingtons, 1874.

Barth, Karl. *The Epistle to the Philippians.* Richmond: John Knox Press, 1962.

Beare, F.W. *A Commentary on the Epistle to the Philippians.* London: Adam & Charles Black, 1959.

Davidson, F. "The Epistle to the Philippians." NBC1. Edited by F. Davidson, A.M. Stibbs, and E.F. Kevan. Grand Rapids: Eerdmans, 1954.

Guthrie, Donald. *New Testament Introduction: The Pauline Epistles.* Chicago: Inter-Varsity Press, 1961.

Hendriksen, William. *Exposition of Philippians.* Grand Rapids: Baker, 1962.

Johnstone, Robert. *Lectures Exegetical and Practical on the Epistle of Paul to the Philippians.* Grand Rapids: Baker, repr. of 1875 ed.

Kennedy, H.A.A. "The Epistle to the Philippians." *The Expositor's Greek Testament.* Edited by W. Robertson Nicoll. London: Hodder & Stoughton, 1917.

Lenski, R.C.H. *The Interpretation of St. Paul's Epistles to the Galatians, to the Ephesians and to the Philippians.* Columbus: Wartburg Press, 1946.

Lightfoot, J.B. *Saint Paul's Epistle to the Philippians.* Grand Rapids: Zondervan, repr. of 1913 edition.

Martin, Ralph P. *Carmen Christi: Philippians 2:5–11 in Recent Interpretation and in the Setting of Early Christian Worship.* Cambridge: Cambridge University Press, 1967.

_____. *The Epistle of Paul to the Philippians.* Grand Rapids: Eerdmans, 1959.

Motyer, J.A. *Philippian Studies: The Richness of Christ.* Chicago: Inter-Varsity Press, 1966.

Moule, H.C.G. *The Epistle to the Philippians.* Cambridge: Cambridge University Press, 1873.

Mounce, Robert H. "The Epistle to the Philippians." *Wycliffe Bible Commentary.* Edited by C.F. Pfeiffer and E.F. Harrison. Chicago: Moody, 1962.

Muller, Jac. J. *The Epistles of Paul to the Philippians and to Philemon.* Grand Rapids: Eerdmans, 1955.

Ramsay, W.M. *St. Paul the Traveller and the Roman Citizen.* 3rd ed. London: Hodder & Stoughton, 1897. Repr. Grand Rapids: Baker, 1949.

Scott, Ernest F. and Wicks, Robert R. "The Epistle to the Philippians." *The Interpreter's Bible.* vol. 11. Edited by George A. Buttrick. New York: Abingdon Press, 1955.

Vincent, Marvin R. *The Epistles to the Philippians and to Philemon.* Edinburgh: T. & T. Clark, 1897.

Walvoord, John F. *Philippians: Triumph in Christ.* Chicago: Moody, 1971.

Periodicals:

Jewett, Robert. "The Epistolary Thanksgiving and the Integrity of Philippians." *Novum Testamentum.* vol. 12, fac. 1 (January, 1970): 40–53.

Mackay, B.S. "Further Thoughts on Philippians." *New Testament Studies.* vol. 7, no. 2 (January, 1961): 161–170.

Marshall, I. Howard. "The Christ-Hymn in Philippians 2:5–11." *Tyndale Bulletin.* 1968, no. 19: 104–127.

McClain, Alva J. "The Doctrine of the Kenosis in Philippians 2:5–8," *The Biblical Review Quarterly* (October, 1928). Reprinted in *Grace Journal,* vol. 8, no. 2 (Spring, 1967): 3–13.

Rahtjen, B.D. "The Three Letters of Paul to the Philippians." *New Testament Studies.* vol. 6, no. 2 (January, 1960): 167–173.

Walvoord, John F. "The Humiliation of the Son of God." *Bibliotheca Sacra.* vol. 118, no. 470 (April, 1961): 99–106.

8. Outline

Introduction (1:1–11)
    1. Greeting (1:1, 2)
    2. Thanksgiving (1:3–8)
    3. Prayer (1:9–11)
  I. The Situation of Paul in Rome (1:12–26)
    1. Paul's Circumstances Had Advanced the Gospel in Rome (1:12–18)
    2. Paul's Circumstances Would Turn Out for Salvation (1:19–26)
  II. First Series of Exhortations (1:27–2:18)
    1. Exhortation to Unity and Courage in View of External Foes (1:27–30)
    2. Exhortation to Unity and Humility Toward Those in the Church (2:1–11)
    3. Exhortation to Work Out Their Salvation (2:12–18)
  III. Two Messengers of Paul to the Philippians (2:19–30)
    1. Timothy (2:19–24)
    2. Epaphroditus (2:25–30)
  IV. Warning Against Judaizers and Antinomians (3:1–21)
    1. The Judaizing Danger (3:1–16)
    2. The Antinomian Danger (3:17–21)
  V. Second Series of Exhortations (4:1–9)
    1. Exhortation to Stand Firm in Unity (4:1–3)
    2. Exhortation to Maintain Various Christian Virtues (4:4–9)
  VI. The Philippians' Gifts to Paul (4:10–20)
    1. The Recent Gift (4:10–14)
    2. The Previous Gifts (4:15–20)
Closing Salutation (4:21–23)

Text and Exposition

Introduction (1:1–11)

1. Greeting

1:1, 2

¹Paul and Timothy, servants of Christ Jesus,

To all the saints in Christ Jesus at Philippi, together with the overseers and deacons:

²Grace and peace to you from God our Father and the Lord Jesus Christ.

1 "Paul and Timothy" are associated in the greeting, not because they were co-authors of the letter, but because Timothy was a well-known Christian leader, especially at Philippi, and was now with Paul. It is certain that Paul alone was the author, in view of the singular verb and pronouns in 1:3, 4, as well as the discussion in 2:19–23. Timothy had been present at the founding of the church at Philippi (Acts 16:1–12) and on several subsequent occasions (Acts 19:22; 20:3–6). Perhaps he served as Paul's amanuensis for the letter.

Paul does not use his title "apostle," perhaps because he is not stressing his authority but is rather making a personal appeal. The circumstances may be compared to those in the Epistle to Philemon, where Paul also does not mention his apostleship. In marked contrast is the Epistle to the Galatians, where Paul stresses his authority.

Both Paul and Timothy are designated as "servants of Christ Jesus." This description emphasizes submission and dependence on their Lord. It is not a technical reference to a specific office, but characterizes their willing service of Christ, their divine Master. The same designation appears in the Epistles of James, 2 Peter, and Jude.

The addressees are named as "all the saints in Christ Jesus" who resided in the Macedonian city of Philippi. Paul places no special emphasis on "all," as though he were counteracting some viewpoint that would exclude some in the church. Paul frequently employed "all" in addressing the various churches he wrote to (cf. Rom 1:7; 1 Cor 1:2; 2 Cor 1:1; 1 Thess 1:2). All believers are "saints" through their spiritual union with Christ, a fact Paul often expressed by the phrase "in Christ Jesus" (Rom 8:1, 2; Eph 2:6, 10, 13; 3:6) or "in Christ" (Rom 12:5; 2 Cor 5:17). This use of the term emphasizes not personal holiness, though the believer's conduct should correspond increasingly to his standing, but the objective status each believer possesses because the merits of Christ are imputed to him. Nor does it refer to a condition after death, for these "saints" were very much alive at Philippi.

Though "overseers and deacons" were the two orders of officers in the local NT churches (1 Tim 3:1–3), Philippians is the only Epistle to mention them in its greeting. (On "overseers" NIV has a footnote: "Or *bishops*.") Why Paul includes them here is nowhere stated, but several observations suggest themselves. It is clear that the church at Philippi was organized and that Paul was not by-passing its local order. Doubtless his mention of overseers and deacons was an endorsement of their authority. Also, the Epistle would have been delivered first to the church officers for reading to the congregation. Because Epaphroditus had previously been sent with a monetary gift (2:25), the

11

deacons as well as the overseers may have been particularly involved in the project of aiding Paul (4:14-16).

2 The familiar blessing, "grace and peace," combines Greek and Hebrew expressions but transforms them into a thoroughly Christian greeting. Exactly the same wording was used by Paul in six other Epistles (Rom, 1 and 2 Cor, Gal, Eph, Philem). God's "grace" is his favor, needed by men in countless ways and bestowed without regard to merit. "Peace" is here a reference not to the cessation of hostilities between sinners and God (Rom 5:1), but to the inner assurance and tranquility that God ministers to the hearts of believers and that keeps them spiritually confident and content even in the midst of turmoil (4:7). The source of these blessings is "God our Father and the Lord Jesus Christ." Paul understands that Jesus the Messiah is the divine Lord, ascended to the Father's right hand and equal to him in authority and honor. Just as Christ and the Father joined in the sending of the Holy Spirit (John 14:26; 15:26), so they will jointly convey these blessings.

Notes

1 The term δοῦλοι (douloi, "servants") is explained by Adolph Deissmann as a Hellenistic usage, based on the practice of a freed slave's becoming a devotee of the deity (Deiss LAE, pp. 323-330). It is more likely, however, that Paul drew his terminology from the OT, where LXX used δοῦλος (doulos) of Moses (Ps 105:26) and other prophets (Jer. 25:4; Amos 3:7), as well as of the divine Servant of Jehovah.

The dative πᾶσιν (pasin, "to all") is used with an articular substantive ἁγίοις (hagiois, "saints") and denotes totality without any particular contrast in view (Eugene Van Ness Goetchius, *The Language of the New Testament* [New York: Scribner's, 1965], pp. 216-218). Thus, "all the saints" denotes each believer in Philippi, but without any particular emphasis that it is *all* and not just *some*.

"Overseers" (ἐπισκόποις, episkopois) denoted the chief administrative officers in local churches. Other versions (e.g., KJV, RSV, NEB) translate the term "bishops" (cf. footnote in NIV); JB has "presiding elders." The term seems to have been interchangeable with "elders" (πρεσβύτερος, presbyteros) in the NT (Acts 20:17, 28; Titus 1:5, 7). The former term designated the office as to its function, and the latter, as to its dignity, being a title doubtless derived from the synagogue. "Deacons" (διακόνοις, diakonois) were the secondary officers in the church (1 Tim 3:1-13). The office was probably derived from that of the seven men referred to in Acts 6:1-7. Although the name διάκονος (diakonos, "deacon") was not used of the seven, the cognates διακονία (diakonia, "service"; NIV, "distribution of food") and διακονέω (diakoneō, "to serve"; NIV, "to wait on [tables]") appear three times in the passage. The deacons were charged with various temporal concerns of the church, such as the dispensing of aid to the needy.

2 The usual Greek salutation in a letter was χαιρεῖν (chairein, "greetings"; cf. Acts 23:26; James 1:1). Paul changed this to χάρις (charis), and thus adds a spiritual dimension to his greeting to the church. The word meant "grace" or "favor" and in Christian contexts developed the special sense of the favor that God bestowed on sinners, saving them and providing for their every need.

2. Thanksgiving

1:3-8

[3]I thank my God every time I remember you. [4]In all my prayers for all of you, I always pray with joy [5]because of your partnership in the gospel from the first day

until now, [6]being confident of this, that he who began a good work in you will carry it on to completion until the day of Christ Jesus.
[7]It is right for me to feel this way about all of you, since I have you in my heart; for whether I am in chains or defending and confirming the gospel, all of you share in God's grace with me. [8]God can testify how I long for all of you with the affection of Christ Jesus.

3 Paul begins his letter by thanking God for his readers. He follows this pattern in all his Epistles except Galatians, where the absence of such sentiment forebodes the serious discussion to follow. With the Philippians Paul had a warm relationship, and this tone is established at the outset of the letter. By stating his thanks to "my God," the author reveals his personal devotion. This was no stereotyped formula, but the natural outflow from the heart of a deeply spiritual man. The thanksgiving was prompted by the joyous memory Paul had of his Philippian friends. It was not that every single memory caused him to thank God, but that his whole remembrance of them was good.

4 These happy memories were reflected in Paul's prayers (root: *deēsis*) for the Philippians. Joy permeated his prayers even while he prayed for their needs.

5 What caused Paul the deepest satisfaction was the Philippians' "partnership in the gospel." The rich term *koinōnia* denotes participation or fellowship, and expresses a two-sided relation (Friedrich Hauck, *Koinōnos*, et al., TDNT, 3:798). In its NT uses it includes the believer's participation in the life of God (1 Cor 1:9; 1 John 1:3) and also the sharing of a common faith. Thus it assumes the existence of a brotherly relationship among believers (2 Cor 8:4; Gal 2:9; 1 John 1:7). Although some have seen here a specific reference to the Philippians' recent gift, it is likely that the apostle's intent was broader. The gift was one expression of their partnership, but Paul was grateful and filled with joy over the frequent evidences of the Philippians' sharing in the work of the gospel. These had been shown to him "from the first day" he had preached the gospel in Philippi about ten years before. At that time he had experienced the hospitality of Lydia (Acts 16:15) and the jailer and his family (Acts 16:33, 34). Later he had received gifts sent him at Thessalonica (Phil 4:16) and at Corinth (2 Cor 11:9), as well as the more recent one brought by Epaphroditus.

6 Of course, it was God who had produced their transformed lives by the work of regeneration. So Paul was confident that God would continue this work until Christ's return. Even though he rejoiced in the Philippians' generous gift and their evidences of spiritual growth, his confidence did not rest ultimately on the Philippians themselves, but on God, who would preserve them and enable them to reach the goal. The "good work" refers to the salvation begun at their conversion. To see it as a direct and limited reference to their monetary gift is unwarranted. Paul would not have hinted that their gift was only a beginning, and that more should follow.

God not only initiates salvation, but continues it and guarantees its consummation. The apostle's thought relates not to the end of life but to the glorious coming of Jesus Christ that will vindicate both the Lord and his people. So Paul is asserting that God will bring his work to completion. Nothing in this life or after death will prevent the successful accomplishment of God's good work in every Christian.

"The day of Christ Jesus" is a phrase occurring with only slight variations six times in the NT, three of them in Philippians (1 Cor 1:8; 5:5; 2 Cor 1:14; Phil 1:6, 10; 2:16). The expression is similar to the "day of the Lord" (1 Thess 5:2) and the OT "day of Jehovah" (Amos 5:18–20). However, in contrast to the OT emphasis on judgment, the "day of Christ Jesus" is mentioned in all cases with reference to the NT church. It will be the time when Christ returns for his church, salvation is finally completed, and believers' works are examined and the believer rewarded.

7 Paul was right in regarding the Philippians so highly, because in a sense they had become partners in his imprisonment and his current legal obligations. To say they were in his "heart" was to use a figure denoting not mere emotions or sentiment, but the essence of consciousness and personality. "Heart" among the Greeks and Hebrews included both mind and will, referring to a person's innermost being (Friedrich Baumgärtel and Johannes Behm, *Kardia*, TDNT, 3:605–614).

The reference to Paul's imprisonment ("I am in chains") belongs with the following rather than the preceding words, as giving evidence of the Philippians' partnership in God's grace. Even when it might have been dangerous to identify themselves openly with Paul, they had treated his misfortunes as their own and had come to his assistance with their gifts. "Defending and confirming the gospel" could be understood as negative and positive aspects of Paul's preaching ministry—i.e., defending the gospel from attacks and proclaiming its message with proofs. There are reasons, however, for regarding these words as legal terminology. The use of *te ... kai* ("both ... and") ties the concept of imprisonment (*desmois*) with that of "defending and confirming." Furthermore, "defending" (*apologia*) is used elsewhere in the NT of a legal defense (Acts 22:1; 25:16; 2 Tim 4:16), and "confirming" (*bebaiōsis*) was a legal technical term (Heb 6:16) for guaranteeing or furnishing security (BAG, p. 138). So Paul may be thinking primarily of his approaching hearing in which he must give a defense of the gospel he preached and in which he hoped also to have occasion to offer clear proofs of the truth of the gospel. In Paul's view, all Christians were on trial with him, for the outcome could ultimately affect them all. The Philippians' assistance by their warm fellowship was a clear reminder that they felt the same way, and thus were sharers of the same grace of God (salvation) as was Paul.

8 Only God could truly vouch for Paul's feelings about his Philippian friends, because they ran so deep. This was not an oath but a statement of fact. Paul's yearnings for this church were not merely the human longing to be with friends but were prompted by the very "affection of Christ Jesus," with whom Paul was in vital union. It was the indwelling Christ who was producing the fruit of love in Paul by the Holy Spirit and who thus enabled him to yearn for their welfare with the compassion of his Lord.

Notes

3 Πάσῃ (*pasē*, "all") is used with τῇ μνείᾳ, (*tē mneia*, "remembrance") in the predicate position, and thus stresses totality, as in 1:1.

The pronoun ὑμῶν (*hymōn*, "of you") can be understood either as a subjective genitive or an objective genitive. If the former, Paul's thanks are based on the Philippians' remembrance of him ("your remembrance") and is a direct reference to the gift that had been sent. It is more likely, however, that the genitive is objective here and that Paul is thankful for all the memories he has of his Philippian friends ("remembrance of you"). This would be consistent with his usage elsewhere, for whenever he uses μνεία (*mneia*) with a genitive, the genitive is always objective (Rom 1:8, 9; 1 Thess 3:6; Philem 4). Also, the passage seems to be naming Paul's activity (the verb is εὐχαριστῶ [*eucharistō*, "I thank"]), rather than the Philippians'.

4 Is 1:4 a parenthesis, as Lightfoot, Hendriksen, and Martin claim? If so, then 1:5 is dependent on εὐχαριστῶ (*eucharistō*, "I thank") of 1:3, and Paul's thanksgiving stems from the Philippians' fellowship in the gospel. But there appears to be no compelling reason why 1:5 cannot be construed with what immediately precedes; "joy because of your fellowship" is a readily understood concept. This makes unnecessary the insertion of parentheses and does not require that 1:5 be related to the somewhat distant *eucharistō*. This is the sense assumed by NIV and NEB. The view that 1:4 is a parenthesis is reflected in RSV. KJV and NASB leave the matter ambiguous.

Verse 4 contains the first of five uses of χαρά (*chara*, "joy") in Philippians (others are 1:25; 2:2, 29; 4:1). In addition, the verb χαίρω (*chairo*, "rejoice") appears seven times (1:18; 2:17, 18, 28; 3:1; 4:4 [twice]), and the compound συγχαίρω (*synchairō*, "rejoice [with]") occurs twice (2:17, 18). Joy is clearly the prevailing atmosphere of the Epistle.

5 The use of ἐπί (*epi*, "because of") is more naturally attached to the phrase immediately preceding than to εὐχαριστῶ (*eucharistō*, "I thank") of 1:3. Otherwise, awkwardness results from the use of two *epi* phrases dependent on *eucharistō*.

6 Absence of the article with ἔργον ἀγαθὸν (*ergon agathon*, "good work") argues for a wider sense than just the recent gift from the Philippians. The same verbs ἐνάρχομαι (*enarchomai*, "begin") and ἐπιτελέω (*epiteleō*, "carry to completion") are used in Galatians 3:3 in reference to the entire Christian life. The "good work," therefore, should be regarded as God's transforming grace in salvation—a grace that provides for continuing manifestations.

7 Most versions have treated με (*me*, "I," "me") as the subject of the infinitive phrase τὸ ἔχειν με ἐν τῇ καρδίας ὑμᾶς (*to echein me en tē kardias hymas*), thus giving the sense: "I have you in my heart." In contrast, NEB regards ὑμᾶς (*hymas*, "you") as the subject: "You hold me in such affection." Word order decidedly favors *me* as the subject, and the sense of this rendering fits the context well.

"Chains" is δεσμοῖς (*desmois*, "bonds," "fetters"). The term can refer to literal shackles, or to imprisonment in general (BAG, p. 175). Βεβαίωσις (*bebaiōsis*, "confirmation") was a technical legal term used of a seller who confirmed a purchase to a buyer and guaranteed it to him in the face of the claims of a third party. It referred to such confirming proof. Thus, Paul regards his proclamation of the gospel even in prison as a legally valid statement. (Deiss BS, pp. 104–109; Heinrich Schlier, *Bebaios*, et al., TDNT, 1:602, 603.)

8 Σπλάγχνοις (*splanchnois*, "affection[s]") originally denoted in early Gr. the inward parts of an animal sacrifice, particularly the heart, liver, lungs, and kidneys, as distinct from the "intestines" (ἔντερα, *entera*). The term seems to have entered Jewish writings during the intertestamental period. In the NT it is used once in the physical sense of entrails (Acts 1:18), and in all other instances with the figurative sense of the seat of emotions or the feeling itself (Helmut Köster, *Splangchnon*, TDNT, 7:548–559).

---

3. Prayer

1:9–11

> 9And this is my prayer: that your love may abound more and more in knowledge and depth of insight, 10so that you may be able to discern what is best and may be pure and blameless until the day of Christ, 11filled with the fruit of righteousness that comes through Jesus Christ—to the glory and praise of God.

9 Paul's genuine thanks for the fellowship of the Philippian saints caused him to pray for their continued spiritual progress. Concern for others should express itself first in prayer, as one recognizes the importance of the divine factor in any lasting spiritual

growth. The basic petition of Paul's prayer is that his readers' love might abound more and more. Love is a fruit of the Spirit (Gal 5:22) that enables all other spiritual virtues to be exercised properly (1 Cor 13:1-3). Without it no Christian is spiritually complete (Col 3:14). No reason appears in the passage to limit this to love for God, for each other, or for Paul. Most likely, it is unrestricted and refers to the continuing demonstration of this spiritual fruit in any and all ways. The Philippians had already displayed their love in generously giving to Paul, but love never reaches the saturation point.

Love must be intelligent and morally discerning, however, if it would be truly *agapē*. What is encouraged here is not a heedless sentiment, but love based on knowledge, the intellectual perception that has recognized principles from the Word of God as illuminated by the Holy Spirit. Spiritual knowledge, gained from an understanding of divine revelation, enables the believer to love what God commands and in the way he reveals. The joining of the expression "depth of insight" to "knowledge" stresses moral perception and the practical application of knowledge to the myriad circumstances of life. Spiritual knowledge is thus no abstraction but is intended to be applied to life. In this instance it will serve to direct the believers' love into avenues both biblically proper and pure.

10 The discerning atmosphere in which their love should operate will require them continually "to discern what is best." Some things are clearly good or bad. In others the demarcation is not so readily visible. In Christian conduct and the exercise of love, such factors as one's influence on others, as well as the effect on oneself, must be considered (1 Cor 10:32). The question should not only be "Is it harmful?" but "Is it helpful?" (1 Cor 10:23).

The goal in view is the day of Christ, in which every believer must stand before his Lord and give an account of his deeds (2 Cor 5:10). This sobering and joyous prospect for the believer should have a purifying effect on his life (1 John 3:3).

11 The conduct that will receive Christ's commendation must be characterized by "the fruit of righteousness." Transformed lives are the demonstration that God works in believers. Paul desires that when his readers stand before Christ, their lives will have been filled with the right kind of fruit. He is not talking about mere human uprightness measured by outward conformity to law (3:9). He is rather speaking of the spiritual fruit that comes from Jesus Christ, produced in them by the Holy Spirit sent by Christ (Gal 5:22). Consequently, all the glory and praise belongs not to believers but to God, for he has redeemed them by the work of his Son and has implanted within them his Spirit to produce the fruit of righteousness. The thought is similar to that in Ephesians 1:6, 12, 14, where Paul says that the entire plan of redemption should result in praise of God's glory.

Notes

9 The compound form ἐπίγνωσις (*epignōsis*, "knowledge") is often used with no discernible difference in meaning from γνῶσις (*gnōsis*) in LXX, the papyri, and the NT. Only when both forms are used in the same context with evident contrast between them is it certain that the slight differences in their connotation are being stressed (cf. Rom 1:21, 28, verb and noun; 1 Cor 13:12, verbs). *Epignōsis* came to be almost a technical term for "the decisive knowledge

of God which is implied in conversion to the Christian faith" (Rudolf Bultmann, *Ginōskō*, TDNT, 1:707). In Phil 1:9 the sense involved is that of thorough and genuine knowledge, but without any attempt to contrast it with something less.

Ἀισθησις (*aisthēsis*, "depth of insight") is part of a word group whose meanings range from sensual perception to intellectual understanding. In LXX it is used mostly for the Hebrew דעת (*da'at*) and is comparable to "wisdom." There is an element of moral discrimination in the term (Prov 1:7). *Aisthēsis* appears only this once in the NT, but the context clearly points to the idea of moral and ethical discernment (1:10). The cognates that occur in Luke 9:45 and Heb 5:14 likewise convey this sense (Gerhard Delling, *Aisthanomai*, et al., TDNT, 1:187, 188).

10 Δοκιμάζειν (*dokimazein*) may mean either "to test" or "to approve after testing"; διαφέρειν (*diapherein*) means "to differ," or "to excel" (i.e., to differ to one's advantage). Hence Paul's statement can be read, "to test the things that differ" (ASV mg.) or "to approve what is excellent" (KJV, ASV, RSV, NASB). Ultimately, the sense in this passage is the same, for the testing of various matters is with the intention of finding the best and performing it.

Although the derivation of εἰλικρινής (*eilikrinēs*) is a matter of disagreement, the most likely explanation traces it to ἥλιος (*hēlios*, "sun") and κρίνω (*krinō*, "judge," "test"). Hence, the meaning is "tested by the light of the sun, completely pure, spotless" (Friedrich Büchsel, *Eilikrinēs*, TDNT, 2:397, 398). The other term in the phrase, ἀπρόσκοποι (*aproskopoi*), may denote either the passive sense of "undamaged" or "blameless," or the active sense of "giving no offense." Probably the former is in view here, as in Acts 24:16.

The tr. "until the day of Christ" uses εἰς (*eis*) in the sense of time (so KJV, Ph, NASB, NIV). Yet it is possible that the apostle's purpose was not to state how long this conduct was to be maintained, but to name the greatest incentive for Christian discerning. Hence, "for" or "with a view to" the day of Christ would then convey this meaning, and is a legitimate handling of *eis*. RSV, NEB, and JB understand the phrase in this way.

11 "Fruit of righteousness" is an OT expression (Amos 6:12); it occurs in NIV as "harvest of righteousness" also in Heb 12:11 and James 3:18. If the genitive δικαιοσύνης (*dikaiosynēs*) is regarded as indicating source, the reference is to imputed righteousness from which practical righteousness is to flow. More likely, it is a genitive of apposition, identifying this fruit as the righteous acts of believers. This usage is similar to the other NT occurrences of the phrase noted above.

I. The Situation of Paul in Rome (1:12-26)

1. *Paul's Circumstances Had Advanced the Gospel in Rome*

1:12-18

> [12]Now I want you to know, brothers, that what has happened to me has really served to advance the gospel. [13]As a result, it has became clear throughout the whole palace guard and to everyone else that I am in chains for Christ. [14]Because of my chains, most of the brothers in the Lord have been encouraged to speak the word of God more courageously and fearlessly.
>
> [15]It is true that some preach Christ out of envy and rivalry, but others out of good will. [16]The latter do so in love, knowing that I am put here for the defense of the gospel. [17]The former preach Christ out of selfish ambition, not sincerely, supposing that they can stir up trouble for me while I am in chains. [18]But what does it matter? The important thing is that in every way, whether from false motives or true, Christ is preached. And because of this I rejoice. Yes, and I will continue to rejoice,

12 "I want you to know" is a variation of a common statement in Paul's letters. It invariably introduces an important assertion and may imply that misunderstanding has

arisen over the matter or that inquiry has been made regarding it. In this instance, the significance of Paul's immediate circumstances was the important matter. On the assumption that the Epistle was written from a Roman imprisonment (see Introduction), Paul is saying that his recent circumstances had not been detrimental but advantageous to the gospel. Verse 12 does not seem to be a reference to his imprisonment, about which previous communication with the Philippians had informed them, but to more recent developments. Perhaps Paul had been moved from his hired house (Acts 28:30) to the Praetorian camp or to some place more accessible to the trial scene. This could easily have been interpreted as bad news, but it had "really served to advance the gospel" in ways to be mentioned subsequently. Paul does not imply that his case has been settled, nor that any official action favoring Christianity had been taken. Nevertheless, his immediate circumstances were to be viewed as a plus for the gospel, not a disaster. The term "to advance" (*prokopēn*) originally denoted making headway in spite of blows and so depicted progress amid difficulties (Gustav Stählin, *Prokopē*, TDNT, 6:704).

13 There were at least two ways in which the gospel had been advanced through Paul's circumstances. The first was that it had been made clear throughout the whole palace guard that Paul's imprisonment was "for Christ." During the first century, prisoners who were sent to Rome from the provinces in cases of appeal were entrusted to the care of the *praefectus praetorio* (F.J. Foakes Jackson and Kirsopp Lake, *The Beginnings of Christianity* [Grand Rapids: Baker Book House, reprint 1966], 5:321, 322). As the guards were assigned in succession to Paul, it soon became clear to them that he was no ordinary captive. The words "for Christ" (*en Christō*) are connected with "clear" (*phanerous*) in the Greek text. Thus Paul was not merely describing his imprisonment as being in the service of Christ ("my chains for Christ"), but was claiming that his relationship to Christ had been made clear to his guards.

The term *praitōriō* ("palace guard") admits of several meanings. In addition to this passage, it is used in the Gospels for Pilate's headquarters in Jerusalem, probably to be identified with the Antonia fortress (Matt 27:27; Mark 15:16; John 18:28 [twice], 33; 19:9). In Acts 23:35 it is used of the Roman governor's headquarters at Caesarea. In Lightfoot's extended note (in loc.) four possibilities are suggested: (1) The emperor's palace in Rome. It may be objected, however, that this term, suggestive of a military despotism, would not likely have been used by Roman citizens for their emperor's residence. Furthermore, no contemporary instance of such use can be cited. (2) The barracks of the praetorian guard attached to the imperial palace. (3) The praetorian camp outside the city wall. These suggestions regard *praitōrion* as a place, but this conflicts with the phrase in 1:13, *kai tois loipois pasin*, literally "and to all the rest," which clearly points to persons. (4) The praetorian guards themselves. This remains the most likely meaning, agreeable to both current usage and to context.

Paul's bold testimony to the gospel of Christ had also been borne "to everyone else" who came to his quarters, including members of the Jewish community (Acts 28:17ff.), at least one Gentile (Philem 10), and many Christian co-workers. Paul was able to get the gospel out from inside prison walls. Instead of falling into self-pity, he took every opportunity to make the gospel known.

14 The second way the gospel had been advanced was that Paul's circumstances had emboldened other Christians in Rome. One might suppose that his imprisonment would have dampened any evangelizing efforts and have caused the believers in Rome to "go underground," but exactly the opposite was true. They drew courage from Paul's example and laid their fears aside. A literal rendering of the clause in the latter part of v.14 is "to a much greater degree they are daring to speak the word of God without fear." That it was "daring" indicates no lessening of the danger but a new infusion of courage. The present tense shows it was no momentary enthusiasm that quickly passed but that it was still the situation as Paul wrote his letter. Surely the apostle's own attitude to his chains must have been largely responsible for these results. If he had become depressed by developments, the effect on others would have been far different. It was Paul's use of the change in his circumstances as a fresh opportunity to spread the Word of God that encouraged the Christians in Rome to do likewise.

15 Not all of the "preachers" in Rome, however, were responding with the highest of motives. Some were proclaiming the message of Christ "out of envy and rivalry." In the light of 1:16, 17, it is clear that their wrong spirit was directed against Paul. Who were these disappointing preachers? Some commentators, like Hendriksen (in loc.), insist that Paul has changed the subject and is no longer speaking of those in 1:14. It has been urged that opponents of Paul (1:15) would not have been reticent to speak out as those of 1:14 had been (Mounce, in loc.). Nevertheless, the most natural way to understand these words is by relating them to 1:14, and to interpret Paul as saying that the newly courageous preachers were of two types. It is not difficult to imagine that even those jealous of Paul could well have been intimidated at first by Paul's imprisonment and have kept quiet to protect themselves.

These opposing preachers have been identified as the Judaizers of 3:1–16 (Lightfoot, pp. 88, 89; Walvoord, *Philippians*; pp. 38, 39). But it is difficult to imagine that Paul would commend such people for speaking "the word of God" (1:14) and then denounce them as "dogs," doers of "evil," and "mutilators of the flesh" (3:2). In Paul's view, Judaizers preached another gospel (Gal 1:6–9). It is more likely that he was referring to a part of the group mentioned in 1:14. They were doctrinally orthodox, but at the same time mean and selfish, using the occasion of Paul's confinement to promote themselves. Because they were envious of Paul, they stirred up discord within the Christian community and hoped to gain a larger following for themselves.

Others, to their credit, were moved by feelings of good will for Paul. Their renewed vigor in proclaiming Christ was a true joining with Paul in the great enterprise of the gospel.

16 These nobler preachers recognized the apostle's sincerity and unselfishness. They realized that his present circumstances were part of a larger divine program and that he had never deviated from it. He had been "put here" (*keimai*), not by his own miscalculations, nor by chance, but by the operation of God's sovereignty. God had brought him to this place and time "for the defense of the gospel." By ways that could never have been foreseen by man alone, God had accomplished within the short space of thirty years the spreading of the gospel of Jesus Christ from its humble beginnings in obscure Judea to its defense before Caesar at the center of the Empire. No doubt it was with some sense of awe that Paul evaluated his situation with the comment, "I am put here." Recognition of the nature of Paul's imprisonment caused many stalwart Christians to respond out of love for him and for the cause he represented. They stepped into the breach and took their stand with him, eager to insure that the gospel did not fail to be proclaimed while Paul was in prison.

17 The former group of preachers (1:15a) were guilty of insincerity, particularly toward

Paul. That they "preach Christ" and that Paul found no fault with the content of their message shows that their problem was not primarily doctrinal but personal. They were not unbelievers or perverters of Christian truth. They were self-seeking opportunists, promoting themselves at Paul's expense. Perhaps they had enjoyed some prominence in the church before he arrived, but had been eclipsed since he came to the city. By taking advantage of Paul's imprisonment, they may have hoped to recover their former popularity. They may have supposed that he would bitterly resent their success (just as they did his) and his imprisonment would become all the more galling to him. If so, they failed to reckon with the greatness of the man.

18 Paul's conclusion, "But what does it matter? . . . ," reveals his sense of values. The importance of the gospel and its proclamation so outweighed any personal considerations that he would not cloud the issue by insisting on settling personal grievances. He was convinced that "Christ is preached" even by these preachers whose motives were suspect. They must have been faithful to the basic message of Christ. They could not have been Judaizers, at least not in the usual sense of that designation. With Paul, to preach "Christ" meant to proclaim the good news of salvation provided freely by God's grace through the redemptive work of Christ and received by men through faith without "works of righteousness" of any kind. It is inconceivable that any Judaizing message with its insistence on performance of Jewish rites would be characterized by Paul as preaching "Christ."

As long as the antagonism was only personal, Paul could rejoice that the greater purpose of disseminating the gospel was being served. Even when some of the preaching was actually a pretext (*prophasei*), utilized to camouflage attacks on Paul, the apostle took the magnanimous view that affronts to himself could be ignored, provided that the truth of the gospel of Christ was proclaimed. He rejoiced in this and intended to maintain this wholesome magnanimity, which rose above all personal feelings.

Although *prophasei* has the sense of pretext, pretense, or "false motives" (NIV), it does not necessarily imply that the antagonistic preachers did not believe what they were preaching, but that their preaching was a pretext to cover other, less-worthy purposes.

Notes

12 The precise formula γινώσκειν δὲ ὑμᾶς βούλομαι (*ginōskein de hymas boulomai*, "Now I want you to know") does not occur again in the NT, but a similar Pauline clause θέλω δὲ ὑμᾶς εἰδέναι (*thelō de hymas eidenai*) appears in 1 Cor 11:3 and Col 2:1, and the negative statement οὐ θέλω δὲ ὑμᾶς ἀγνοεῖν (*ou thelō de hymas agnoein*, "I do not want you to be ignorant") occurs in Rom 1:13; 11:25; 1 Cor 10:1; 12:1; 2 Cor 1:8; and 1 Thess 4:13.

14 The words ἐν κυρίῳ (*en kyriō*, "in the Lord") may be understood either with the preceding phrase τῶν ἀδελφῶν (*tōn adelphōn*, "of the brothers") or the following πεποιθότας (*pepoithotas*, "being confident"). Construing it with the former has led to the objection that "the brethren in the Lord" is a redundancy and has no parallel in the NT (Lightfoot, p. 88). However, there is no more incongruity with this expression than with the reference to ἀδελφοῖς ἐν Χριστῷ (*adelphois en Christō*, "brothers in Christ") in Col 1:2. It is true that "being confident in the Lord" is common Pauline terminology (Rom 14:14; Gal 5:10; Phil 2:24; 2 Thess 3:4), but in every instance *en kyriō* follows rather than precedes the form of πείθω (*peithō*, "to be confident") on which it depends. It is best, therefore, to treat the expression as referring to "the brethren in the Lord," that is, fellow Christians.

Textual variation occurs at 1:14—λόγον τοῦ θεοῦ λαλεῖν (logon tou theou lalein, "to speak the word of God"). The Byzantine text-type, supported in this instance by P[46], omits τοῦ θεοῦ (tou theou, "of God"). The longer reading is supported by א A B P, as well as by early witnesses among the ancient versions. The sense is not materially affected, for with either reading the reference is to the Word of God.

15-17 NIV accords with RV, ASV, RSV, NEB, and NASB, along with the Gr. texts of WH, Nestle, and UBS, in preserving the chiasma of 1:15-17. KJV, however, follows the TR and transposes vv.16 and 17, presumably to keep the sequence parallel with v.15. But the literary structure of chiasma (in which in a series of four items, item one is paired with item four, and two is paired with three) appears elsewhere in the NT (e.g., Philem 5). Of course, the ultimate sense of the passage is the same, regardless of the sequence:

The word ἐριθείας (eritheias) in v.17 was apparently thought to be derived from ἔρις (eris, "strife") by the translators of KJV, and thus rendered "contention." However, the term is distinguished from eris in 2 Cor 12:20 and Gal 5:20. It is more likely, therefore, that it is related to ἐριθεύω (eritheuō, "to work as a day-laborer") and ἔριθος (erithos, "a day-laborer"). The development of its meaning as "self-seeking" or "selfish ambition" reflects aristocratic disdain for one who had to earn his daily living instead of being free to donate his services as one of the nobility (Friedrich Büchsel, Eritheia, TDNT, 2:660, 661). The meaning "selfish ambition" fits well the six other NT uses of ἐριθεία (Rom 2:8; 2 Cor 12:20; Gal 5:20; Phil 2:3; James 3:14, 16).

18 The expression τί γάρ (ti gar) is elliptical and conveys such ideas as "what, then [is the situation]?" or "what does it matter?" (NIV) or "what business is it of mine?" See Rom 3:3; 1 Cor 5:12. (BAG, p. 827.) The elliptical statement continues with πλὴν ... ὅτι (plēn ... hoti), which grammatically introduces the clause beginning with Χριστός (Christos) and indicates the important issue in response to the rhetorical question posed by ti gar.

The employment of ἀλλά (alla; NIV, "yes") to join the two clauses stating Paul's rejoicing illustrates the emphatic use of ἀλλά with the sense of "certainly," "indeed," or "in fact" (H.E. Dana and J.R. Mantey, A Manual Grammar of the Greek New Testament [New York: Macmillan, 1946], pp. 240, 241). Whether the clauses should be separated by a full stop, with the second clause regarded as introductory to v.19 (RSV, NEB, NIV), or treated as part of the same statement and both as properly a part of v.18 (KJV, ASV, NASB) is of minor consequence. All will agree that a transition is being made at this point, and the transitional statement at the close of v.18 serves so well to tie both parts together that the exact point of the division is open to debate.

---

2. Paul's Circumstances Would Turn Out for Salvation

1:19-26

> [19]for I know that through your prayers and the help given by the Spirit of Jesus Christ, what has happened to me will turn out for my deliverance. [20]I eagerly expect and hope that I will in no way be ashamed, but will have sufficient courage so that now as always Christ will be exalted in my body, whether by life or by death. [21]For to me, to live is Christ and to die is gain. [22]If I am to go on living in the body, this will mean fruitful labor for me. Yet, what shall I choose? I do not know! [23]I am torn between the two: I desire to depart and be with Christ, which is better by far; [24]but it is more necessary for you that I remain in the body. [25]Convinced of this, I know that I will remain, and I will continue with all of you for your progress and joy in the faith, [26]so that through my being with you again your joy in Christ Jesus will overflow on account of me.

19 Paul moves to the second encouraging aspect of his present situation in Rome, which was the prospect it held for his "deliverance" (sōtērian). Is this a reference to deliver-

ance from his present imprisonment? It is true that Paul expressed confidence of release in 1:25 and 2:24, but the immediate context puts the "deliverance" as somewhat apart from either life or death (1:21), and the inner struggle described in 1:22–24 makes it questionable whether he would have stated the anticipated result of his Roman trial with this sort of certainty. The other possibility is to treat "deliverance" in the sense of spiritual salvation. Paul viewed salvation as having several aspects—past (Eph 2:8), present (Phil 2:12), and future (Rom 13:11). Here the present and future aspects may be fused into one as the apostle looks to the unfolding of his Christian life and his ultimate hope of standing unashamed both before human judges and before his Lord (cf. v.20).

Paul viewed his deliverance as being accomplished by two means. The first was the effective prayers of the Philippians on his behalf. The second was the support furnished by the Holy Spirit, who is here called "the Spirit of Jesus Christ." These two means were not necessarily unrelated, inasmuch as Paul may have regarded the Philippians' prayers as being answered by the Spirit's increased activity on his behalf.

20 If we interpret "deliverance" in the broadest sense, we understand Paul to say that regardless of the outcome of his immediate physical circumstances, he has every reason to expect spiritual victory to be his. In the Greek text "eagerly expect" and "hope" are nouns, not verbs, and are grammatically joined so as to indicate that they are aspects of a single concept. The noun *apokaradokia* is made up of *kara* ("head") and *dechomai* ("to take," or perhaps originally, "to stretch"). The term denotes "stretching the head forward" (Gerhard Delling, *Apokaradokia*, TDNT, 1:393). The prefix *apo* may suggest looking away with concentration, ignoring other interests (Kennedy, in loc.). Only in Christian literature is the term found, and not earlier than Paul. The only other NT use is in Romans 8:19. The term is linked with *elpis* ("hope") by the use of one article and *kai* ("and"), thus implying an inner connection. Delling states that *elpis* denotes "well-founded hope" and *apokaradokia* means "unreserved waiting" (TDNT, 3:393).

In this time of waiting for the settlement of his case, Paul had a well-founded hope that he would "in no way be ashamed." This is a broad statement referring first to his appearance before the authorities for the final disposition of his case. There may also be overtones of his ultimate appearance before Christ, because he speaks of the possibility of death and of the advantage of being with Christ. He has the confident hope that he will continue to maintain the sort of courage characteristic of his ministry in the past.

The expression *en pasē parrēsia* ("sufficient courage," NIV) conveys the thought of openness, courage, boldness, or confidence, whether toward God or people. Prominent are instances in which this quality is viewed in relation to speech. In 1:20 Paul may be thinking in terms of his coming testimony before his imperial judges. It would not be as easy to give a courageous witness in those circumstances, apart from the help of the Holy Spirit.

Paul wants Christ "to be exalted," regardless of whether "life" (physical) or "death" would be the verdict on his "body." The passive voice of the verb "to be exalted" (*megalunthēsetai*) should be noted. Paul did not say, "I will exalt Christ," but "Christ will be exalted in my body." The apostle was not relying on his own courage, but on the action of the Holy Spirit who would produce this result in response to the prayers of Paul and the Philippians (1:19).

21 "For to me" is placed in the emphatic position, stressing the fact that Paul's own faith was unshaken, regardless of the circumstances. No adverse decision from the court nor the alarm of his friends could alter his firm belief about his present or his future. "To live is Christ." The very essence of Paul's present life was Christ and all that this entailed. From the theological fact that Paul was identified with Christ in a vital spiritual union (Gal 2:20) issued far-reaching practical implications. Christ had become for him the motive of his actions, the goal of his life and ministry, the source of his strength. "To die" after such a life could only mean "gain." Not only would Paul's state after death bring gain, inasmuch as he would be with Christ (1:23), but the act itself of dying at the hands of Rome was no tragedy in Paul's eyes. Such a death would bear added witness to the gospel; it would confirm that Paul's faith was steadfast to the end and it would serve as the gateway to Christ's presence.

22 Nevertheless, if he should continue to live as a result of a favorable disposition of his case in Rome, this would provide continued opportunity for him to labor fruitfully in the cause of Christ. For Paul this never meant an easy life. His labors in establishing churches and nurturing them toward maturity were characterized by frequent opposition, physical hardships, and much spiritual anguish. Yet he looked on his apostolic ministry as a challenge to be grasped and as fruit to be harvested. (The same metaphor appears in Rom 1:13.)

"To go on living in the body" employs *sarki* ("flesh") rather than *sōmati* ("body"). Although this may be merely a synonym employed for literary variety inasmuch as *sōmati* was used in 1:20, it may also have been adopted to convey the thought of the earthly, physical sphere with its limitations and weaknesses.

When the verb *haireomai* occurs in the NT, it is used exclusively in the middle voice with the sense of "choose" or "prefer." The term is used of the election of believers by God (2 Thess 2:13) and of the choice by Moses in aligning himself with his own people (Heb 11:25). In Philippians 1:22 it does not mean that Paul literally had the prerogative of choosing his fate, but it is a reference to his personal preference.

The verb *gnōrizō* ("know," NIV) means "to make known" in each of its other twenty-four NT occurrences (including seventeen other uses by Paul), and the presumption is strong in favor of its having this sense here. Thus, the meaning would be "I cannot tell" or "I cannot declare [to you]." The meaning "to know" does occur in the papyri and LXX, however, and so is a possibility for 1:22 (Rudolf Bultmann, *Gnōrizō*, TDNT, 1:718).

Paul was so positively committed to the will of God that both life and death held certain attractions. If the choice were left to him, he would not know what to decide. How fortunate that God does not force us to make such choices!

23 As Paul thought of his prospects, he felt himself in a dilemma, though in his case either alternative was a good one. The two possibilities were continued life or sudden death inflicted by Rome. "I am torn" suggests the divided nature of his thinking about this matter. The Greek word (*sunechomai*) depicts a person or object held under pressure from two sides so that movement in either direction is difficult or impossible ("I am hard pressed," NASB; "I am in a strait," KJV).

The basic sense of *sunechō* is "to hold something together" (Helmut Köster, *Sunechō*, TDNT, 7:877). Of its twelve NT uses, two are by Paul, nine are by Luke (including Acts), and one is in Matthew. The term is sometimes used of diseases that are viewed as seizing, gripping, or controlling their victims. It also depicts someone occupied with or absorbed in something (Acts 18:5). In the present instance, the idea of distress may be present, as in the cases where the word is used in reference to diseases (cf. Luke 4:38).

From the standpoint of what would be an advantage for him, he had the desire to leave this life and be with Christ. Death for him would be a departure (*analusai*) from his

23

present state, like the release of a prisoner from his bonds (Acts 16:26, *analuthē* [ℵ D]) or the departure of a guest from a wedding feast (Luke 12:36, *analusē*). It would be no catastrophe, since it would cause Paul to "be with Christ." He foresaw no soul-sleep while awaiting the resurrection, nor any purgatory. As he had already explained to the Corinthians, absence from the body means for the believer immediate presence with the Lord (2 Cor 5:8). There was no question in Paul's mind as to the ultimate superiority of this. It was "better by far" (*pollō mallon kreisson*), because it would bring him to the goal of his Christian life (3:8-14). It would bring rest from his labors (Rev 14:13) and the joy of eternal fellowship in the very presence of the Lord whom he loved.

24 Yet the apostle also recognized another standpoint from which his future might be viewed. His remaining alive would offer a certain advantage to his Philippian readers. He does not state specifically what this advantage was but the obvious reference is to the ministry he might still perform for them.

25 Paul was confident that his situation was in the Lord's hands (1:19-24) and that what occurred would bring glory to God, regardless of the specific turn it might take. Furthermore, his confidence now prompted him to say, "I know that I will remain." What was the basis of this confidence? Was it the result of a favorable development in the legal proceedings, or of a special revelation from God? Against the idea of a new legal development is the necessity of supposing some sort of break between this verse and those immediately preceding, during which fresh information came to Paul. Yet no hint appears of such a momentous happening. The word "know" (*oida*) cannot be pressed to mean infallible knowledge and it is doubtful whether Paul would have spoken as he did in 1:20-24 if he knew by prophetic inspiration that he would be set free. It is far more likely that the statement represents his personal conviction based on what seemed to be probable in the light of all the factors. The need of many for his apostolic ministry outweighed his own need to be with Christ immediately. Furthermore, he must have known that the case against him was not strong (Acts 23:29; 25:25; 26:31, 32), and thus his hope of release was well-founded. Nevertheless, because likelihood of release was only personal conviction, he makes allowance in his previous explanation for the possibility that things might turn out adversely. Evidence from the pastoral Epistles, confirmed by considerable early historical testimony, indicates that Paul was released from this first Roman imprisonment and had opportunity for travel, including a trip through Macedonia (and presumably Philippi), before being reimprisoned and suffering a martyr's death.

That "know" (*oida*) does not mean infallible knowledge is well indicated by comparison with another Pauline use of it in Acts 20:25, as Lightfoot has pointed out. If both instances demand certainty of knowledge, one of them failed of fulfillment, for Acts 20:25 says Paul "knew" he would not see the Ephesian elders again because of his approaching capture. Yet Philippians 1:25 indicates that he "knew" he would be released from that imprisonment (p. 94). The hypothesis of two Roman imprisonments with a period of freedom between them in which he visited both Ephesus and Macedonia is supported by 1 Timothy 1:3 and other passages in the pastoral Epistles. Among the early Fathers, considerable testimony is found for Paul's release from the first Roman imprisonment (Clement of Rome, *First Epistle to the Corinthians*, ch. 5; Muratorian Canon; Eusebius, *Ecclesiastical History*, II.22).

Paul's continued ministry among the Philippians would be aimed at advancing their spiritual growth and deepening their joy in the Christian faith. The believers' experience should not be static but characterized by a growing understanding of spiritual truth. This in turn would increase their joy as they entered more fully into the understanding of their privileges and prospects in Christ.

26 The "joy" in Paul's thought here was their "ground for boasting or glorying" (*kauchēma*). The emphasis is not on the action itself, but on the basis for it. As the Philippians would experience the progress and joy that Paul's labors among them would produce, they would have new and greater reasons for overflowing (*perisseuē*) with joy. This reason for glorying would be found "in Christ Jesus," of course, but its immediate occasion would be "on account of me" (*en emoi*), said Paul. His ministry among them would enable them to see more clearly the riches of their salvation in Christ.

Notes

19 The wording τοῦτό μοι ἀποβήσεται εἰς σωτηρίαν (*touto moi apobēsetai eis sōtērian*, "this will result in my salvation") is exactly the same as Job 13:16 (LXX). There Job was responding to his accusers by stating that he would be vindicated when he would ultimately stand before God. Paul may have used this language not only because the wording was appropriate for his purposes, but also because the context of ultimate vindication before God was also relevant.

The genitive τοῦ πνεύματος (*tou pneumatos*, "of the Spirit") is probably subjective here, though in this instance both subjective and objective aspects are intertwined and indistinguishable from a practical standpoint. The Spirit would help Paul successfully face these unpleasant experiences and accomplish God's will in his life. By referring to the Spirit as τοῦ πνεύματος Ἰησοῦ Χριστοῦ (*tou pneumatos Iēsou Christou*, "the Spirit of Jesus Christ"), Paul reflects the fact that the Holy Spirit has been bestowed on men by Christ as well as by the Father (John 15:26).

21 The two infinitive phrases are in the present tense: τὸ ζῆν (*to zēn*, "to live"), and the aorist: τὸ ἀποθανεῖν (*to apothanein*, "to die"). The former understandably stresses the progressive nature of living. The aorist looks simply at the fact of dying. It is difficult to see Lightfoot's grammatical justification for stating (p. 92), "The tense denotes not the act of dying but the consequence of dying, the state after death." Such an idea would have been better conveyed by the perfect tense. The aorist names the act in the simplest possible way. Anything more must be drawn from the context. It is best to regard the expression as Paul's reference to his possible death at the hands of Rome. Any connotation of the state after death must be inferred from the mention of "gain," not the tense of ἀποθανεῖν (*apothanein*, "to die").

23 "Better by far" utilizes a triple comparative πολλῷ μᾶλλον κρεῖσσον (*pollō mallon kreisson*), found nowhere else in the NT in this precise form. It employs the comparative form of the adjective κρατύς (*kratys*, "more excellent"), which is commonly used as the comparative of ἀγαθός (*agathos*, "good"), the comparative adverb μᾶλλον (*mallon*, "to a greater extent"), and the dative adjective πολλῷ (*pollō*, "much") used adverbially.

24 The use of τῇ σαρκί (*tē sarki*, "in the flesh") is in the physical sense and as such is virtually synonymous with σῶμα (*sōma*, "body"), as in 1:22. The ethical sense in which this term is sometimes used by Paul to denote the sinful nature of man is not involved here.

25 The verbs μενῶ (*menō*) and παραμενῶ (*paramenō*) convey the idea of remaining, the former in the general sense of "remain alive," and the latter more specifically "to remain with you." Hauck suggests that παραμενῶ (*paramenō*) means "to stay with someone ... with a hint of service" (F. Hauck, *Menō*, et al., TDNT, 4:578).

26 The noun καύχημα (*kauchēma*, "joy") is found in the NT only in the Pauline Epistles and Hebrews. In all cases it denotes either the grounds or cause for boasting (i.e., the thing of which

one is proud), or the content of one's boasting. A cognate καύχησις (*kauchēsis*) depicts the action of boasting. (Rudolf Bultmann, *Kauchaomai*, TDNT, 3:648, 649.)

II. First Series of Exhortations (1:27–2:18)

1. *Exhortation to Unity and Courage in View of External Foes*

1:27–30

> 27Whatever happens, conduct yourselves in a manner worthy of the gospel of Christ. Then, whether I come and see you or only hear about you in my absence, I will know that you stand firm in one spirit, contending as one man for the faith of the gospel 28without being frightened in any way by those who oppose you. This is a sign to them that they will be destroyed, but that you will be saved—and that by God. 29For it has been granted to you on behalf of Christ not only to believe on him, but also to suffer for him, 30since you are going through the same struggle you saw I had, and now hear that I still have.

27 As citizens of a spiritual realm, the Philippians should stand firm in one spirit. This should be true "whatever happens" to Paul, for the responsibility for their spiritual growth rested ultimately with them and their appropriation of the riches in Christ. Whether Paul would be released and thus enabled to visit them in person, or be forced to remain away from them and learn of their progress through the reports of others, his exhortation was the same. They must conduct their lives in a manner appropriate to the gospel of Christ.

In this connection, Paul used a verb that meant literally "to live as a citizen" (*politeues-the*). Although none of its NT uses relate to the political side of life in society as such, it was an apt term for a letter written to a church in a city whose inhabitants were proud of their status as Roman citizens (Acts 16:12, 20, 21). The earliest members of the Philippian church would have known that Paul had used his Roman citizenship to bring about a speedy and dignified release from imprisonment there (Acts 16:36–40). Out of this cultural background the readers were challenged to live as those who had a higher and vastly more significant citizenship (Phil 3:20).

The readers are urged to "stand firm in one spirit." It is possible to regard "spirit" as a reference to the Holy Spirit (Eph 4:3), but the explanatory phrase "as one man" (*miā psychē*, "with one soul") strongly suggests that both are descriptions of Christian unity of thought and action, similar to the expression in Acts 4:32, "of one heart and of one soul." Of course, true unity must be produced by the Holy Spirit; however, the source is not what is stressed here, but the result. It is doubtful whether Paul was trying to draw sharp psychological distinctions between these terms. If such are to be sought to any degree, the former term (*pneumati*) probably denotes man's highest center of motivation, and for the Christian this would be quickened by the Holy Spirit. The latter term (*psychē*) would denote the area of sensory experience.

This exhortation to unified thought and action has in view the goal of contending "for the faith of the gospel." The reference is to the objective faith (i.e., the body of truth) embodied in the gospel message. They are to be "contending" for it, a positive statement of their need to promote and protect the message of Christ, while at the same time implying that adversaries must be faced. The use of the compound form *synathlountes* ("contending together") conveys the need for joint effort. The athletic metaphor of teamwork reinforces the previous references to "one spirit" and "one soul," and is a reminder that a unified effort is needed if they are to be victorious in the contest.

28 Paul does not want the Philippians to be terrified in any respect by their opponents. The noble character of their cause and the recognition that Christ is on their side should cause believers to avoid the unreasoning terror that prevents intelligent effort. Who were these opponents? Some have insisted that the reference could not have been to Jews because the Jewish population of Philippi was too small (Lenski, p. 755). This ignores the fact that hostile Jews often dogged Paul's steps and caused trouble in the churches he founded. Such was the case in other Macedonian churches (Thessalonica: Acts 17:5; Berea: Acts 17:13). In the light of Paul's discussion in 3:2–6, it seems clear that Jewish hostility was present. But there is nothing in 1:28 that restricts the reference to Jewish opponents. What is virtually certain is that these were external foes, not false teachers within the church. It is most likely that Paul was speaking generally of adversaries of the church of whatever kind. Whether Jewish or pagan, they usually employed the same tactics, and the need for unity and courage among the believers was crucial.

Failure of the church to be intimidated by enemies was a token of the ultimate failure of the enemies of God. The adversaries may not have recognized this, but it was nonetheless a sign that their attacks were futile and that the church would prevail. This sign or token was intended for the adversaries (not to the adversaries *and* the believers, as the rendering in KJV based on an inferior textual reading suggests), but it was a sign to them of two things: their ultimate destruction and the salvation of the believers. "And that by God" refers grammatically neither to "salvation" nor to "sign" (both of which are feminine nouns, for which the feminine form of "that" would be required, rather than the neuter, which was used), but to the entire fact that believers have been granted courage from God to stand firm in their struggles and so are demonstrating their salvation.

29 The whole situation was part of God's gracious provision for those enlisted in the cause of Christ. The privileges enjoyed by Christians included the ability not only to believe in Christ initially at regeneration and subsequently throughout the Christian life, but also to suffer for him. If we question the propriety of referring to suffering as a privilege and a "gracious gift" (*echaristhē*), we must remember that the NT regards suffering as God's means of achieving his gracious purposes both in his own Son (Heb 2:10) and in all believers (James 1:3, 4; 1 Peter 1:6, 7).

30 In this matter of suffering, the Philippians were experiencing the same sort of struggle Paul had endured throughout his ministry. They had seen some of Paul's sufferings when he had been in Philippi (Acts 16:19–24). They had heard of others he had undergone more recently in Rome (perhaps from reports of travelers or other messengers, including those who conveyed the information about Epaphroditus, 2:26).

In Hellenistic usage *agōn* ("struggle," NIV) originally meant a place of assembly, then a place where athletic contests were held, and later the contest itself. The term also developed a metaphorical use for any kind of conflict. Ethelbert Stauffer has shown the various motifs in which the term appears in the NT. In Philippians 1:28 the thought of "antagonists" appears, and this is consistent with the idea expressed elsewhere of the obstacles, dangers, and even catastrophes that the Christian may face (E. Stauffer, *Agōn*, TDNT, 1:134–140).

27

Notes

27 The verb πολιτεύομαι (politeuomai, "to conduct oneself ") occurs twice in the NT (Acts 23:1; Phil 1:27). Strathmann shows how the term had been influenced by Hellenistic Judaism and denotes a life shaped by religion (Hermann Strathmann, *Polis*, et al., TDNT, 6:534, 535). The cognate πολίτευμα (politeuma, "citizenship") in 3:20 makes it clear that the citizenship Paul had in mind was not Roman but heavenly.

The εἴτε ... εἴτε (eite ... eite, "whether ... or") construction is somewhat irregular. One would have expected ἀκούων (akouōn, "hearing") or ἀκούσας (akousas, "having heard") following ἀπὼν (apōn, "being absent"), and then a finite verb such as μανθάνω (manthanō, "I understand"). Yet Paul's meaning is not obscured. Whether he comes and sees for himself or is absent and only hears reports, the results, he hopes, will be the same—viz., that his readers are standing firm.

28 The passive participle πτυρόμενοι (ptyromenoi) is from πτύρω (ptyrō), which occurs only here in the NT. It means "to frighten" or "terrify" and was used in referring to the terror of a startled horse (M.R. Vincent, *Word Studies in the New Testament* [Grand Rapids: Eerdmans, reprinted 1946], 3:427). Diodorus Siculus used it when he wrote about the frightened chariot-horses of Darius at the battle of Issus (17:34).

Various forms of ἀντίκειμαι (antikeimai, "to oppose") are used in the NT to denote opposers of the Christian faith, including opponents of Jesus (Luke 13:17), as well as adversaries of the church, both Jewish and Gentile (1 Cor 16:9; 2 Thess 2:4; 1 Tim 5:14).

The words ἀπωλείας (apōleias, "of destruction") and σωτηρίας (sōtērias, "of salvation") are used in obvious contrast. Ἀπώλεια (apōleia) is the regular NT term for eternal destruction and is so used in the Synoptics (Matt 7:13), Paul (Rom 9:22), Peter (2 Peter 2:1, 3), and John (John 17:12). "What is meant is not a simple extinction of existence ... but an everlasting state of torment and death" (Albrecht Oepke, *Apōleia*, TDNT, 1:397). This sense is made all the more certain by the contrasting parallel in the verse with σωτηρία (sōtēria), which surely refers here to the spiritual state of believers.

29 The article τὸ (to) with ὑπὲρ Χριστοῦ (hyper Christou) makes a substantive of the phrase, thus: "this matter for the sake of Christ." The two occurrences of ὑπέρ (hyper) in this verse are with the sense of "on behalf of," "for the sake of," or "because of," denoting the moving cause or reason (BAG, p. 846. 1.d).

30 The nominative participle ἔχοντες (echontes, "having") is apparently dependent on πολιτεύεσθε (politeuesthe, "conduct yourselves") or στήκετε (stēkete, "you stand") in 1:27. The only objection to this explanation is the rather considerable distance involved. However, the thought of contending in the struggle resumes the concept of conducting their lives, and the grammar is regular. The alternative is to treat *echontes* as an anacoluthon or as an independent nominative.

2. Exhortation to Unity and Humility Toward Those in the Church

2:1-11

¹If you have any encouragement from being united with Christ, if any comfort from his love, if any fellowship with the Spirit, if any tenderness and compassion, ²then make my joy complete by being like-minded, having the same love, being one in spirit and purpose. ³Do nothing out of selfish ambition or vain conceit, but in humility consider others better than yourselves. ⁴Each of you should look not only to your own interests, but also to the interests of others.

⁵Your attitude should be the same as that of Christ Jesus:

6Who, being in very nature God,
did not consider equality with God
something to be grasped,
7but made himself nothing,
taking the very nature of a servant,
being made in human likeness.
8And being found in appearance as a man,
he humbled himself
and became obedient to death—
even death on a cross!
9Therefore God exalted him to the highest place
and gave him the name that is above every name,
10that at the name of Jesus every knee should bow,
in heaven and on earth and under the earth,
11and every tongue confess that Jesus Christ is Lord,
to the glory of God the Father.

1 The following exhortation also concerns unity, but this time the focus is turned on problems within the church. To encourage the fulfillment of this injunction, Paul listed four incentives. All are stated as "if " clauses (with the verb understood), but the condition is assumed to be true. Thus, the sense of the first clause is "If there are any grounds for exhortation because you are in Christ, as indeed there are . . . ." As Christians, they were in a vital union with Christ and this placed obvious obligations on them. They were responsible to heed the orders of Christ as issued by him either directly during his ministry or through his apostles. Second, the comfort and encouragement provided by love should prompt the Philippians to join hands in common action. Their love for Christ and for their fellow believers (including Paul) ought to impel them to desist from divisiveness in any form. Third, the fellowship produced by the Holy Spirit should stimulate the practical exercise of unity. They have been made one by the Spirit (cf. 1 Cor 12:13) and thus are partners with him and with each other. Recognition of this theological truth would find expression in their lives. Fourth, the existence of tenderness and compassion among them would make the unity that was being called for the normal and expected thing.

Paraklēsis ("encouragement," NIV) may be translated as either "exhortation" or "consolation." To understand the term in this context as implying more than just comfort is consistent with other Pauline statements on unity. In Ephesians 4:1-3 the unity of the believers is made the subject of an exhortation. The translation "encouragement" can convey both ideas.

In the third of the conditional statements in this verse, pneumatos ("Spirit") can be either objective or subjective. If objective, the sense is "fellowship with the Spirit," as reflected in RSV and NIV and supported by scholars such as Martin (Epistle of Paul to the Philippians, pp. 48, 49, 91). Others, such as Beare and Hendriksen, understand the expression more broadly to include both aspects—the participation in the Spirit and the common life produced by the Spirit to form the Christian community (Beare, in loc.; Hendriksen, p. 98 n.). That the subjective aspect ("fellowship produced by the Spirit") should be included in the concept is strongly suggested by two of the other clauses, in which the exhortation comes from their being in Christ, and their comfort comes from love.

2 The exhortation itself is first stated and then elaborated on. Paul exhorted the Philip-

pians to make his joy full by minding the same thing. He was already experiencing joy because of his associations with this church (1:3, 4; 4:10), but one thing was yet needed to make his joy "complete" (*plērōsate*). They needed to be "like-minded" (literally, "mind the same thing"). Of course, this was not a command for unity at the expense of truth. It assumes that "the same thing" is also "the right thing."

The enjoinder to maintain unity in their thought and action is elaborated on in four participial phrases. By complying with these instructions, the readers would create a climate where true unity would flourish. First, they should be possessing a mutual love. Inasmuch as it is assumed that all were believers indwelt by the same Spirit (2:1), the love that is the fruit of the Spirit (Gal 5:22) ought to be demonstrated in every life. Second, they should be setting their minds on unity with oneness of soul. This phrase repeats the thought appearing earlier in the verse and reinforces the conclusion that there was a problem of disharmony within the congregation. It may be unfair to center the problem on Euodia and Syntyche (4:2), but they were at least involved.

3 Third, they should avoid selfish ambition and conceit and consider others above themselves. Paul had experienced adverse effects from this sort of selfish ambition among some unworthy preachers at Rome (1:17). Persons who seek to advance themselves usually enjoy glorying in their success, but all such glory is "vain conceit" (*kenodoxian*). The Christian attitude should reveal itself in "humility" (*tē tapeinophrosunē*). This concept was not highly regarded in Greek literature. Grundmann observes that the Greek concept of a free man led to contempt for any sort of subjection, whereas the Bible proposes that we should be controlled by God and thus assumes that to subject ourselves to God is praiseworthy (Walter Grundmann, *Tapeinos*, et al., TDNT, 8:11, 12). This paved the way for the Christian ethic that calls for believers to be humble toward one another, mindful of their spiritual brotherhood and their ultimate subjection to Christ. In the exercise of humility, Paul instructed his readers to "consider others better than yourselves." This does not mean that we must have false or unrealistic views of our own gifts as compared with those of others. Moral superiority is not in view. What Paul means is that our consideration for others must precede concern for ourselves (Rom 12:10). This will go far toward removing disharmony.

4 Fourth, they should be looking not only to their own interests but also to those of others. The self-centeredness that considers only one's own rights, plans, and interests must be replaced by a broader outlook that includes the interests of one's fellows. "But also" indicates that our own affairs need not be totally ignored, but that the interests of others must also form a part of our concern. The believer should not neglect the welfare of himself and his family (1 Tim 5:8) in order to involve himself in the good of others. What Paul is calling for is a Christian concern that is wide enough to include others in its scope. When each member of the Christian community exercises this mutual concern, problems of disunity quickly disappear.

5 The great example of humility is Christ Jesus. Although verses 5 to 11 contain one of the outstanding Christologies in the NT, they were written to illustrate the point of humility and selflessness. Another instance where Paul makes a sublime statement about Christ almost incidentally in illustrating a practical point is Ephesians 5:25-27.

The literary form of the beautiful passage before us leads many to regard it as an early Christian hymn that Paul incorporated into his Epistle (see Introduction, 5). But Paul himself was quite capable of a highly poetic style (cf. 1 Cor 13), and may well have composed these exalted lines. Regardless of their precise origin, the passage provides a masterly statement of Christology, and serves well the author's purpose of illustrating supreme condescension.

The exhortation comes first: "Your attitude should be the same as that of Christ Jesus." Here the Greek text could be literally rendered "Keep thinking this among you, which [attitude] was also in Christ Jesus." This rendering fits the context better than another suggestion that has been offered: "Have the same thoughts among yourselves as you have in your communion with Christ Jesus" (BAG, p. 874). Believers, of course, cannot duplicate the precise ministry of Jesus but they can display the same attitude.

6 Christ's preincarnate status is then stated. Two assertions are made: He existed in the form of God and he did not regard his existing in a manner of equality with God as a prize to be grasped or held onto. "Being in very nature God" is, literally, "existing in the form of God." The term *morphē* denotes the outward manifestation that corresponds to the essence, in contrast to the noun *schēma* (2:7), which refers to the outward appearance, which may be temporary.

The participle *hyparchōn* ("being" [NIV], in the sense of "existing") is in the present tense and states Christ's continuing condition. To say that he was existing in the essential metaphysical form of God is tantamount to saying that he possessed the nature of God. The phrase is elaborated on by the words "equality with God" (*isa theō*). It should be noted that *isa* is an adverb (not the substantive *ison*), and hence describes the manner of existence. This does not need to be regarded as precisely the same as "the form of God," for one's essential nature can remain unchanged, though the manner in which that nature is expressed can vary greatly through changing times and circumstances.

The noun *harpagmon* ("something to be grasped") has been variously interpreted. Does it mean something that has been seized, or something to be seized? This uncertainty has led to three possibilities: (1) The preincarnate Christ already possessed equality with the Father and resolved not to cling to it. (2) Christ had no need to grasp at equality with God, for he already possessed it. (3) Christ did not reach for his crowning prematurely, as Adam had, but was willing to wait till after his suffering.

Understanding that *harpagmos* can be used passively in the same sense as *harpagma* to mean "prize," the interpreter must look to the context for guidance. That the preexistent state is in view seems evident from the movement of the passage (see also the parallel at 2 Cor 8:9). Inasmuch as he already existed in "the form of God," the mode of his existence as equal with God was hardly something totally future and thus as yet unexperienced but must rather be something he divested himself of. Hence, view 3 above does not fit the context so well as view 1. View 2, though expressing a truth, does not provide an adequate basis for the statements that follow.

7 The description then moves to Christ's incarnate state. Two clauses carry the main thoughts: "[he] made himself nothing" and "he humbled himself " (v.8). The first clause is literally "but himself he emptied"; it uses a verb (*ekēnosen*) that has lent its name to the so-called "kenosis" theories that probe the nature of Christ's "emptying" himself. Although the text does not directly state that Christ emptied himself "of something," such would be the natural understanding when this verb is used. Furthermore, the context has most assuredly prepared the reader for understanding that Christ divested himself of something. What it was the following phrases imply.

The one who was existing in the form of God took on the form of a servant. The word "taking" (*labōn*) does not imply an exchange, but rather an addition. The "form of God" could not be relinquished, for God cannot cease to be God; but our Lord could and did take on the very form of a lowly servant when he entered human life by the Incarnation. It is sometimes suggested that the term "servant" refers to the exalted Servant of Jehovah, but this passage seems intended to emphasize his condescension and humble station. What an example our Lord provides of the spirit of humility (cf. 2:3–5)! Inasmuch as angels also are servants, the statement makes it clear that Christ became part of humanity: "being made in human likeness." The word "likeness" (homoiōmati) does not bear the connotation of exactness as does eikōn, or of intrinsic form as does morphē. It stresses similarity but leaves room for differences. Thus Paul implies that even though Christ became a genuine man, there were certain respects in which he was not absolutely like the other men. (He may have had in mind the unique union of the divine and human natures in Jesus, or the absence of a sinful nature.)

In summation, Christ did not empty himself of the form of God (i.e., his deity), but of the manner of existence as equal to God. He did not lay aside the divine attributes, but "the insignia of majesty" (Lightfoot, p. 112). Mark Twain's novel The Prince and the Pauper, describing a son of Henry VIII who temporarily changed positions with a poor boy in London, provides an illustration. Christ's action has been described as the laying aside during the incarnation of the independent use of his divine attributes (A.J. McClain, "The Doctrine of the Kenosis in Philippians 2:5–8," Grace Journal, vol. 8, no. 2; reprinted from The Biblical Review Quarterly, October, 1928). This is consistent with other NT passages that reveal Jesus as using his divine powers and displaying his glories upon occasion (e.g., miracles, the Transfiguration), but always under the direction of the Father and the Spirit (Luke 4:14; John 5:19; 8:28; 14:10).

8 After describing the fact of the Incarnation, Paul turns to the consideration of the depths of humiliation to which Christ went: "he humbled himself " and went to "death on a cross." The concluding phrase in 2:7 states what Christ actually was; the opening phrase of 2:8 looks at him from the standpoint of how he appeared in the estimation of men. He was "found" by them, as far as his external appearance was concerned (schēmati), as a mere man (hōs anthrōpos). Outwardly considered, he was no different from other men. Even this was great condescension for one who possessed the form of God, but Christ's incomparable act did not end here. He further humbled himself by "becoming obedient to death." He was so committed to the Father's plan that he obeyed it even as far as death (Heb 5:8). Nor was this all, for it was no ordinary death, but the disgraceful death by crucifixion, a death not allowed for Roman citizens, and to Jews indicative of the curse of God (Deut 21:23; Gal 3:13).

The mention of staurou ("cross") connoted probably the cruelest form of capital punishment. Crucifixion had been practiced by the Phoenicians and Persians and was taken over by the Romans. In Rome it was a punishment reserved for slaves and foreigners. (Pierson Parker, "Crucifixion," IDB, A–D, pp. 746, 747.)

9 The final movement of thought in this sublime illustration describes Christ's subsequent exaltation. The nature of this exaltation was God's elevating Christ to the highest position and granting him the name above all names. "Exalted . . . to the highest place" renders the Greek word hyperypsōsen, which might be translated "superexalted." The reference is to the resurrection, ascension, and glorification of Jesus following his humiliating death, whereby all that he had laid aside was restored to him and much more besides. Implicit in this exaltation is the coming consummation mentioned in the next verses, when his triumph over sin and his lordship will be acknowledged by every being.

In view of the chronological pattern exhibited in this passage, the giving of "the name" must have been subsequent to the Cross. This would appear to be sufficient to rule out the identity of the name in view as being "Jesus." A more likely identification of "the name" is "Lord," the equivalent many times of the Old Testament "Jehovah," and supported by the thought of v.11. Christ's exaltation is expressly stated as manifesting his lordship in Acts 2:33–36. Another explanation takes "the name" in the sense of position, dignity, or office, similar to the OT use of the word *šēm* ("name"). Other NT uses of "name" in this sense may be in Ephesians 1:21 and Hebrews 1:4. There are also instances where "the name" is used alone as a reference to God or Christ (see Acts 5:41; 3 John 7). This use had clear precedent in the OT (Lev 24:11, 16, ASV, RSV; 2 Sam 7:13).

10 The purpose of Christ's exaltation is that all beings might bow in acknowledgment of the name that belongs to Jesus (v.10), and confess that Jesus Christ is Lord (v.11). Because of what the name of Jesus represents, a time is coming when every knee shall bow before him in recognition of his sovereignty. The statement is built on the wording of Isaiah 45:23, a verse quoted by Paul in Romans 14:11 also (cf. Rev 5:13). This universal acknowledgment will include angels and departed saints in heaven, people still living on earth, and the satanic hosts and lost humanity in hell.

The form *Iēsou* (Jesus) can be either genitive or dative, allowing the phrase to be rendered either as "at the name of Jesus" or "at the name Jesus." The former appears to be the more probable, inasmuch as the exaltation is said to be at the time when God granted his Son the "name," and this occurred considerably after the name Jesus was given to Christ. Hence, the expression should be understood as "at the name that belongs to Jesus."

The genitives *epouraniōn*, ("in heaven"), *epigeiōn* ("on earth"), and *katachthoniōn* ("under the earth") are either masculine or neuter. If the latter is meant, Paul's statement was intended to include all of creation, animate and inanimate. Undoubtedly this would agree with Paul's teaching elsewhere regarding the submission of all creation to the Son of God (Rom 8:19–22). However, the mention of "knee" and "tongue" certainly suggests personal beings, unless the passage is highly figurative (cf. Ps 148). But since the context is not figurative, the likelihood is that the terms are masculine here.

11 Submission will be expressed not only by bending the knee, but also by verbal confession. The mention of "tongue" and "confess" suggests a restriction to moral beings, but "every" indicates a universal acknowledgment of Christ's sovereignty, even by his enemies. Paul does not imply by this a universal salvation, but means that every personal being will ultimately confess Christ's lordship, either with joyful faith or with resentment and despair.

This ultimate confession that Jesus Christ is Lord is apparently Paul's indication of the "name" granted Jesus at his exaltation following the Cross (v.9). The name "Lord" with all the dignity and divine prerogatives this implies will eventually be recognized by every creature. Of course, the Son in his *nature* was always deity, but the exaltation following the Cross granted him the dignity of station commensurate with his nature and far superior to his humble state while on earth.

"To the glory of God the Father" is Paul's closing doxology to this remarkable Christology. He has never lost sight of the divine order and of the grand scheme in which the incarnation of Christ must be viewed. Recognition of Christ's lordship fulfills the purpose of the Father and so brings glory to God.

This picture of Christ's humiliation and subsequent exaltation was intended by Paul

33

to encourage in his readers an attitude of Christlike humility. If they were to be identified as Christ's followers, they must demonstrate his characteristics. The appeal, however, was not only to a life of lowliness and hardship; it also contained the reminder that victory followed humiliation and that God's glory will ultimately prevail.

Notes

1 The masc.-fem. form τις (*tis*, "any") in the fourth clause poses the problem of grammatical disagreement with the neuter σπλάγχνα (*splanchna*, "viscera"). Attempts to solve it have elicited some imaginative explanations. Bengel urged that "joy" be understood with *tis* as the predicate of each clause: "if bowels and mercies be any joy," etc. (John Albert Bengel, *New Testament Word Studies*, trans. C.T. Lewis and M.R. Vincent [Grand Rapids: Kregel, repr. 1971], 2:431). Lenski (p. 761) translates: "if any fellowship, (let it be) of spirit; if any (such fellowship), (let it be) tender mercies and compassions!" This separates *tis* from *splanchna* and avoids the grammatical disagreement, but at the cost of considerable manipulation. *Tis* is found in all ancient MSS (including ℵ A B C D E F G K L P) except for a few minuscules, and must be considered the best-attested reading. The most likely conjecture is that the original form was the neuter τι (*ti*) and that the sigma (ς) was accidentally assimilated early from the following word (*splanchna*) by a scribal error of dittography (Kennedy, pp. 432, 433; Hendriksen, p. 98 n.). The error must have occurred prior to our earliest extant MSS.

2 The use of ἵνα (*hina*, "so that") here introduces the content of the injunction, not just the purpose of it. It is one of those instances where the more common telic use of *hina* is absorbed into the subject of the wish.

Τὸ αὐτὸ φρονῆτε (*to auto phronēte*, "think the same [thing]"; NIV, "being like-minded") and τὸ ἓν φρονοῦντες (*to hen phronountes*, "thinking the one [thing]"; NIV, "being one in . . . purpose") mean essentially the same thing. It is usually suggested that the latter is stronger than the former and serves to reinforce the injunction.

Σύμψυχοι (*sympsychoi*, "one in spirit") may be regarded as an independent item in the series of phrases or as belonging to the words immediately following. Favoring the latter is the conserving of the literary parallelism utilizing four participles in Paul's elaboration (2:2–4)—a parallelism that would otherwise be marred by the intrusion of an additional item that is not a participle.

3 No verb is expressed in the opening part of v.3, perhaps in the interests of preserving the fourfold participial construction. The reader must supply "do" or "doing."

4 The MSS vary between the sing. and pl. forms of ἕκαστος (*hekastos*, "each") in the two occurrences in this verse. Some have both as singulars; some, both plurals; and others, one sing. and one pl. Inasmuch as the adjective can be used substantively in either sing. or pl., it is not difficult to see how variation could occur. The Nestle text (25th ed.) adopts both plurals; UBS gives the first as sing., the second as pl.

5 The active form φρονεῖτε (*phroneite*, "think") is found in the major uncials (ℵ A B C* D E F G), and is to be preferred. The passive φρονείσθω (*phroneisthō*) is the reading of TR and was the basis of the KJV rendering.

6 All the verb forms in this passage are aorists, except for ὑπάρχων (*hyparchōn*, "being") and εἶναι (*einai*, "to be"), the two that refer to Christ prior to when he "emptied himself." The use of the two present forms is most appropriate for describing the timeless existence of the preincarnate Christ. Although these two verbs often seem interchangeable, the distinctive sense of each would be assumed in a context where both appear. "In the one instance we have *existence* as such, in the other we have *being* in a condition which comports with that existence" (Lenski, in loc.).

The noun μορφή (*morphē*, "nature") refers to that external form that represents what is intrinsic and essential. It indicates not merely what may be perceived by others, but what is objectively there (J. Behm, *Morphē*, TDNT, 4:743). In this passage it refers to the intrinsic form

34

which was chiefly against God, was used elsewhere by Paul to instruct the church (1 Cor 10:10). On the other hand, the problem of disunity in the congregation has already been seen in this letter (2:2), and more is to come (4:2). Perhaps the command is sufficiently general to cover both.

Emphasis in the command falls on the word *everything* (literally, "all things"), which is actually the first word of the verse in the Greek text. Most Christians are able to do some things without complaint. It is when we are exhorted to be doing "all things" with a joyful spirit that the difficulty comes. Yet the outworking of our Christian faith in daily life lays this responsibility upon us.

15 The purpose of the exhortation to work out their salvation was that the readers might be pure and uncontaminated light-givers in the world. By regeneration they had already become children of God in nature and position. Now as they progressed in sanctification, they would become "children of God without fault," particularly as viewed by the world around them. By faithfully adhering to the word of God as contained in Scripture and taught them by Paul, their lives would be free from anything blameworthy (*amemptoi*, "blameless"), as well as devoid of matters foreign or improper in the heart (*akeraioi*, "pure"). Their nature as God's children would be clearly evident, with no obvious flaws (*amōma*, "without fault") to disfigure their witness. The apostle is mindful of their location within a corrupt society. In OT language (Deut 32:5) he depicts mankind generally as "a crooked and depraved generation." By "generation" he was probably thinking of mankind as morally the product of one sinful stock (John 8:44), rather than merely a group of contemporaries. Amid this moral blackness, the children of God should stand out as stars at midnight. Believers are the possessors of Christ, the Light of the world (John 8:12), and so are now light-givers to the world (Matt 5:14). "You shine" states the present fact. They are not told to shine, but are reminded that they already do. The challenge was to let the light shine out unhindered.

16 As luminaries in a world of spiritual darkness, they were to "hold out the word of life." The present participle *epechontes* can be understood either as "holding fast" or as "holding forth." Those who regard the preceding clause as parenthetical (e.g., Lightfoot) explain what follows as in contrast to the "crooked and depraved generation" and so adopt the meaning "holding fast the word of life." On the other hand, the figure of "stars" supports the idea of "holding out" or "holding forth," and there is no real reason to treat it as a parenthesis. Furthermore, this latter sense assumes the former, for those who hold out the word of life to others are understood to have first received it themselves. The word of life is, of course, the gospel, which brings eternal life when it is received by faith (John 6:68).

Faithful living by the Philippians will provide Paul with added reason to rejoice when he appears before Christ. "Boast" (*kauchēma*) refers to the occasion or grounds for boasting (see note on 1:26). "The day of Christ" is the time when Christ will return for his church, and when believers will have their works inspected and rewarded (see note on 1:6). Paul wants the content or basis of his boast at that time to be that his labors for the Philippians had not been useless. He desires that all his efforts to win them to Christ and to nurture their faith will be vindicated at Christ's judgment seat by the victorious presence of the Philippian believers. "Run" expresses Paul's energetic activity, and "labor" depicts its toilsome aspects.

17 The prospect of standing before Christ reminded Paul that it might be soon. By the vivid metaphor of a drink offering, he explained that even though he was presently in a dangerous situation that could lead to a martyr's death, it was the climax of his ministry and a cause for rejoicing. Both Jewish and Greek religious practice included the use of wine poured out ceremonially in connection with certain sacrifices (Num 15:1–10; Homer, *Illiad*, 11:775), and it is fruitless and unnecessary to determine which was most influential in Paul's figure. What is important is to see that Paul regarded his own life as a sacrifice in the interests of the spiritual advancement of such persons as the Philippian believers. He used the same metaphor in 2 Timothy 4:6. "The sacrifice and service" employs only one article with the two nouns, and probably is a hendiadys meaning "sacrificial service." The apostle is thinking of their various Christian ministries performed as a spiritual sacrifice to God (4:18; Heb 13:15) and springing from their faith.

Paul was not embittered but was rejoicing in his present labors and sufferings. He was willing not only to endure his present sufferings but also to lay down his life, and the prospect of being with Christ and of having his ministry among the Philippians seen as successful filled him with joy. Enduring his present danger would be a demonstration that he had learned something of the "mind of Christ" (2:5). (As it turned out, he was probably not executed until some years later during a second Roman imprisonment.) Furthermore, he rejoiced not only for his own sake, but jointly with the Philippians as he contemplated his relation to their faith. He was its planter and nourisher, and thus their victories were his also. He conveys this idea not only by the words "rejoice with all of you," but also by the figure depicting his life as being poured out as a sacrifice along with the Philippians' own sacrifice. They were priests together, making spiritual sacrifices to God as a result of their faith in Christ. Their sacrifices consisted of themselves, presented by faithful service during life, and if need be, by a martyr's death.

18 Likewise the Philippians should display the same attitude as Paul. They must not wring their hands, nor bewail their own trials and Paul's. They must learn to find real joy as they work out their salvation and must also learn to share Paul's attitude about his situation.

Notes

---

12 The use of μὴ (*mē*, "not") is governed by the imperative κατεργάζεσθε (*katergazesthe*, "continue to work out"), rather than the indicative ὑπηκούσατε (*hypēkousate*, "you obeyed"); hence, the intervening phrases regarding Paul's presence and absence must be construed with the exhortation to "work out" rather than with the reference to their previous obedience.

The compound *katergazesthe* may have its distinctive sense here, which looks to the successful accomplishment of a task. Kennedy points to a Pauline instance where both simple and compound forms are used (2 Cor 7:10) and concludes that "ἐργ. refers to a process in its mediate workings, while κατεργ. looks solely at the final result" (p. 440).

13 The Greek word-family to which ἐνεργῶν (*energōn*, "working"; NIV, "works") belongs conveys the thought of energy as fully active, effective in reaching its goal. It is not mere resident energy, but energy in operation (William Barclay, *More New Testament Words* [New York: Harper & Brothers, 1958], pp. 46ff.). Hence, Paul depicts God as actively and continually putting forth his energy in believers to insure the accomplishment of their task.

14 The remaining NT uses of the noun γογγυσμός (*gongysmos*, "complaining") have to do with grumbling complaints against others, a factor suggesting that such would also be the case here. However, the analogy with Israel's murmuring makes it inadvisable to rule out the possibility

that the apostle may have in view complaints against God as well. The term διαλογισμῶν (*dialogismōn*, "arguing") is used in the NT predominantly of evil thoughts, or else of anxious reflection or doubt (G. Schrenk, *Dialogismos*, TDNT, 2:97, 98).

15 The active verb φαίνω (*phainō*) means "shine," and the middle form φαίνομαι (*phainomai*) means either "shine" or "appear" (BAG, p. 859). It does not seem warranted, therefore, to allege that φαίνεσθε (*phainesthe*) can only be rendered "appear" in this passage. Such uses as in Matt 24:27 and Rev 18:23 are legitimate parallels with the sense of "shine." Φωστῆρες (*phōstēres*) refers to light-giving bodies, especially the heavenly bodies such as the sun and stars (BAG, p. 880). The metaphorical uses have this as the background.

16 The verb ἐπέχω (*epechō*) occurs five times in the NT, but in none of the other instances is the sense precisely what is called for in Phil 2:16 (cf. Luke 14:7; Acts 3:5; 19:22; 1 Tim 4:16). Neither "hold fast" nor "hold forth" (or "hold out") fits the other uses. Both of these senses, however, are found in other literature, and the choice must be made on contextual grounds.

17, 18 The verb σπένδω (*spendō*, "pour out") occurs only twice in the NT, both times as passives and both as metaphors of Paul's suffering and eventual martyrdom (Phil 2:17; 2 Tim 4:6). Although Gr. custom generally called for the liquid offering to be poured on top of the sacrifice and Jewish procedure required it to be poured around it (Jos. Antiq., III.9.4), the preposition ἐπί (*epi*) is broad enough in meaning to cover both practices (and is so used in LXX of the drink offering, as well as in pagan literature).

In nonbiblical Gr., the word-family of λειτουργία (*leitourgia*, "service") denoted official service to the political body. It also developed a cultic use, and it was this use that found further development in LXX, where it was used of priestly functions (R. Meyer, *Leitourgeō*, *Leitourgia*, TDNT, 4:215-225). Paul is using the term here in harmony with his metaphor of sacrifice. (See also H. Strathmann, *Leitourgeō*, TDNT, 4:226-231.)

Lightfoot (p. 119) has insisted that συγχαίρω (*synchairō*) be understood as "congratulate" rather than "rejoice with" in v.17, since the latter would imply the Philippians were already rejoicing and hence the command for them to do so in v.18 would be strange. While admitting the possibility, one may also note that there are other plausible explanations for the meaning "rejoice with" (as in the exposition above). "Congratulate" seems extremely awkward.

III. Two Messengers of Paul to the Philippians (2:19-30)

1. *Timothy*

2:19-24

> [19] I hope in the Lord Jesus to send Timothy to you soon, that I also may be cheered when I receive news about you. [20] I have no one else like him, who takes a genuine interest in your welfare. [21] For everyone looks out for his own interests, not those of Jesus Christ. [22] But you know that Timothy has proved himself, because as a son with his father he has served with me in the work of the gospel. [23] I hope, therefore, to send him as soon as I see how things go with me. [24] And I am confident in the Lord that I myself will come soon.

19 The somber note sounded in the previous two verses is balanced by the more optimistic tone that follows. Paul planned to send Timothy to Philippi with a report and hoped to come shortly himself. His hope was "in the Lord Jesus." Every believer is "in Christ," and this vital union should influence every thought and activity. Thus Paul loves in the Lord (1:8); grounds his confidence in the Lord (2:24); rejoices in the Lord (3:3; 4:10); and desires that others rejoice in Christ (1:26; 3:1), welcome Christian leaders in the Lord (2:29), and always stand firm in the Lord (4:1). It may

be that Paul was uncertain of the outcome of his case at Rome and therefore the more obviously submitted all his plans and hopes to the lordship of Jesus.

Timothy was named in the opening of the letter (1:1), but his mention here in the third person shows that he was not a co-writer. Paul refers to Timothy and his proposed trip to Philippi with graciousness and delicacy. One might suppose that Paul would have explained that the purpose of the trip was to tell the Philippians about Paul's situation. But he only hints at that idea by the word "also" and by the clause "as soon as I see how things go with me" (v.23), because his main purpose is to hear about the Philippians, though he assumes that his readers will be cheered by a favorable report of him. The spiritual advancement of the churches was always uppermost in Paul's mind.

Paul must have expected Timothy not to remain at Philippi but to bring him word about the church immediately. Conceivably, they could have planned to meet at Ephesus after Paul's release. At least, they were presumably together at Ephesus subsequent to this time (1 Tim 1:3). This would require that before leaving for Philippi, Timothy knew with certainty the date of Paul's release. (Perhaps 2:23 implies this.) Otherwise, Timothy would have been expected to return to Paul at Rome before the apostle left the city.

20 Paul's glowing testimony about Timothy was not to introduce his young associate, for he was already well known at Philippi (see comment on 1:1). It did serve, however, to avert possible disappointment that Paul himself could not come at once and indicated that he had the fullest confidence in his younger associate. "No one else like him" is literally "no one of equal soul" (*isopsychon*). In the light of what follows, it seems best to take the comparison as being between Timothy and Paul's other available associates (so Lightfoot, Beare, Hendriksen), rather than between Timothy and Paul (so Alford). In the matter of "a genuine interest in your welfare," no one that Paul might conceivably have sent had the same interest in the Philippians as did Timothy. How appropriate that two of the pastoral Epistles were later written to him as he exercised his pastoral concerns in another city.

21 These words must be understood in harmony with other statements in the letter. They must not be denied their force, but neither must they be understood with undue harshness. Paul had already noted that some among his acquaintances at Rome were more concerned with furthering their own interests (1:14-17). Yet his reference to them was a temperate one (1:18). Furthermore, he must have been on good terms with many of the brethren who are included in his comment in 2:21, for he conveys their greeting in 4:21. Nevertheless, some restriction in Paul's reference would seem legitimate, for he is surely not including Epaphroditus or Luke or Aristarchus as not seeking the interests of Christ. It is best to regard Paul as referring solely to all those around him who might conceivably have undertaken the trip to Philippi. Some of them he may have asked and they had refused him in favor of their own pursuits. Others he may have considered but not asked because of what he knew about them. Luke and Aristarchus may have been away on other missions and so have been unavailable. That they are not mentioned in 1:1 suggests their absence at the time the letter was written.

22 The proved character of Timothy, however, put him in a class apart. By the thorough test of his repeated presence and ministry in Philippi, as well as by his reputation achieved elsewhere, the Philippian Christians knew him as a man of God (cf. comment on 1:1). Paul also vouches for him on the basis of many years of personal experience. He and the younger Timothy had a father-son relationship. Together they had served Christ for the furtherance of the gospel, beginning with Paul's second missionary journey more than ten years earlier.

23 The Greek sentence begins with *touton* ("this one"), which gathers up all that has just been said regarding Timothy and emphasizes that he is the one to be sent to Philippi. He will not be the bearer of the letter, however, because Paul wants to retain him until he has more definite information about the outcome of his case ("as soon as I see how things go with me"). This implies that Paul thinks there will soon be some kind of legal decision regarding him. This letter will alert the Philippians to Timothy's coming and will also let them know the reason why he did not come with Epaphroditus. They will also know that when Timothy does come, he will be bringing word about the crucial developments in Paul's legal case.

24 Although granting that the decision might go either way (not because his legal grounds were weak, but because justice is not always served in human courts), Paul was still confident that release was in prospect, and that he would fulfill his wish to visit the Philippians (cf. comments on 1:25). This confidence in the Lord must be similar to that implied in 2:19—"I hope in the Lord Jesus. . . ." All the acts, thoughts, and attitudes of Christians should spring from the fact that they are "in the Lord" and are prompted by the Spirit's energy. Everything they do should be consistent with, and submitted to, the Lord's will.

The Book of Acts does not record Paul's release from his Roman imprisonment. Nor does it record his execution at the end of it. But evidence furnished by the pastoral Epistles supports the hypothesis of a release during which Paul did additional traveling in Crete, Asia Minor, Macedonia, and Achaia. There is good reason, therefore, to believe that Paul's hope was realized.

Notes

19 The verb εὐψυχῶ (*eupsychō*) occurs only here in the NT. Its meaning of "be glad, have courage, be cheered" is well established in the papyri. The imperative εὐψύχει (*eupsychei*) is frequently found on grave inscriptions, meaning "farewell" (BAG, p. 330).

20 The tr. "of like soul or mind" for ἰσόψυχον (*isopsychon*) has the support of classical usage, though the word does not appear elsewhere in the NT (BAG, p. 382). With this meaning in view, Lightfoot is probably right in understanding Paul to mean "no one of a mind equal to Timothy," for if Paul had meant "equal to me," he would have said "no one *else*" or "no one except Timothy" (pp. 120, 121). Barth (p. 85) chooses the meaning "close associate," based on the meaning of the word in LXX of Ps 54:13 (Heb.: Ps 55:13). Beare, however, points out that Paul could hardly have been consciously indebted to this LXX passage, inasmuch as the context uses the word in an unflattering way in referring to a betrayer (p. 96). The meaning of "confidant" is advocated by P. Christou ("Isopsuchos, Phil 2:20," JBL, vol. 70 [1951]: 293–296).

21 The name Jesus Christ appears in the order Ἰησοῦ Χριστοῦ (*Iēsou Christou*) in P[46], D, and the Alexandrian family (except B), and is adopted in the UBS text. The alternate reading transposes the words to Χριστοῦ Ἰησοῦ (*Christou Iēsou*), and is found in B and TR. This reading was adopted by Nestle (25th ed.).

22 It is possible to understand a shift in Paul's thought after the words ὡς πατρὶ τέκνον (*hōs patri teknon*, "as a son with his father"). The sense would then be: "as a child serves a father, he served with me." Paul is thought to have begun with the concept of a child serving his father, but to have shifted the wording slightly to indicate that in the ministry both he and Timothy were actually serving Christ. He then inserted the words "with me" to show this (Beare, p. 86). But the thought is certainly clear enough if the dative πατρί (patri, "[with] father") is treated as parallel with σὺν ἐμοί (syn emoi, "with me"); hence, "as a child [serves with] a father, he served with me" (Hendriksen, note, p. 136).

23, 24 The verb ἀφοράω (aphoraō), occurring here as the aorist subjunctive ἀφίδω (aphidō), is used one other time in the NT (Heb 12:2). The latter use shows clearly the basic meaning of "look away at something in the distance." This sense may also be implicit in the usage here, as Paul looks ahead to the time when a decision will be reached in his case. The adverb ἐξαυτῆς (exautēs, "immediately"; NIV, "as soon as") occurring at the end of v.23 should probably be construed with πέμψαι (pempsai, "to send"). It was added because Paul did not want to leave the impression that the delay until he should see how things turned out would be a long one.

---

2. Epaphroditus

2:25-30

25But I think it is necessary to send back to you Epaphroditus, my brother, fellow worker and fellow soldier, who is also your messenger, whom you sent to take care of my needs. 26For he longs for all of you and is distressed because you heard he was ill. 27Indeed he was ill, and almost died. But God had mercy on him, and not on him only but also on me, to spare me sorrow upon sorrow. 28Therefore I am all the more eager to send him, so that when you see him again you may be glad and I may have less anxiety. 29Welcome him in the Lord with great joy, and honor men like him, 30because he almost died for the work of Christ, risking his life to make up for the help you could not give me.

25 The second of Paul's messengers to Philippi, and the one whose forthcoming trip was the immediate occasion for this Epistle was Epaphroditus (see Introduction, 4). He is mentioned in the NT only in Philippians (2:25; 4:18). There is no reason to identify him with Epaphras of Colosse (Col 1:7; 4:12; Philem 23), though the names are similar. Epaphroditus had brought the Philippians' gift to Paul. He is identified by the apostle in a series of glowing terms. He was "my brother" (ton adelphon), a sharer of spiritual life with Paul and so his brother in Christ. He was a "fellow worker" (synergon), a participant with Paul in the labors of the gospel. Paul said he was also "my ... fellow soldier" (systratiōtēn mou), a sharer of the dangers involved in standing firm for Christ and in proclaiming the gospel. The next terms tell of Epaphroditus's relation to the Philippians. He had acted as their "messenger" (apostolon), the duly appointed and commissioned delegate to convey the Philippians' gift to Paul. (The broader use of the term apostle without the addition of the phrase "of Jesus Christ" is used also of Barnabas [Acts 14:14] and apparently of Silas and Timothy [1 Thess 2:7; cf. 1:1], and James the Lord's brother [Gal 1:19; 1 Cor 15:7]. For this less-restricted use of apostolon, see also 2 Cor 8:23.)

In this capacity Epaphroditus had served as their "minister" (leitourgon), functioning officially on their behalf in performing a sacred service to Paul. The noun leitourgos appears five times in the NT (Rom 13:6; 15:16; Phil 2:25; Heb 1:7; 8:2) and in several of these a priestly sort of ministry is in view. It is used of Christ's priestly ministry in the heavenly tabernacle (Heb 8:2) and of Paul's sacred service in the evangelizing of Gentiles and presentation of them to God (Rom 15:16). Hence, the use in Philippians 2:25 has overtones of a priestly act, that of Epaphroditus's presenting to Paul the Philippians' offering, "an acceptable sacrifice, pleasing to God" (4:18).

Now Paul had decided that Epaphroditus should be sent home to Philippi for the reasons he next explained.

26 The verb *epipotheō* ("to long for") used here of Epaphroditus, was used by Paul regarding his own feelings toward the Philippians in 1:8. It is also used of the Spirit's strong yearning for the total allegiance of man's heart (James 4:5), and of a newborn baby's longing for milk (1 Peter 2:2).

The addition of *adēmonōn* ("distressed") to the mention of Epaphroditus's longings emphasizes the intensity of his feeling. The only other NT uses of this word describe our Lord's emotions in Gethsemane (Matt 26:37; Mark 14:33). The etymology of the word is not certain, although it is most commonly traced to *adēmos* ("away from home") and thus "beside oneself, distressed, troubled." Epaphroditus had become deeply distressed when he learned that the Philippians knew of his illness. One must beware of reading too much between the lines, but it is a fair inference that more is involved than merely mutual concern. The strong word "distressed" and Paul's emphasis on the point that Epaphroditus had really been seriously ill and should be given a hero's welcome may imply that some misunderstanding had arisen in Philippi, and that word of it had gotten back to Rome. Perhaps there were rumors that he was a malingerer, or that he had been more of a burden than a help to Paul.

27 Paul therefore said that Epaphroditus had "indeed" been "ill" and had "almost died." The precise nature of his ailment is not indicated but it was related to his labors in the Lord's service, perhaps from the hazards or the exertions of the journey to Rome (v.30). The illness was so severe that Paul regarded the recovery as an intervention of God. It is clear that even though at times he exercised "the signs of an apostle" (2 Cor 12:12), Paul himself did not miraculously heal Epaphroditus. Apparently not even apostles could do miracles at will, but only when miracles were in God's purpose. In the case of Epaphroditus, God produced the recovery and by so doing displayed his mercy both on Epaphroditus and on Paul. The restoration of health to the sick man spared Paul "sorrow upon sorrow." He felt keenly the misfortunes of his friends, and though he had been distressed over the illness of this courageous emissary, he was spared the additional sorrow that his death would have brought.

28 The verb *epempsa* ("send") is an epistolary aorist and refers to the present sending of Epaphroditus with this letter. In view of the circumstances noted above, Paul was sending him more hastily than he would otherwise have done. If the serious illness and the apparent misunderstanding at Philippi had not occurred, Paul might have retained him longer, perhaps till the end of the trial. This may also have been part of the intention of the Philippians in sending Epaphroditus to Paul. It was important, then, that this letter should accompany Epaphroditus, so that the Philippians would rejoice at his safe return. Paul was concerned also about the feelings of Epaphroditus (v.26). Thus the return of the messenger to the church, along with the true explanation of what had happened, should bring a happy conclusion to the whole affair and satisfy both parties. At the same time, Paul himself would benefit by being relieved from further anxiety, for knowing that his friends were relieved always brought a lessening of his painful concern over problems in the churches.

29 Paul therefore exhorted the Philippians to welcome Epaphroditus with joy as fellow Christians should. He had fulfilled his mission with distinction and deserved an appropriate homecoming. Paul's words imply that more was involved in Epaphroditus's disturbed feelings than simple affectionate concern, otherwise no such urging from the apostle to welcome him would have been necessary. Some sort of alienation had arisen. The church was also to do more than refrain from criticism of Epaphroditus. They were to give him due recognition for his faithful and sacrificial service to Paul.

30 The reason why a genuine welcome was deserved by Epaphroditus was twofold. First, he had been engaged in the work of Christ and had actually risked his life to accomplish it. Second, he had been trying by his labors to make up for the Philippians' absence from Paul, and so they owed him their gratitude. Epaphroditus's close call with death is to be explained in relation to his sickness (v.27), and was not the result of persecution or of adverse judicial proceedings. Furthermore, the ailment was directly due to his Christian labors on behalf of Paul. Perhaps it resulted from the rigors of travel and was compounded by his efforts to continue ministering to Paul in spite of being sick. It was not merely an unavoidable circumstance but was a risking of his life in the interests of his ministry. Paul strongly commended Epaphroditus to the church that had sent him. The church should be grateful, because Epaphroditus had actually been representing them and was doing for Paul what they could not do. Inasmuch as 4:14-18 reveals that the Philippians had done more than other churches for the apostle, the "lack of service" (KJV) here must be the lack of their physical presence with him. This Epaphroditus had supplied by his presence and personal care. This explanation of the "lack" (*hysterēma*) is supported by the use of the same word describing the Corinthians' absence from Paul as compensated for by the coming of Stephanas, Fortunatus, and Achaicus (1 Cor 16:17).

Notes:

---

25 The verb ἡγησάμην (*hēgēsamēn*) is an epistolary aorist, viewing the action from the standpoint of the reader rather than the writer. English would use the present "I think" (NIV) or the perfect "I have thought."

27 The initial καὶ γὰρ (*kai gar*, "for indeed") implies that the previous statement that Epaphroditus had become ill was really an understatement (Lightfoot), since the man had nearly died. So the report of illness that had reached Philippi had not been exaggerated. The phrase λύπην ἐπὶ λύπην (*lupēn epi lupēn*, "sorrow upon sorrow") is sometimes explained as the sorrow of bereavement added to the miseries of his imprisonment (so Martin, *Philippians*, p. 131). The view expressed in the exposition seems preferable, however.

28 In classical and Hellenistic Gr., the word group σπουδάζω-σπουδαῖος (*spoudazō-spoudaios*) means "to make haste" or "be zealous, active, concerned." In LXX the use is largely confined to "haste." Josephus, however, uses it also in the sense of being zealous, concerned, or showing interest. Both senses are found in NT usage. (Gunther Harder, *Spoudazō*, TDNT, 7:559-568.) The comparative adverb σπουδαιοτέρως (*spoudaioterōs*) could have either sense here, but the idea conveyed by "more hastily" may best suit the context, where Paul explains why he is sending Epaphroditus home at this particular time.

Whether πάλιν (*palin*) should be understood with the preceding ἰδόντες (*idontes*) as meaning "having seen him again" or with the following verb χαρῆτε (*charēte*), with the meaning "again you may rejoice," cannot be settled on grammatical grounds. Paul elsewhere uses *palin* both after and before the verb, though he shows a decided preference for placing it before the verb. If that should be the case here, the sense is that the Philippians would once again rejoice over their brother after seeing him returned and in good health.

29 Although the pl. τοὺς τοιούτους (*tous toioutous*, "men like [him]") is used, we need not conclude that the reference is to companions of Epaphroditus, for Paul returns immediately to the sing. in the next verse. The pl. is a generalization, in which the treatment requested by Paul is the sort that is appropriate for all similar cases.

30 The reading τὸ ἔργον Χριστοῦ (*to ergon Christou*, "the work of Christ") is one of several variations among the MSS at this point. This reading has been adopted by Nestle and UBS, and is reflected in KJV, ASV, and NIV. It has the early support of P[46] B G. D and K are similar, differing only by including the article τοῦ (*tou*). The uncials ℵ A P read κυρίου (*kuriou*, "of the Lord") instead of Χριστοῦ, (*Christou*, "of Christ"), and minuscule 1985 has τοῦ θεοῦ (*tou theou*, "of God"). The most interesting variant appears only in C, in which *to ergon* ("the work") stands alone. This rather abrupt usage is paralleled by the terminology in Acts 15:38 and explains how the other variants could have arisen, but its meager documentary support makes it questionable. It is the reading preferred by Lightfoot and Kennedy.

The verb παραβολεύομαι (*paraboleuomai*, "to risk, to expose to danger") appears in a second-century A.D. inscription at Olbia on the Black Sea, honoring a certain Carzoazus, son of Attalus. Deissmann has tr. as follows: ". . . but also to the ends of the world it was witnessed of him that in the interests of friendship he had exposed himself to dangers as an advocate in (legal) strife (by taking his clients' causes even) up to emperors" (Deiss LAE, p. 88).

IV. Warning Against Judaizers and Antinomians (3:1-21)

1. The Judaizing Danger

3:1-16

¹Finally, my brothers, rejoice in the Lord! It is no trouble for me to write the same things to you again, and it is a safeguard for you.
²Watch out for those dogs, those men who do evil, those mutilators of the flesh. ³For it is we who are the circumcision, we who worship by the Spirit of God, who glory in Christ Jesus, and who put no confidence in the flesh—⁴though I myself have reasons for such confidence.
If anyone else thinks he has reasons to put confidence in the flesh, I have more: ⁵circumcised on the eighth day, of the people of Israel, of the tribe of Benjamin, a Hebrew of Hebrews; in regard to the law, a Pharisee; ⁶as for zeal, persecuting the church; as for legalistic righteousness, faultless.
⁷But whatever was to my profit I now consider loss for the sake of Christ. ⁸What is more, I consider everything a loss compared to the surpassing greatness of knowing Christ Jesus my Lord, for whose sake I have lost all things. I consider them rubbish, that I may gain Christ ⁹and be found in him, not having a righteousness of my own that comes from the law, but that which is through faith in Christ—the righteousness that comes from God and is by faith. ¹⁰I want to know Christ and the power of his resurrection and the fellowship of sharing in his sufferings, becoming like him in his death, ¹¹and so, somehow, to attain to the resurrection from the dead.
¹²Not that I have already obtained all this, or have already been made perfect, but I press on to take hold of that for which Christ Jesus took hold of me. ¹³Brothers, I do not consider myself yet to have taken hold of it. But one thing I do: Forgetting what is behind and straining toward what is ahead, ¹⁴I press on toward the goal to win the prize for which God has called me heavenward in Christ Jesus.
¹⁵All of us who are mature should take such a view of things. And if on some point you think differently, that too God will make clear to you. ¹⁶Only let us live up to what we have already attained.

1 By the use of "finally" (*to loipon*), Paul seems to be drawing his Epistle to a close. Inasmuch as over forty percent of the letter is yet to come, some assume that a combination of several letters makes up the Epistle, and suggest that 3:1 is the conclusion of one of them (see Introduction, 2). However, the introductory *to loipon* cannot be confined to the one sense of "finally."

Because of the wide variation in the use of this expression by Paul and other writers, in the New Testament and outside, it may be best to understand the meaning here in a nontechnical and very natural way. A speaker may use the word "finally" when he passes the midpoint of an address, and then continue on for a rather long time. This poses no real problem for the English listener, and even less for a Greek reader for whom the expression could also mean simply "furthermore" or "in addition."

On the assumption that the Epistle is a unity, Paul's exhortation to "rejoice in the Lord" should be understood as belonging with what follows. The readers are to maintain the joyful spirit that has characterized this letter, though Paul now goes on to speak of some unpleasant matters. He repeats some of his former instructions ("to write the same things to you again"), but this is "no trouble" to him, for it has in view the worthy goal of safeguarding them from entrapment in wrong doctrine.

How specifically should "the same things" be understood? Surely it does not refer to the command to rejoice, for this would not have been thought to be a troublesome task or a safeguard against something dangerous. Because there has been no earlier warning against Judaizers in this letter, some have referred "the same things" to prior correspondence with the Philippians. This is certainly possible, though little evidence exists to support it. If, however, Paul meant the words to refer to previous warnings against opponents generally, then 1:27-30 would be an earlier instance in this letter.

2 The verses that follow warrant the identification of these opponents with the Judaizers —those who dogged the trail of the apostles and endeavored to compel Gentile converts to submit to circumcision and other Jewish practices in order to be saved. Three epithets designate them. "Dogs" denotes the wild, vicious, homeless animals that roamed the streets and attacked passersby. Used figuratively, it was always a term of reproach (cf. Deut 23:18; 1 Sam 17:43; 24:14; Prov 26:11; Isa 56:10, 11). Jesus used it in reference to opponents of God's truth (Matt 7:6), and Jews often used it similarly of Gentiles. Paul turns the figure back upon the Judaizing teachers and castigates them with the very term they probably used of others. "Men who do evil" is literally "the evil workers" (*tous kakous ergatas*). If the word *workers* is stressed, the epithet may emphasize their energetic labors and perhaps their concentration on performing deeds of law rather than trusting God's grace.

In the last term, "mutilators of the flesh" (NIV), literally "the mutilation" (*tēn katatomēn*), Paul deliberately parodies the Judaizers' insistence on circumcision by sarcastically calling it mutilation. (An even bolder term ["emasculate themselves," NIV] appears in Gal 5:12). For those who had lost the significance of circumcision and insisted on it as a rite for Christians, it was nothing more than a mutilation of the flesh.

3 Paul follows the above warning with an explanation. Christians are the real "circumcision," not the Judaizers who insisted on the physical rite. He refers to those who have received the circumcision of the heart, whether they be Jew or Gentile (Rom 2:25-29; Col 2:11). This concept was no innovation, for the OT spoke of it frequently (Lev 26:41; Deut 10:16; 30:6; Jer 4:4; Ezek 44:7). The Judaizers misunderstood OT doctrine as well as Christian teaching. Elsewhere Paul equates this circumcision performed without

46

hands with the believer's removal from spiritual death to spiritual life (Col 2:11, 13). Thus it is virtually synonymous with regeneration.

Just as Paul characterizes the Judaizing teachers by three terms in the previous verse, so in v.3 he explains the true circumcision by three descriptive clauses. First, such persons worship by the Spirit of God, not by human traditions or some external rite. Second, they glory in Christ Jesus. Satisfaction comes from recognizing that their hope is found in Christ alone, not through meticulous conformity to the external demands of the Mosaic law. They have understood that Christ's sacrifice has fulfilled the law for them. These words of Paul echo Jeremiah 9:23, 24, and are used by him also in 1 Corinthians 1:31 and 2 Corinthians 10:17. Third, they put no confidence in the flesh. This states the negative aspect of the previous positive phrase. "Flesh" (*sarx*) refers to what man is outside of Christ. Paul often uses the term in controversy with Judaizers, especially in Romans and Galatians (e.g., Rom 3:20; 7:18, 25; Gal 2:16; 3:3; 5:19, 24). He teaches that sinful humanity has no grounds for confidence before God, because man unaided is powerless to achieve righteousness before God. The true believer, however, puts all of his trust in Christ and so removes any grounds for human pride or boasting.

4 Paul's personal testimony shows that he is not reacting against the Judaizers because he is jealous of their supposed strengths. In stating that true believers put no confidence in the flesh, he has in mind the contrary teaching of those opponents who stressed the importance of conformity to Jewish practices. For the sake of argument, therefore, he temporarily adopts one of their attitudes ("confidence in the flesh") and shows that his rejection of certain Jewish "advantages" was not because he did not possess them. He used the same approach in writing to the Corinthians, when for the moment he "made a fool" of himself in order to make his point (2 Cor 11:26–12:12). If any one of these opponents should claim an advantage because of his Jewish heritage and practices, Paul wanted it known that in such matters he could stand on equal footing with any Judaizer. He disavowed such as reasons for confidence before God, not because he did not possess them, but because he had found them inadequate to provide the righteousness God requires (cf. vv.7–9).

5 Now he enumerates some of those reasons for confidence in the flesh. First on the list is physical circumcision, perhaps because the Judaizers so greatly stressed it. Proselytes received this rite at the time they adopted Judaism. (Were some of the Judaizing teachers of this sort?) Others submitted to it in adulthood for various reasons (Acts 16:3). But Paul had been circumcised as a Jewish boy in accord with the instruction given to Abraham (Gen 17:12) and in accord with what the law later prescribed (Lev 12:3). Furthermore, he was born of Israelite stock. He was no proselyte; the blood of Jacob flowed in him. He belonged to the tribe of Benjamin, a fact he proudly acknowledged on more than one occasion (Acts 13:21; Rom 11:1). This tribe alone had been faithful to the Davidic throne at the time of the division of the kingdom. It had given the nation its first king, after whom Paul had been named by his parents. By calling himself a "Hebrew of Hebrews," he may have meant he had no mixed parentage but was of pure Jewish ancestry from both parents. The phrase may also refer to his linguistic and cultural upbringing, which involved the Hebrew and Aramaic languages (in distinction from that of the Hellenist Jews), even though he had been born in the Diaspora (Acts 6:1; 22:2, 3).

It is often averred that Paul mentions his connection with Benjamin because that tribe was especially honored among the tribes of Israel. In addition to the distinctions of Benjamin mentioned in the exposition, this patriarch was the only one born in the Promised Land, he was the offspring of Jacob's favorite wife, and the feast of Purim commemorated the national deliverance by Mordecai, a Benjamite. Furthermore, some suggest that this tribe held the post of honor in the armies of Israel ("following you, Benjamin," Judg 5:14). We must recognize, however, that the tribe of Benjamin also had its share of disappointing episodes, King Saul left much to be desired as a spiritual leader. The shameful episode of the Levite and his concubine (Judg 19–20), the kidnapping of women at Shiloh (Judg 21), and the cursing of David by Shimei (2 Sam 16:5–14), are blots upon the name of Benjamin and should caution us against elevating this tribe unduly. Paul's point may simply have been that he was an Israelite by birth—a Benjamite as a matter of fact—and thus was certainly a genuine Jew.

In addition, it had been his own choice to belong to the most orthodox of the Jewish parties, the Pharisees. This party contained the most zealous supporters and interpreters of OT law, and Paul had studied under Gamaliel, its most celebrated teacher (Acts 22:3; cf. 5:34).

6 When measured for its zeal, Paul's pre-Christian life had been noted for promoting Judaism and condemning Christians. He had become the archpersecutor of the church, and his reputation had gone far beyond Jerusalem (Acts 9:13, 21). His had been no half-hearted Judaism. When judged by men in accord with the righteousness the law demands, he had been blameless. As an earnest Pharisee, he had paid meticulous attention to the requirements of the Mosaic law, and no one could have charged him with failure to keep it. Of course, a distinction must be drawn between external conformity to the law in areas where men can judge and inflict legal penalties, and the perfect spiritual conformity to it that God alone can truly assess, and by which "no one will be justified" (Gal 2:16; 3:11).

7 Through his conversion on the Damascus road, Paul had learned to count such "advantages" as liabilities because of Christ. "Whatever" indicates that the previous listing was not exhaustive but illustrative. He once had regarded such things as "profit" (or "gains" —the Greek word *kerdē* is plural) toward his goal of achieving righteousness by the law, but now he has come to the settled conviction that they were actually a detriment. They had not provided him with true righteousness at all. By trusting falsely in human performance, he had not only failed to make any progress toward the righteousness God requires but had also let his Jewish "advantages" drive him to persecute the church, which proclaimed the message of the righteousness of God received by faith, the only kind of righteousness God accepts.

8 "What is more" introduces a clause stressing that Paul's experience on the Damascus road had produced a strong and lasting impression. The merits of Christ counted for everything. By using *panta* ("all things") rather than *tauta* ("these things," v.7), Paul's thought broadens from his Jewish advantages just mentioned to include everything that might conceivably be a rival to his total trust in Christ. The "surpassing greatness" can be understood of Christ in an absolute sense, though it likely includes at least a sidelong glance at the list of supposed advantages he had once trusted in. Christ is far superior to them in every respect—so much so that Paul had cast them away as nothing but rubbish.

For Paul, the knowledge of Christ Jesus as his Lord meant the intimate communion with Christ that began at his conversion and had been his experience all the years since then. It was not limited to the past (as v.10 shows), but was a growing relationship in which there was blessed enjoyment in the present and the challenge and excitement of increasing comprehension of Christ in personal fellowship. In the interests of this sublime goal, Paul had willingly suffered the loss of all those things (*ta panta*) about which he had spoken, and continues to regard them as "rubbish" in order that he might "gain Christ." Although at regeneration a person receives Christ, this is only the beginning of his discovery of what riches this entails. In Christ all the treasures of wisdom and knowledge are hidden (Col 2:3), but to search them out and appropriate them personally requires a lifetime.

9 Paul's desire to "be found in him" probably has an eschatological aspect. Paul wants the divine scrutiny he will undergo at Christ's return to reveal unquestionably that he had been in vital spiritual union with Jesus Christ. For this to be so, it could not be on the basis of a righteousness he could call "my own" (*emēn*), that is, the kind of righteousness one might achieve through general conformity to the Mosaic law. Such might win the admiration of men, but it could never achieve the absolute perfection God requires (Gal 3:10, 11; James 2:10). In strong contrast (*alla*, "but"), to be found in Christ requires the righteousness that has its source not in man but in God who has provided Jesus Christ, the "Righteous One" (Acts 3:14; 1 John 2:1).

This righteousness of God provided in Christ is received by man "through faith" (*dia pisteōs*) and thus man acquires it "by faith" or "on the basis of faith" (*epi tē pistei*). It is not man's achievement as accomplished by doing the law's requirements but is God's provision freely offered men in Christ (Rom 3:20–22). "Faith" is the very opposite of human works; it is the reception of God's work by those who acknowledge the futility of their own efforts to attain righteousness.

10 The phrase "to know him" (NIV, "to know Christ") resumes the thought of v.8 and explains in more detail what is involved in "knowing Christ Jesus." Paul wants to know experientially the power of Christ's resurrection. He is not thinking only of the divine power that raised Christ from the dead, but of the power of the resurrected Christ now operating in the believer's life. This power enables believers to "live a new life" (Rom 6:4) because they have been "raised with Christ" (Col 3:1; Eph 2:5, 6).

Closely associated in the apostle's thought is "the fellowship of sharing in his sufferings." No reference to Christ's expiatory sufferings is meant, for those were Christ's alone. But each believer, by identifying himself with Christ, incurs a measure of Christ's afflictions (Col 1:24). These may be of varying kinds and degrees, both inward and external, as believers find themselves in a world that is hostile because of their allegiance to Christ. Paul has already expressed this thought to the Philippians in 1:29, where he regards suffering in some sense as an inevitable consequence of believing in Christ (cf. Matt 16:24).

"Becoming like him in his death" further elaborates the previous phrase. For a believer to share Christ's sufferings involves such a complete identification with him that it can only be explained as a death to the former life (cf. Rom 6:4–11). The theological import of union with Christ must be experientially demonstrated. This is the process of sanctification and is intended to bring the believer's present state into ever-increasing conformity to Christ (Rom 8:29; 2 Cor 3:18; Phil 3:21). Therefore, those who died with him and rose with him (Col 2:20; 3:1–3) must exhibit this truth by a separation from their old life and a continual walking in the power supplied by Christ's resurrection life.

49

11 The form of this statement poses a problem for the interpreter, suggesting as it does in many versions that, though Paul is hopeful of experiencing the resurrection, he has some doubt about it. This is difficult to harmonize with his strong affirmations of faith elsewhere (e.g., 1 Cor 15:1–34). Some have explained the expression as an indication of Paul's humility (Muller, pp. 117, 118; Hendriksen, p. 170). Others regard the apparent doubt as relating not to the fact but the manner in which Paul would be involved (Lenski, p. 841). The verse reflects his uncertainty as to whether he would be among the dead to be raised or among the living to be transformed without dying (Walvoord, *Philippians*, p. 88.) But it is also possible to regard the clause as expressing expectation rather than doubt. See the NIV translation "and so, somehow, to attain to the resurrection from the dead."

"The resurrection from the dead" (*tēn exanastasin tēn ek nekrōn*) is not the usual NT expression. Usage of the preposition *ek* ("out of") twice in the expression strongly suggests a partial resurrection "out from" other dead ones. Hence Paul must be thinking not in terms of a general resurrection of righteous and wicked, but of believers only (cf. Rev 20:4–15). Some interpreters have seen this expression as a reference to the "rapture" of living believers (S.L. Johnson, "The Out-Resurrection from the Dead," BS, vol. 110, no. 439 [July, 1953]; Walvoord, *Philippians*, p. 88). However, it is not clear that *exanastasis* means anything other than "resurrection." The only uncertainty in Paul's mind is whether he will participate in the resurrection because he will have died by then, or whether he will receive his transformed body without dying because the Lord might come before he dies (1 Thess 4:14–17).

12 Having stated that his conversion brought about a new assessment of his goals and gave him the overwhelming desire to know Christ ever more fully, Paul then explains how his present life is a pursuit in this new direction. But he does not want to be misunderstood. He is not claiming that his conversion has already brought him to his final goal. He has not already received all he longs for nor has he been brought to that perfect completeness to which he has aspired. Perhaps there were perfectionists in Philippi who had resisted the Judaizers with their emphasis on works and ceremonies by going to the extreme of claiming to have acquired already the consummation of spiritual blessings. Paul understands clearly that he has a continuing responsibility to pursue the purposes Christ had chosen him for. Spiritual progress is ever the imperative Christians must follow.

13 In this statement Paul addresses the Philippians by the endearing title "brothers," as he repeats the thought of v.12. The emphatic *egō emauton* ("I ... myself") might conceivably introduce his response to what some at Philippi were saying about him. Absence of any other indication that Paul was being accused of espousing perfectionism makes it more likely that his emphasis was in contrast with what some Philippians were claiming about themselves. Paul did not regard himself as having obtained the final knowledge of Christ and the fullest conformity to him. Some may have taught that performance of Jewish rites could bring such perfection, but Paul knew it was not so. One thing, therefore, was the consuming passion of his life.

Using the metaphor of a footrace, Paul describes his Christian life as involving the continual forgetting of "what is behind," and the relentless centering of his energies and interests on the course that is ahead of him. "Forgetting" did not mean obliterating the memory of the past (Paul has just recalled some of these things in vv.5–7), but a conscious refusal to let them absorb his attention and impede his progress. He never allowed his

Jewish heritage (vv.5–7) nor his previous Christian attainments (vv.9–12) to obstruct his running of the race. No present attainment could lull him into thinking he already possessed all Christ desired for him.

14 Continuing the metaphor, Paul likens his Christian life to pressing onward to the goal so as to win the prize. In applying the figure, the goal and the prize are virtually identical, though viewed perhaps from different aspects. Paul's goal was the complete knowledge of Christ, both in the power of his resurrection and the fellowship of his sufferings (v.10). When the goal was reached, this prize would be fully his. As Hendriksen expresses it, "goal" rivets attention on the race that is being run, whereas "prize" centers the thought on the glory that follows (p. 175). E.M. Blaiklock concludes that Paul has the chariot races of Rome in mind (*Cities of the New Testament* [London: Pickering & Inglis, 1965], pp. 43, 44). The "upward calling" could then refer to the summons to the winner to approach the elevated stand of the judge and receive his prize. It is possible that the prize is to be understood as the "upward call of God" (NASB), interpreted as the "rapture" of the church. However, the word *klēsis* ("calling") is always used elsewhere by Paul, not in reference to Christ's return but to denote the effective call of God that brings men to salvation (1 Cor 1:26; 7:20; Eph 1:18; 4:1, 4; 2 Thess 1:11; 2 Tim 1:9). The expression *anō klēseōs* ("upward call"; NIV, "called me heavenward") is similar to *klēseōs epouraniou* ("heavenly calling") in Hebrews 3:1, which certainly refers to the divine call to salvation. Hence, it is preferable to regard Paul as speaking of the goal and prize for which believers have been called to salvation in Christ.

15 In concluding this section, Paul exhorts those who are mature to think in harmony with what he has just said, and promises that those who think differently about minor points will be enlightened by God if their attitude is right. "Mature" (NIV; KJV, "perfect") is the correct rendering of *teleioi*, as Paul's other five uses of the term referring to persons attest (1 Cor 2:6; 14:20; Eph 4:13; Col 1:28; 4:12). He does not mean "sinless," but is referring to a certain level of spiritual growth and stability in contrast to infants. By using the word *teleioi* Paul is not making a sarcastic reference to perfectionists. Instead, he is calling those who have progressed in the faith to recognize the truth he has just voiced (cf. 3:13, 14 and also the entire explanation in 3:2–14). If the Philippian believers are lax in their pursuit of spiritual goals or erroneously suppose they have already arrived, they need to understand Paul's declaration. And if they generally agree but still differ on some isolated point, Paul is confident that God will lead them to the truth if their minds are open to his leading.

16 No one, however, must wait for God to reveal the truth on all points before he begins to give himself to spiritual growth. Each believer should exercise fully the degree of maturity he already possesses. "Live up to" is the verb *stoichein* ("to keep in line with") and calls for Christians to maintain a consistent life in harmony with the understanding of God's truth they already have. Paul recognizes that Christians, though proceeding along the same path, may be at different stages of progress and should be faithful to as much of God's truth as they understand.

Notes

1 The adverbial use of τὸ λοιπόν (*to loipon*) with the sense of "in addition" or "furthermore" provides a transition to something new. Near the end of a work, it may have the sense of "finally," but it does not always appear at the close of a letter. Paul uses it elsewhere near the middle, such as at 1 Thess 4:1 (without the article) and 1 Thess 3:1 (with the article). In the former instance, nearly one-half of the letter still remained, and in the latter, fully one-third was yet to be written.

The tr. of the imperative χαίρετε (*chairete*) as "goodbye" by Goodspeed in 3:1 and 4:4 (twice) reflects his view that the present Philippians was not originally a unity (*The New Testament, An American Translation*, [Chicago: Univ. of Chicago Press, 1923]). There are, however, no other clear uses of the verb carrying this meaning in the NT, though it does have this sense in sepulchral inscriptions (E.J. Goodspeed, *Problems of New Testament Translation* [Chicago: Univ. of Chicago Press, 1945], pp. 174, 175). It is frequently used in greetings at the beginning of letters.

2 The use of the noun κύων (*kuōn*, "dog") in the disparaging sense in which it appears throughout the NT must be distinguished from κυνάριον (*kynarion*), the dimunitive form, which denoted the " 'house dog' as distinct from the 'yard dog' or the 'dog of the streets' " (Michel, *Kunarion*, TDNT, 3:1104). Jesus referred to the *kynarion*, or house dog, in his discourse with the Gentile woman (Matt 15:26, 27; Mark 7:27, 28).

Paul's use of κατατομή (*katatomē*, "concision"; NIV, "mutilators of the flesh") is a play on περιτομή (*peritomē*, "circumcision") in v.3. The noun does not occur elsewhere in Scripture but the corresponding verb appears in LXX to denote the pagan practice of cutting the flesh for religious purposes (Lev 21:5; 1 Kings 18:28; Isa 15:2).

3 The preferred reading θεοῦ (*theou*, "of God") is supported by א A B C Dᶜ G K and yields the tr. "who worship by the Spirit of God" (NIV). This seems preferable to another grammatical possibility: "who worship the Spirit of God." Without at all denying the full deity of the Holy Spirit, it is still doubtful whether any instance can be found in Scripture authorizing believers to worship the Spirit directly in distinction from the Father and the Son. Lightfoot (in loc.) shows that the verb λατρεύω (*latreuō*, "to worship") had come to have a technical sense referring to the worship of God, and therefore one does not need to regard πνεύματι θεοῦ (*pneumati theou*, "the Spirit of God") as the object of the verb (i.e., recipient of the worship). The alternate reading θεῷ (*theō*) found in D P and a corrector of א may have been due to failure to recognize that the verb did not necessarily require an object. This alternate reading gives the sense: "worship God by the Spirit/spirit." Following the preferred reading, it is best to regard *pneumati* as a dative (instrumental) of agency (as in Rom 8:14; Gal 5:18; see Dana, H.E. and Mantey, J.R., *A Manual Grammar of the Greek New Testament* [New York: Macmillan, 1946], p. 91). The oldest witness to this passage (P⁴⁶) omits *theou*.

4 The noun πεποίθησις (*pepoithēsis*, "confidence") may have either a subjective or an objective sense and may thus denote confidence or grounds for confidence (BAG, p. 649). Having denied in v.3 that believers have "confidence in the flesh," Paul would hardly have contradicted himself in the very next sentence. It is better, therefore, to regard the noun as being used objectively to refer to the reasons or basis for confidence in the flesh. Of course, Paul had learned through his conversion that regardless of one's advantages in the flesh, flesh cannot win the approval of God.

6 Ζῆλος (*zēlos*, "zeal") may be either masc. or neuter, with no apparent difference in meaning. The neuter accusative occurs here. The use of νόμῳ (*nomō*, "law") without the article is thought by some to refer to the Mosaic law in the abstract sense as a principle of action (Lightfoot, pp. 147, 148). Paul, however, usually means the Law of God as contained in the OT, whether or not the article is employed (W.D. Davies, "Law in the NT," IDB, vol. K–Q, p. 99), and it is at least questionable whether this feature is to be pressed with a term that is virtually a proper name.

7 The verb tenses here and in the succeeding verses are important. The imperfect ἦν (ēn, "was") depicts the continuing attitude of Paul regarding his Jewish "advantages" prior to his conversion. The perfect tense ἥγημαι (hēgēmai, "I consider") describes his present settled condition of mind toward those matters that began at the crisis experience when he saw Christ, and that continued unchanged ever since.

8 The combination of the five conjunctions and particles ἀλλὰ μενοῦν γε καὶ (alla menoun ge kai) provides a subtle shading of the thought that English is ill-equipped to translate. "What is more" (NIV) or "more than that" is an approximation. "Ἀλλά [alla] suggests a contrast to be introduced, μέν [men] adds emphasis, while οὖν [oun], gathering up what has already been said, corrects it by way of extending the assertion; γε [ge] can scarcely be translated, representing, rather, a tone of the voice in taking back the limitations implied in ἅτινα ... κέρδη (hatina ... kerdē)." (H.A.A. Kennedy, "Philippians," EGT, 3:452.)

The etymology of σκύβαλον (skybalon, "rubbish") is uncertain, but in usage it was employed of excrement, of scraps or leavings after a meal, or of general refuse. In the NT it appears only here. The less offensive sense of refuse or rubbish fits the context well; however, if Paul is understood to be rising to a crescendo in his explanation, replacement of ζημία (zēmia, "loss") with a bolder term denoting "dung" would not be unlike him (cf. v.2; Gal 5:12).

The purpose clause with ἵνα (hina, "so that") was related to the verb ἡγοῦμαι (hēgoumai, "consider") in the exposition. Another view construes the clause with the aorist verb ἐζημιώθην (ezēmiōthēn, "I have lost"), and thus explains the subjunctive verbs that follow hina as referring to events connected with Paul's conversion (e.g., Lenski, pp. 837, 838). This alternative fits the thought of v.9, which speaks of forensic, not personal, righteousness and provides a legitimate and probably easier explanation of the clause "that I may gain Christ" and what follows. This view, however, makes the clause "and I consider [them] rubbish" parenthetical. In spite of these attractions, the other view is preferable, since it requires no manipulation of the text. There is no clear warrant for seeing any parenthesis in this passage.

9 It is possible that εὑρεθῶ (heurethō) may be used in the general sense of "be shown as" or simply as "be." Note such uses as "Philip was found [εὑρέθη, heurethē] at Azotus" (Acts 8:40) and "if ... we ourselves also are found [εὑρέθημεν, heurethēmen] sinners" (Gal 2:17). Thus, Phil 3:9 would mean "and be in him," without any particular reference to the Second Coming. But the mention of resurrection (v.11) makes the eschatological sense here a natural one.

The possessive adjective ἐμὴν (emēn, "of my own") is more emphatic than μου (mou, "my") would have been and shows that the contrast is intended to be strong between "my own righteousness" and "the righteousness of God."

10 One article is used with δύναμιν (dynamin, "power") and κοινωνίαν (koinōnian, "fellowship"), denoting them as aspects of a single entity—in this case, facets of Paul's concept of what is involved in knowing Christ.

The participle συμμορφιζόμενος (symmorphizomenos, "being conformed"; NIV, "becoming like") has no other NT use, but the cognate σύμμορφος (symmorphos) is used twice, both by Paul and both times in reference to the believer's likeness to Christ (Rom 8:29; Phil 3:21). This word-family differs from its synonyms by denoting the essential form, rather than mere outward appearance, which may be temporary. Paul is thus stating his desire to duplicate in his experience the essence of the Christ-life in an ever-increasing way.

11 Εἴ πως (ei pōs, "if somehow"; NIV, "and so, somehow") occurs four times in the NT (Acts 27:12; Rom 1:10; 11:14; Phil 3:11). In each of these there is some uncertainty about the matter stated, whether regarding its ultimate achievement or the manner in which it will be accomplished. The sense of expectation, however, is stressed by BDF, p. 375. Burton considers the statement an omitted apodasis that is virtually contained in the protasis. The protasis then expresses the object of hope and has nearly the force of a purpose clause (Syntax of the Moods and Tenses [Chicago: Univ. of Chicago Press, 1897], p. 276).

The NT hapax legomenon ἐξανάστασιν (exanastasin, "resurrection") not only has the article, but is followed by a prepositional phrase that is tied to it attributively by a second article. Whether this term is to be differentiated from ἀνάστασις (anastasis) of v.10 or was merely a stylistic variation is debatable. S.L. Johnson suggests that the sense of "rising up" as found in Polybius would fit admirably the rapture of the church, and its greater vividness than *anastasis* also argues for interpreting it as the rapture ("The Out-Resurrection from the Dead," BS, 110:145). Hendriksen argues for the sense of being "raised completely above sin and selfishness" (pp. 169, 170), although there is little NT warrant for such a use of *anastasis* or its cognate (the only time in the NT that *anastasis* does not refer to physical resurrection is in Luke 2:34, a highly figurative passage). The majority view regards the word as denoting physical resurrection, however, on the basis of its cognate, and from the sense of "from the dead," which follows.

12 The aorist indicative ἔλαβον (*elabon*, "I received"; NIV, "I have ... obtained") points to the experience on the Damascus road nearly thirty years before. The perfect tense of τετελείωμαι (*teteleiōmai*, "have ... been made perfect") depicts the settled condition resulting from that previous occurrence. Paul knew that the culmination of his spiritual progress had not occurred at the beginning (nor at any other time in the past), nor had he arrived at such a state since. The present tense of διώκω (*diōkō*, "I press on") denotes the constant pursuit of the goal.

Whether ἐφ᾽ ᾧ (*eph' hō*) should be treated as "because" or "inasmuch as," naming the reason why Paul feels obligated to pursue the goal (same use as in Rom 5:12; 2 Cor 5:4), or as "with a view to which" (NIV, "for which") referring to the unstated object of καταλάβω (*katalabō*, "to take hold"), is uncertain (C.F.D. Moule, *An Idiom Book of New Testament Greek* [Cambridge: Cambridge Univ. Press, 1953], p. 132). Both fit the context easily. The latter use is the best choice in Phil 4:10, and is adopted in KJV, ASV, Ph, NEB, and NIV. The alternative appears in RSV.

13 The MSS vary between the negatives οὐ (*ou*, UBS) and οὔπω (*oupō*, Nestle). The meaning of the passage is not altered, however, because either "not" or "not yet" must be understood in the light of Paul's claim that he does not presently possess, but that he ultimately will.

"One thing I do" reproduces the phrase ἐν δέ (*hen de*), which uses no verb, and the literal sense "but one thing" is even more forceful and dramatic.

14 Of the eleven NT occurrences of κλῆσις (*klēsis*, "calling"), the only non-Pauline uses are Heb 3:1 (dependent upon one's view of authorship) and 2 Peter 1:10. All eleven have reference to the call of God to salvation. The phrase ἐν Χριστῷ Ἰησοῦ (*en Christō Iēsou*, "in Christ Jesus") should be construed with "calling," not with the more remote "I press on."

15 Paul must be using τέλειοι (*teleioi*, "mature") in a different sense from his use of the verb τετελείωμαι (*teteleiōmai*, "made perfect") in v.12. There the reference was to the culminating and complete perfection toward which each believer must strive. The adjective, however, denotes a relative perfection (maturity) that can be a present possession. Other NT writers using the adjective in this way are Matthew (5:48), the writer of Hebrews (5:14), and James (1:4; 3:2).

16 The infinitive στοιχεῖν (*stoichein*) is used here as an imperative (Dana and Mantey, *Manual Grammar*, pp. 216, 217). Although infrequent, this use of an infinitive does occur elsewhere in the NT (Rom 12:15; Tit 2:2). The verb means "to keep step."

A textual variant is reflected in the KJV, which adds the words "let us mind the same thing" (κανόνι, τὸ αὐτὸ φρονεῖν, *kanoni, to auto phronein*). Numerous other minor variations that occur among the MSS at this point may have been influenced by Gal 6:16 and Phil 2:2.

---

2. The Antinomian Danger

3:17-21

> [17]Join with others in following my example, brothers, and take note of those who live according to the pattern we gave you. [18]For, as I have often told you before and now say again even with tears, many live as enemies of the cross of Christ. [19]Their destiny is destruction, their god is their stomach, and their glory is in their shame. Their mind is on earthly things. [20]But our citizenship is in heaven. And we eagerly await a Savior from there, the Lord Jesus Christ, [21]who, by the power that enables him to bring everything under his control, will transform our lowly bodies so that they will be like his glorious body.

17 In the early years of the church, believers needed practical guides for conduct. So Paul urged the Philippians to join together in imitating his conduct, just as he had done in his exhortation to the church at Corinth—"Follow my example, as I follow the example of Christ" (1 Cor 11:1). Such advice was not egotism, for Paul's emphasis was always strongly christological (e.g., Phil 2:5–8). Furthermore, Paul includes others in this model as he urges his readers to take note of those who were living in conformity with "the pattern we gave you" (v.17)—i.e., the high standard outlined in 3:7–16. Literally, Paul wrote, "you [pl.] have us as a pattern," and the "us" includes not only himself but Timothy and perhaps Epaphroditus also. Hence, he was not claiming a unique superiority.

18 Who were these "enemies of the cross of Christ"? Some regard them as the Judaizers of 3:2, whose emphasis on legalism undermined the effect of the Cross (Lenski, Muller, Barth). Others view them as antinomians, who went to the opposite extreme from the Judaizers and threw off all restraints (Lightfoot, Kennedy, Beare, Hendriksen). By their lawless lives, they too were enemies of the Cross and the new life that should issue from it. Verse 19 is more readily understood of the antinomians.

It is not likely that these men were simply pagans, of whom nothing much better was to be expected. In all probability they were professing Christians, but ones whose lives were so profligate that it was clear to Paul that they had never been regenerated. Presumably, they were not actually members of the Philippian church (the character of the entire Epistle would have been different if "many" such people were in that congregation), but because there were such in the Christian world as a whole, they posed a danger to every church (cf. Rom 16:17, 18; 2 Peter 2:10–22). Paul had already warned of them, perhaps in former visits or letters, and felt real anguish when the churches were threatened with falseness of doctrine or life.

19 The ultimate end for such persons is "destruction" (*apōleia*, the regular NT word for eternal loss, the opposite of *sōtēria*, "salvation"). (See note on 1:28.) "Their god is their stomach." To interpret this as referring to the Judaizers demands relating it to various "kosher" food regulations. It is easier to explain it of sensualists who indulged various physical appetites without restraint (Rom 16:18; 1 Cor 6:13; Jude 11). "Their glory is in their shame." By their indulgence, they actually exulted in what ought to have been shameful to them (Eph 5:12). Those who relate the statement to Judaizers explain the "shame" as a euphemism for one's private parts, specifically the circumcision demanded by the Judaizers. It would be most unusual, however, for Paul to speak of circumcision as a "shame." The final description characterizes the "enemies of the cross of Christ" as continually minding earthly things. Their whole attention is fixed on physical and material interests. They stand in stark contrast to spiritual men, as explained in the following verse.

20 The "our" is emphatic and stresses the distinction between true believers, whose essential relationships belong to the heavenly sphere, and the sensualists just discussed, who are exclusively concerned with earthly things. The Christian's "commonwealth" is in heaven, and for him earthly things must at best be secondary. The Philippians would find this a most apt metaphor, for in a political sense they knew what it was to be citizens of a far-off city (even though most of them had probably never been to Rome) and they were proud of that status (Acts 16:12, 21; see comment on Phil 1:27). On an immeasurably higher plane, believers belong to the "city . . . whose architect and builder is God"

(Heb 11:10), the "Jerusalem that is above" (Gal 4:26), and are themselves "foreigners and strangers on earth" (Heb 11:13; 1 Peter 2:11). As such, their eyes should be heavenward, anticipating the coming of their Savior, who is not a mere earthly emperor but the Lord Jesus Christ. An eager expectation of his return does much to protect the believer from earthly, sensual enticements.

21 Christ at his return will "transform" (*metaschēmatisei*, "change the outward form of") believers' mortal bodies, so that they will conform to the character of his resurrection body. The present body is described literally as "the body of lowliness" (*to sōma tēs tapeinōseōs*), a description calling attention to its weakness and susceptibility to persecution, disease, sinful appetites, and death. At Christ's coming, however, the earthly, transient appearance will be changed, whether by resurrection of those dead or by rapture of the living, and believers will be transformed and will receive glorified bodies that will more adequately display their essential character (*summorphon*) as children of God and sharers of divine life in Christ. This will be accomplished by the same effective operation (*energeian*) that will ultimately bring all things in the universe under the authority of Christ.

The tr. "vile" (KJV) for *tapeinōseōs* conveys a wrong idea. Emphasis is not on sinfulness, but on lowliness or humble status.

In all NT uses of *energeia* ("power"), the working is from a supernatural source, whether God or Satan. Hence, effective power is in view. (See note on 2:13.)

Notes

17 Because συμμίμηται (*symmimētai*, "fellow imitators") takes an objective genitive, the sense is "join with others in imitating me," not "join with me in imitating Christ."

The verb σκοπέω (*skopeō*) means "look out for," or "notice," and whether the object is to be emulated (as here) or avoided (Rom 16:17) must be gleaned from the context. Paul and his associates had furnished themselves as a τύπον (*typon*, "example") for Christian conduct. The noun τύπος (*typos*, [nom.] "example") denoted originally the visible impression made by the stroke of some instrument, then a pattern or model. In the moral realm it can mean "example" (BAG).

18 Identification of these errorists as having some connection with the Christian movement is strengthened by the use of περιπατοῦσιν (*peripatousin*, "walking"), a term most commonly used by Paul to describe the conduct of Christians.

19 On ἀπώλεια (*apōleia*, "destruction"), see note on 1:28. The idea that αἰσχύνη (*aischynē*, "shame") refers to one's private parts is expressed by JB: "'Shame' may be only the traditional euphemism for the circumcised member" (p. 343, note). But there is no evidence for this. The primary LXX usage as "disgrace" (TDNT, 1:189) accords better with relegating the passage to antinomians.

The nominative phrase οἱ φρονοῦντες (*hoi phronountes*, literally, "the ones thinking"; NIV, "their mind") is grammatically governed by πολλοί (*polloi*, "many") of v.18.

20 The noun πολίτευμα (*politeuma*, "citizenship") occurs only here in the NT. The cognate πολιτεία (*politeia*, Acts 22:28; Eph 2:12) can mean either "citizenship" (rights and duties of a citizen) or the "commonwealth" itself, but *politeuma* seems limited to the sense of "commonwealth" (BAG, pp. 692, 693; TDNT, 6:535).

The antecedent of ἐξ οὗ (*ex hou*, "from where"; NIV, "from there") is probably οὐρανοῖς (*ouranois*, "heaven"), with the sing. pronoun having a sense of agreement with the noun, which is commonly pl. (as here) in form but sing. in meaning. It is possible, of course, for the sing. *politeuma* to be the antecedent.

Even though σωτήρ (*sōtēr*, "savior") was a title for various gods in pagan cults and was also applied to various human leaders or to the king, as shown on inscriptions, it was used of God in LXX (Ps 24:5; 26:9); hence, Paul did not need to borrow the usage from any pagan source (BAG, p. 808).

21 On the difference between the related words σχῆμα (*schēma*) and μορφή (*morphē*), see comments and notes on 2:6, 8. The difference is relevant here also. Christ will "transform" the outward, earthly appearance. Then the essential person, regenerated with life from God, will exhibit in his glorified body the form that truly reflects his status in Christ. His body will "conform" to Christ's body.

It is questioned whether αυτῳ (*autō*), which is generally regarded as the preferred reading, should be given the rough breathing and treated as reflexive (αὑτῷ, *hautō*) or should be treated as the personal pronoun (αὐτῷ, *autō*). Lightfoot insists that the aspirated form has no place in the NT (p. 157). However, even if the form is left unaspirated, the personal pronoun is often used with a reflexive sense (RHG, pp. 680, 681; BDF, p. 283; E.V. Goetchius, *The Language of the New Testament* [New York: Scribner's, 1965], p. 375).

V. Second Series of Exhortations (4:1-9)

1. Exhortation to Stand Firm in Unity

4:1-3

> [1]Therefore, my brothers, you whom I love and long for, my joy and crown, that is how you should stand firm in the Lord, dear friends!
> [2]I plead with Euodia and I plead with Syntyche to agree with each other in the Lord. [3]Yes, and I ask you, loyal yokefellow, help these women who have contended at my side in the cause of the gospel, along with Clement and the rest of my fellow workers, whose names are in the book of life.

1 This verse is another of Paul's subtle transitions, so skillfully blended as to make it difficult to decide whether it should be placed with what precedes or what follows. A good transition, however, fits both segments. Inasmuch as the following statements discuss the need for unity among certain individuals, it is appropriate to treat v.1 (as does NIV) as a general exhortation to the whole church to stand firm in the manner Paul has been outlining in the previous verses (especially 17–21). It is of interest that the same verb *stēkō* ("stand firm") was used also at the beginning of the first series of exhortations in this Epistle (1:27).

The reference to the Philippians as "brothers, you whom I love and long for," shows the strong feeling of intimacy the apostle felt toward these readers. Their description as Paul's "joy and crown" echoes his earlier words to another Macedonian church (1 Thess 2:19). The Philippians were his present joy as he received favorable reports of their spiritual growth, and their presence with Christ at his return would be his future crown when Christ comes to reward his servants. The "crown" (*stephanos*) mentioned here is the wreath of victory or celebration.

2 The apostle turns from his general exhortation to an application of it. Two women, Euodia and Syntyche, are instructed to bring their attitudes into harmony. Paul does not indicate which one was in the wrong but knows that if the attitude of each would be formed "in the Lord," the disharmony would vanish. Repetition of the verb may indicate

the need for separate admonitions because the rift between them had become so great. Paul's method of handling the problem suggests that it was not a doctrinal issue, but a clash of personalities.

3 At this point Paul seeks to enlist the aid of a third party, Syzygus ("yokefellow," NIV), whom he challenges to live up to his name and be a "loyal yokefellow" (*gnēsie syzyge*) by bringing these women together (see note). (Another Pauline play on a personal name occurs in Philem 10, 11.) Inasmuch as Euodia and Syntyche had once labored with Paul, they should be able to do so again. Perhaps they had been among the original group of converts at Philippi, for women had been Paul's first hearers there (Acts 16:13–15). Their Christian labors had been in conjunction with Clement and others of Paul's co-workers. This Clement is not otherwise known to us with certainty. Even though some of these names are not recorded in this letter, Paul knows that their service is not forgotten, for their names are recorded in the Book of Life. The reference is to the register in heaven of those who are saved (Rev 3:5; 17:8; 20:12, 15; 21:27; 22:19; cf. Luke 10:20; Heb 12:23). It does not imply that they and Clement were now dead, though they might have been. Paul's memory of these happy associations prompted his concern that the present disunity might be ended so that faithful Christian activity could proceed and prosper.

Notes

1 The most common NT meaning of στέφανος (*stephanos*) is "wreath." In four instances, it refers to the crown of thorns, and though it was doubtless meant to mock Jesus' regal claims, *stephanos* rather than διάδημα (*diadēma*) was probably used here because Paul referred to a wreath rather than a royal circlet of gold. The majority of uses denotes the wreath bestowed on believers as a reward by Christ. One instance utilizes the term to denote Christ's crown (Rev 14:14), indicating that even here the connotation may be victory rather than rulership.

2 Εὐοδία (*Euodia*) and Συντύχη (*Syntyche*) are women, as the fem. pronouns αὐταῖς (*autais*) and αἵτινες (*haitines*) in v.3 show. These names are common in the inscriptions and there is no warrant for allegorizing them to represent parties in the church.

3 The verb ἐρωτῶ (*erōtō*) usually means "to ask a question" but can mean "to request." This latter sense is employed here as Paul requests assistance in healing the breach between the two women.

Some have objected that "Syzygus," "yokefellow" in NIV, has not yet been found elsewhere as a proper name. Nevertheless, it still provides a better sense for σύζυγε (*syzyge*) than the suggested alternatives. A proper name is to be expected among the proper names given before (Euodia, Syntyche) and after (Clement). To regard the term as a reference to Paul's wife (!) or some other woman runs afoul of the masculine adjective γνήσιε (*gnēsie*, "loyal"). Unless this person were the acknowledged head of the congregation at Philippi who would have been the one to receive the letter, it is difficult to see how the Philippians themselves could have identified this "yokefellow." Identifying this person as Epaphroditus is illogical, since he was with Paul at the moment. If we identify him as Luke, we must assume either that the Epistle emanated from an earlier time (from Ephesus, perhaps) when Luke presumably was there (inferred from the "we" passages in Acts 16:10 and 20:6) or that Luke was at Philippi some of the time Paul was in Rome. There is no evidence for the latter.

The phrase μετὰ καὶ Κλήμεντος (*meta kai Klēmentos*, "along with Clement") should be construed with συνήθλησάν (*synēthlēsan*, "contended with") as denoting that Clement labored with these women, rather than referring it to the more distant συλλαμβάνου (*syllambanou*, "help") as though Paul were trying to enlist Clement and others to join Syzygus in uniting the women. Clement was identified by Origen as the well-known Clement of Rome (A.E. Brooke, *The*

Commentary of Origen on St. John's Gospel [Cambridge: Cambridge Univ. Press, 1896], 1:173, 174, on 1:29), but no evidence is given for his conclusion.

---

2. Exhortation to Maintain Various Christian Virtues

4:4–9

[4]Rejoice in the Lord always. I will say it again: Rejoice! [5]Let your gentleness be evident to all. The Lord is near. [6]Do not be anxious about anything, but in everything, by prayer and petition, with thanksgiving, present your requests to God. [7]And the peace of God, which transcends all understanding, will guard your hearts and your minds in Christ Jesus.
[8]Finally, brothers, whatever is true, whatever is noble, whatever is right, whatever is pure, whatever is lovely, whatever is admirable—if anything is excellent or praiseworthy—think about such things. [9]Whatever you have learned or received or heard from me, or seen in me—put it into practice. And the God of peace will be with you.

4 From his previous exhortation to unity and from his attempt to correct a case of disunity, Paul proceeds to exhort the church to maintain certain positive Christian virtues. First, believers are to "rejoice in the Lord always" and "again" to "rejoice." The double emphasis on rejoicing may imply that a single injunction might prompt the question "How can we rejoice, in view of our difficulties?" So he repeats the command, because in all the vicissitudes of the Christian life, whether in attacks from errorists, personality clashes among believers, persecution from the world, or threat of imminent death—all of which Paul himself was experiencing at this very time—the Christian is to maintain a spirit of joy in the Lord. He is not immune to sorrow nor should he be insensitive to the troubles of others; yet he should count the will of God his highest joy and so be capable of knowing inner peace and joy in every circumstance.

5 Second, believers are to be gentle to all. The term *epieikēs* ("gentleness") is difficult to translate with its full connotation. Such words as *gentle, yielding, kind, forbearing,* and *lenient* are among the best English attempts, but no single word is adequate. Involved is the willingness to yield one's personal rights and to show consideration and gentleness to others. It is easy to display this quality toward some persons, but Paul commands that it be shown toward all. That would seem to include Christian friends, unsaved persecutors, false teachers—anyone at all. Of course, truth is not to be sacrificed, but a gentle spirit will do much to disarm the adversary.

As an encouragement, Paul now reminds his readers the Lord is near. His reference is to the Parousia (not just Christ's continuing presence with believers). This seems clear from the context of the letter, where 3:20, 21 focused attention on the glorious prospect in view for believers at Christ's return. A similar connection between a longsuffering spirit and the Lord's coming occurs in James 5:8. The statement is a reminder that at his arrival the Judge will settle all differences and will bring the consummation that will make most of our human differences seem trifling.

6 Third, believers should be prayerful instead of anxious. The verb *merimnate* can mean "to be concerned about" in a proper Christian sense (and is so used by Paul in 2:20), but here the meaning is clearly that of anxiety, fretfulness, or undue concern. Paul is not calling for apathy or inaction, for as we make plans in the light of our circumstances, it is our Christian privilege to do so in full trust that our Father hears our prayers for what we need. The answer to anxiety is prayer. "Prayer" (*proseuchē*) denotes the petitioner's attitude of mind as worshipful. "Petition" (*deēsei*) denotes prayers as expressions of need. "Thanksgiving" (*eucharistias*) should accompany all Christian praying, as the supplicant acknowledges that whatever God sends is for his good. It may also include remembrance of previous blessings. "Requests" (*aitēmata*) refers to the things asked for.

7 Having just given us a classic exhortation to pray, Paul attaches to it the beautiful promise that when we turn from anxiety to prayer and thanksgiving, God will give us his own peace. This peace is for those who are already at peace with God through justification by faith in Christ (Rom 5:1). Although some explain *hē hyperechousa panta noun* ("which transcends all understanding," NIV) as meaning that God's peace accomplishes far more than any human forethought or plan might devise, the comparable expression in Ephesians 3:20 shows that the common rendering is preferable. The NIV rendering or the KJV, "which passeth all understanding," well conveys the sense. For the peace of God not only suffices but far surpasses human comprehension. It acts as a sentry to guard the believer's heart (a biblical symbol for the personality in which the mind resides) and the believer's thoughts from all anxiety and despair.

8 Fourth, believers should keep on thinking and doing what is morally and spiritually excellent. This involves centering their minds on exalted things and then (v.9) putting into practice what they have learned from Paul's teaching and example.

Here (v.8) Paul has set forth in memorable words a veritable charter for Christian thought. Although this beautiful list of virtues is not exclusively Christian, we need not suppose that Paul has borrowed it from pagan moralists. All the terms are found in the Greek versions of the OT (LXX or Symmachus), and most of them appear elsewhere in the NT. "True" (*alēthē*) has the sense of valid, reliable, and honest—the opposite of false. It characterizes God (Rom 3:4) and should also characterize believers. "Noble" (*semna*) is used in the NT only by Paul—here and in 1 Tim 3:8, 11; Tit 2:2—and in the latter passages refers to church officers—i.e., a quality that makes them worthy of respect. "Right" (*dikaia*) refers to what is upright or just, conformable to God's standards and thus worthy of his approval. "Pure" (*hagna*) emphasizes moral purity and includes in some contexts the more restricted sense of "chaste." "Lovely" (*prosphilē*) occurs only here in the NT. It appears in LXX (Esther 5:1) and Josephus (Antiq. I.18.12; XVII.6.22) and relates to what is pleasing, agreeable, or amiable. "Admirable" (*euphēma*) occurs only here, though Paul uses the cognate *euphēmia* in 2 Corinthians 6:8. It denotes what is praiseworthy, attractive, and what rings true to the highest standards.

Suddenly Paul changes the sentence structure to conditional clauses—"if anything is. . . ."—a rhetorical device that forces the reader to exercise his own discernment and choose what is "excellent" (*aretē*) and "praiseworthy" (*epainos*). Paul knows that when we continually center our minds on such thoughts as these, we shall live like Christians.

9 Since Paul himself had been their teacher and example, what they had learned from him they were to keep on practicing. The four verbs in this verse form two pairs. The first pair, "learned" and "received," describes the Philippians' instruction by Paul, from whom they had been taught Christian doctrine and Christian living. The next pair, "heard" and "saw," depicts their personal observation of the apostle—both his speech and his conduct. As Martin aptly remarks, in the early days of the church before the NT writings were written or widely circulated, the standards of Christian belief and behav-

ior were largely taught by being embodied in the words and example of the apostles (*Philippians*, p. 173). Those who follow this apostolic guidance have the additional promise that God, who provides true peace (v.9; cf. v.7), will be with them.

Notes

4 On χαίρετε (*chairete*, "rejoice"), see note on 3:1.
5 Herbert Preisker notes that ἐπιεικής (*epieikēs*, "gentleness") and cognates are used in LXX and Josephus mostly of a quality of God or some human ruler who possesses sovereignty but chooses to display mildness or leniency. In the NT the noun form is used of Christians who are associated with the divine King, but must also display his gentleness to others (2 Cor 10:1). In Phil 4:5 Christians have a special incentive to display this royal virtue because the Lord is at hand and their promised glory will soon be manifested. (H. Preisker, TDNT, 2:588–590.)
6 Of the nineteen NT uses of μεριμνάω (*merimnaō*, "to be anxious, concerned"), only four occur in a favorable sense, and all of these four are by Paul (1 Cor 7:32, 34; 12:25; Phil 2:20). The rest are used of anxiety, as in the teaching of Jesus on this subject (Matt 6:25, 27, 28, 31, 34). A striking instance of this meaning relates to Martha (Luke 10:41).
   On the precise distinctions among the terms for prayer in v.6, see Trench, pp. 188–192.
7 Lightfoot exemplifies those who interpret ἡ ὑπερέχουσα πάντα νοῦν (*hē hyperechousa panta noun*, "which transcends all understanding") as referring to human device or council. He regards νοῦν as denoting man's planning, which is so frequently characterized by anxiety and is thus greatly inferior to God's provision for man's needs. Lightfoot admits, however, that Ephesians 3:20 supports the other interpretation (p. 161).
   In both OT and NT, καρδία (*kardia*, "heart") denotes the innermost part of a person—the seat of one's mental and spiritual powers. Although it may include the feelings and emotions, its more important function is its role as the moral, volitional, and intellectual center of man. A narrower term is νοῦς (*nous*), tr. "understanding" by KJV and NIV. From the *nous* proceed a person's thoughts (νοήματα, *noēmata*), rendered somewhat inexactly as "minds" by KJV and NIV.
   The verb φρουρέω (*phroureō*, "to guard") can mean a kind of guarding that prevents entrance or exit, as well as the more general meaning of simple protecting or keeping. "The peace of God" is here regarded as a military protector preventing anxieties within or satanic doubts from without.
8 Some regard τὸ λοιπόν (*to loipon*) as a resumption of the previous "final" word in v.1, after a digression. Others see in it a combining of two letters. There is no need to adopt either explanation. The expression "the God of peace" clearly ties v.9 with v.7 as part of the same unit. Hence, *to loipon* may be regarded as Paul's concluding exhortation in this series, before he introduces the topic of the Philippians' gift.
   Dana and Mantey (*Manual Grammar*, p. 247) argue for a special use of εἴ τις (*ei tis*) and treat it as equivalent to ὅ τι (*ho ti*) or ὅς τις (*hos tis*). This yields the rendering "whatever is true . . . noble," etc., giving broader applications of faith following the previous particularized examples.
9 The verbs ἐμάθετε (*emathete*, "you learned") and παρελάβετε (*parelabete*, "you received") are virtually synonymous; the former refers to the acquisition of knowledge, the second has the additional connotation of gaining instruction from a teacher.
   The article with εἰρήνης (*eirēnēs*, "peace") probably points to the former reference in v.7; thus it means "the God of this peace."

VI. The Philippians' Gifts to Paul (4:10–20)

1. *The Recent Gift*

4:10–14

> ¹⁰I rejoice greatly in the Lord that at last you have renewed your concern for me. Indeed, you have been concerned, but you had no opportunity to show it. ¹¹I am not saying this because I am in need, for I have learned to be content whatever the circumstances. ¹²I know what it is to be in need, and I know what it is to have plenty. I have learned the secret of being content in any and every situation, whether well-fed or hungry, whether living in plenty or in want. ¹³I can do everything through him who gives me strength.
> ¹⁴Yet it was good of you to share in my troubles.

10 As Paul begins to conclude his letter, he voices his joy over the Philippians' recent contribution to him. This is probably not his first note of thanks to them, for considerable time had elapsed since Epaphroditus had brought the gift and several contacts with the church at Philippi had already been made (see Introduction, 3). Furthermore, it is doubtful that his expression of gratitude would have been left to the end of the letter (see Introduction, 4). Paul retained a vivid memory of their generous act. "At last" (*ēdē pote*) should not be regarded as a rebuke, but merely as showing that communication had again occurred after a period of no contact. (The usage is similar to that in Rom 1:10.) Paul makes it clear that the fault was not theirs but came from a lack of opportunity. Perhaps no messenger had been available. In addition, the apostle's own circumstances had been highly irregular in recent years, in part, at least, because of imprisonment and shipwreck. Now the demonstration of concern had bloomed again, like plants in the spring.

11 The apostle hastens to make clear that though he undoubtedly had a need, it was not relief of this need that primarily concerned him. He had learned to be content with what God provided, irrespective of circumstances. It is significant that Paul had to "learn" this virtue. Contentment is not natural to most of mankind.

In Stoic philosophy, *autarkēs* ("content") described a person who accepted impassively whatever came. Circumstances that he could not change were regarded as the will of God, and fretting was useless. This philosophy fostered a self-sufficiency in which all the resources for coping with life were located within man himself. In contrast, Paul locates his sufficiency in Christ who provides strength for believers.

12 Paul understood what it was to be in want as well as "to have plenty." The latter may refer to his earlier days as a rising figure in Judaism (Gal 1:14) or to the possibility that he had received a sum of money more recently. On the other hand, the expression may be merely relative. It may be that Paul considered the times he was not suffering privation to be times of plenty (e.g., Acts 9:19, 28; 16:15, 33, 34; 18:3; 21:8). He had learned the secret of trusting God "in every [particular] situation" (*en panti*) and in all situations as a whole (*en pasin*).

13 His was no Stoic philosophy, however. He did not trace his resources to some inner fortitude that would enable him to take with equanimity whatever life brought him. Instead, his strength for "everything" lay in the One who continually empowered him.

The name "Christ," to which we are accustomed through the KJV translation of v.13, does not appear in the most reliable manuscripts, but surely Paul has Christ in mind. The apostle was not desperately seeking a gift from the Philippians, because he knew that Christ would give him the strength for whatever circumstances were in God's will for him.

14 Nevertheless, the Philippians must not feel that their gift had been unnecessary. They had responded properly to his need, and Paul was truly grateful—not so much for what the gift did for him as for the willingness of the Philippians to share with him. They had accepted his affliction as their own and had done something about it.

Notes

10 The aorist indicative ἐχάρην (echarēn, "I rejoiced" may be either ingressive, denoting the historical incident that caused Paul's rejoicing, or it may be epistolary. If the latter, the meaning is "I rejoice" (as in NIV).

This sole NT occurrence of ἀναθάλλω (anathallō) may be either transitive, "you caused your thinking concerning me to bloom again," or intransitive, "you bloomed again in regard to your thinking concerning me" (NIV, "you have renewed your concern for me"). The difference in meaning is slight, with the latter being perhaps a bit more tactful, since it avoids the implication that their previous lack of thought for Paul came from their failure.

The antecedent of ᾧ (hō) may be either the masc. ἐμοῦ (emou), thus yielding "about whom you were also thinking," or else the entire neuter infinitive phrase τὸ ... φρονεῖν (to ... phronein), hence, "concerning which [i.e., your thinking about me] you were also thinking."

11 The neuter phrase ἐν οἷς (en hois) is not indefinite and should not be rendered "in whatever state." It refers to his present circumstances in Rome, "in which circumstances." The elaboration in the next verse, however, applies the principle more generally.

12 Ramsay argues that Paul's trial in Rome would have required considerable money, and observes that Felix apparently thought Paul had access to funds. He suggests that he may have inherited some family wealth (pp. 34–37, 310–313).

The double use of καί (kai) is the "both ... and" construction. The irregularity is caused by the repetition of οἶδα (oida, "I know"), but this is apparently for additional emphasis.

It need not be supposed that Paul borrowed the verb μεμύημαι (memuēmai) from the mystery religions. The term was a technical one, "to initiate into the mysteries," but undoubtedly had a general use as well, "to learn the secret" (NIV). If the cultic sense is insisted on, then we must assume that Paul was using it ironically (G. Bornkamm, Mueō, TDNT, 4:828).

13 The form πάντα (panta, "all things") is an accusative of reference after ἰσχύω (ischuō, "I can do"), as in James 5:16. That Christ is to be understood as the one empowering Paul (though MS evidence is against inclusion of the name here) is strongly probable in the light of a similar statement of Paul in 1 Tim 1:12, τῷ ἐνδυναμώσαντί με Χριστῷ Ἰησοῦ τῷ κυρίῳ ἡμῶν (to endynamōsanti me Christō Iēsou tō kyriō hēmōn, "Christ Jesus our Lord, who has given me strength").

14 The adversative πλήν (plēn, "yet") cautions the readers against drawing the conclusion that Paul did not need their gift.

2. The Previous Gifts

4:15–20

15Moreover, as you Philippians know, in the early days of your acquaintance with the gospel, when I set out from Macedonia, not one church shared with me in the matter of giving and receiving, except you only; 16for even when I was in Thessalonica, you sent me aid again and again when I was in need. 17Not that I am looking for a gift, but I am looking for what may be credited to your account. 18I have received full payment and even more; I am amply supplied, now that I have received from Epaphroditus the gifts you sent. They are a fragrant offering, an acceptable sacrifice, pleasing to God. 19And my God will meet all your needs according to his glorious riches in Christ Jesus.
20To our God and Father be glory for ever and ever. Amen.

15 In order to make it clear that he is not minimizing the Philippians' generosity toward him, Paul recalls some earlier demonstrations of their love for him. When the gospel was first preached to them—approximately ten years before (Acts 16)—they were the only church to contribute to him when he left Macedonia. Some commentators are influenced by the succeeding reference to Thessalonica and explain this passage to mean that Paul received the gift in Thessalonica while on his way from Macedonia to Achaia (Corinth), though Thessalonica is itself in Macedonia. But this seems more awkward than to consider the gift as the one sent him by the Philippians while he was in Corinth (2 Cor 11:9). As he mentions this gift, he also recalls two earlier instances of their generosity when he was in Thessalonica.

Paul does not mean that no other church ever assisted him (cf. 2 Cor 11:8), but that on the specific occasion referred to here no other church had come to his aid. He uses business terminology, "an account of giving and receiving" (*logon doseōs kai lēmpseōs*—NIV, "the matter of giving and receiving"), to depict the situation.

16 Not only had the Philippians sent him a gift when he left Macedonia, but even when he was in Thessalonica, shortly after his departure from Philippi (Acts 17:1), they had made a contribution to him on more than one occasion. Presumably these earlier gifts were small and so were in a different category from the one mentioned in v.15. This is also implied by references in the Thessalonian Epistles showing that Paul earned his living there (1 Thess 2:9; 2 Thess 3:7, 8).

17 Paul's readers must not suppose that he is primarily concerned with their gift as such, but rather in the development of the grace of giving among them. Continuing to use business terminology, he says that he regards such displays as interest accruing (NIV, "credited") to their account. Their spiritual growth was the fruit Paul desired, and to this end he directed his ministry.

18 The financial language continues as Paul says, "I have received full payment and even more." The gifts brought by Epaphroditus (2:25–30) had completely met his needs, and Paul considers this contribution a sacrificial offering to God, made to further the Lord's work by helping his servant (cf. Matt 25:40). "A fragrant offering" (*osmēn euōdias*) is used in Ephesians 5:2 of Christ's sacrificial offering of himself to God on man's behalf. It reflects the Levitical ritual (e.g., Lev 1:9, 13, 17; 2:12 [LXX]). Such offerings pleased God, because they came from obedient hearts.

The verb *apechō* appears regularly in business papyri and ostraca in the sense of receiving in full. It was a technical expression in drawing up receipts. Deissmann cites numerous examples with several photographs and also notes that *apechō* is often combined with *panta* ("all") in receipts, as is done in Phil 4:18 (Deiss LAE, pp. 110–112, 166).

19 In words that countless Christians have relied on as one of the great Scripture promises, Paul now reminds his benefactors that "his" God (*ho theos mou*, "my God") will do what he himself is in no position to do; namely, reimburse his benefactors. This assurance of the divine supply of the Philippians' needs implies that they had given so liberally that they actually left themselves in some real "need" (*chreian*). Yet it is true that those who share generously with others, especially to advance the work of the Lord, are promised a divine supply of anything they might lack because of their generosity (Prov 11:25; 19:17; Matt 5:7).

The preposition *kata* ("according to") conveys the thought that God's supply of the Philippians' need will not be merely from or out of his wealth but in some sense appropriate to or commensurate with it. The phrase *en doxē* ("in glory"; NIV, "glorious") is sometimes construed with *plērōsei* ("will fill"; NIV, "will meet") and tr. "gloriously" (Muller), or in a local sense, perhaps with eschatological tones, "by placing you in glory" (Lightfoot). Word order, however, strongly favors relating it to *ploutos* ("riches"), "his riches in glory," or "glorious riches" (Martin, *Philippians*). By this understanding, we are to think of the heavenly glories that Christ now enjoys as explaining the source of our supply.

20 Small wonder that Paul closes this beautiful passage with a doxology. The glory of God's providential care must always be recognized by his children. Even the eternal ages yet to come will not be sufficient to exhaust the praises that belong to him.

Notes

15 Although the spelling Φιλιππήσιοι (*Philippēsioi*) is apparently a Latin form less common than Φιλιππεῖς (*Philippeis*) or Φιλιππηνοί (*Philippēnoi*), it also appears in the title of this Epistle and in that of Polycarp's Epistle (see W.M. Ramsay, "On the Greek Form of the Name Philippians," JTS, I [1900], p. 116).

The aorist indicative ἐξῆλθον (*exēlthon*, "I set out") does not describe a process of leaving, or being "on the way," but an actual departure. This reinforces the view that Paul is referring to his actual removal from Macedonia to some other place. The mention of Thessalonica in v.16 indicates that the sharing in v.15 is a separate incident.

Even though λόγον δόσεως καὶ λήμψεως (*logon doseōs kai lēmpseōs*, "the matter of giving and receiving") is financial language, it is clearly figurative. Paul surely did not keep books on the gifts of his friends, nor did he list anything in the debit column.

16 Some regard the introductory ὅτι (*hoti*, "because"; NIV, "for") as dependent on οἴδατε (*oidate*, "you know") in v.15, thus making the clause explicative of the preceding assertion. This is grammatically possible, but by no means mandatory, and runs into the objection that the mention of Thessalonica hardly explains Paul's departure from Macedonia. It seems better to regard *hoti* in the loose causal sense as "for" (BAG, p. 594).

The phrase ἅπαξ καὶ δίς (*hapax kai dis*) is literally "once and twice" and could easily be so understood here, since Paul was in Thessalonica only a short time (Acts 17:1–10). It has this literal sense in LXX (Deut 9:13; 1 Macc 3:30), and may also have it in its only other NT occurrence (1 Thess 2:18). A more general understanding as "more than once" without expressing the exact number is also possible (L. Morris, *"Kai Hapax kai Dis,"* NovTest, 1:3 [July, 1956], pp. 205–208; L. Morris, *The Epistles of Paul to the Thessalonians* [Grand Rapids: Eerdmans, 1957], p. 58).

17 Οὐχ ὅτι (*ouch hoti*, "not that") is comparable to the same expression in v.11, being a denial of what could have constituted a false conclusion by the readers.

The term λόγον (*logon*, "account") is used in the same financial figure as in v.15. No literal business account is meant, but simply one in which the practical expression of the Philippians' concern for Paul is described as interest accruing to their spiritual investment.

20 The one article with the phrase τῷ δὲ θεῷ καὶ πατρὶ ἡμῶν (*tō de theō kai patri hēmōn*) makes it certain that only one person is meant, one who is both God and Father. Hence, the meaning is "to even our Father."

The concluding ἀμήν (*amēn*) is a transliteration of the Hebrew אָמֵן (*'āmēn*), often used at the close of a doxology (1 Chron 16:36; Neh 8:6). It denotes assent to the doxology as valid (H. Schlier, *Amēn*, TDNT, 1:335–338).

Closing Salutation

4:21-23

> ²¹Greet all the saints in Christ Jesus. The brothers who are with me send greetings. ²²All the saints send you greetings, especially those who belong to Caesar's household.
> ²³The grace of the Lord Jesus Christ be with your spirit.

21 It is likely that the remaining words of the Epistle were written by Paul's own hand, after the pattern announced in 2 Thessalonians 3:17 (see also Gal 6:11; Col 4:18). He sends greetings to every believer at Philippi, to be conveyed to them no doubt by the leadership of the church to whom the letter was initially delivered. Paul's associates also send their greetings. They are to be distinguished from the resident Roman Christians who are mentioned in the next verse. These "brothers who are with me" (*hoi sun emoi adelphoi*) include Timothy and perhaps Epaphroditus (1:1; 2:19–30), and possibly even some of those mentioned in 1:14. The inclusion of these greetings is a caution against interpreting 2:21 as an indictment of all Paul's associates except Timothy (see comment on 2:21).

22 "All the saints" refers to members of the church at Rome. Paul also extends special greetings from "those who belong to Caesar's household." This expression denotes those engaged in imperial service, whether as slaves or freedmen, in Rome or elsewhere. Among them may have been the palace guard (1:13). It is most unlikely that Nero's immediate family is meant, but the expression could refer to persons of considerable importance on the emperor's staff. Paul does not say why they were singled out for special mention. Presumably the Philippians would understand. Perhaps some of these government servants had come from Philippi or had once been stationed at that Roman colony.

23 The concluding benediction is exactly the same as Philemon 25 and similar to Galatians 6:18. It invokes on the Philippian church the continuing favor of Christ to be with their spirits. The realization of this benediction would increase the harmony of the congregation by causing the spirit of each believer to cherish the grace of the Lord Jesus

Christ and by bringing a joyous peace among them, fulfilling the apostle's opening wish (1:2).

Notes

21 "All the saints" (NIV) is actually the sing. "every saint" (πάντα ἅγιον, *panta hagion*) and considers the believers separately. The pl. form πάντες οἱ ἅγιοι, (*pantes hoi hagioi*) in the following verse looks at the saints in Rome collectively.

The phrase ἐν Χριστῷ Ἰησοῦ (*en Christō Iēsou*, "in Christ Jesus") can be construed with either ἀσπάσασθε (*aspasasthe*, "greet") or with ἅγιον (*hagion*, "saint"). In favor of the latter is the analogy with 1:1, and the word order.

22 Lightfoot's extended note explains how οἰκία Καίσαρος, (*oikia Kaisaros*, "Caesar's household") is the Gr. terminology for the Lat. *domus* or *familia Caesaris* and includes the whole of the imperial household. From inscriptions (chiefly sepulchral), lists have been compiled of the varied functions of its members. Vast numbers of these imperial servants were foreign slaves, and if the surmise is correct that many of the earliest converts in Rome were drawn from these classes, the mention of such persons by Paul becomes readily understandable (pp. 167, 171–177). Josephus uses the expression *oikia Kaisaros* in the same way (Antiq. 17.5.8).

23 TR has πάντων (*pantōn*, "all") rather than τοῦ πνεύματος (*tou pneumatos*, "spirit").

COLOSSIANS
Curtis Vaughan

COLOSSIANS

Introduction

1. Destination
2. Authorship
3. Place of origin
4. Occasion
5. Purpose
6. Theme
7. Relation to Ephesians
8. Bibliography
9. Outline

1. Destination

Colosse was a small town situated on the south bank of the Lycus River in the interior of the Roman province of Asia (an area included in modern Turkey). Located about a hundred miles east of Ephesus, its nearest neighbors were Laodicea (ten miles away) and Hierapolis (thirteen miles away). Both of these cities, the more important of which was Laodicea, are named in the Epistle as having communities of believers (cf. 2:1; 4:13). Colosse and Laodicea were probably evangelized during the time of Paul's extended ministry in Ephesus (Acts 19:10). During the periods of the Persian and Greek empires, Colosse was a city of considerable importance. Both Herodotus (fifth century B.C.) and Xenophon (fourth century B.C.) speak of this fact, the former calling Colosse "a great city of Phrygia" and the latter describing it as "a populous city, wealthy and large." But the road system was later changed, and a decline in the social and commercial importance of Colosse set in. In Paul's day it was only an insignificant market town. Lightfoot therefore speaks of the Colossian church as "the least important to which any epistle of Paul is addressed."[1]

We have no record of the establishment of the Colossian church; indeed, Colosse is not even mentioned in Acts. All our information about the church, therefore, must be found in this letter and in incidental allusions in the companion letter to Philemon.

2. Authorship

The authenticity of Colossians has sometimes been questioned. Today, however, there is broad agreement that it is, as it purports to be (1:1; 4:18), from the hand of Paul—or that it is at least substantially Pauline. Evidence in support of Pauline authorship comes

---

[1]J.B. Lightfoot, *St. Paul's Epistles to the Colossians and to Philemon* (London: Macmillan, 1879), p. 16.

not only from within the Epistle but also from the witness of early Christian writers. Admittedly, the external testimony to Colossians is not equal to that of some other Pauline Epistles; nevertheless, it is quite strong. Allusions to it in Ignatius, Polycarp, and Barnabas are open to question, but Justin (c.100–c.165) seems to have used it. Irenaeus (c.125–c.202), Clement of Alexandria (d. c.215), and Origen (c.185–c.254) explicitly refer it to Paul, and it is cited in Marcion's list (c.146) and in the Muratorian Canon (c.170). Colossians is also found in second-century Old Latin versions. Moreover, it is included in the Chester Beatty codex of the Pauline Epistles (P46), which originated in Egypt near the end of the second century. So far as we can determine from extant writings, Colossians was never suspect in ancient times. In fact, the external testimony for it is so ancient and consistent as to obviate any doubts regarding its authenticity.

Pauline authorship appears not to have been seriously questioned until near the middle of the nineteenth century, when T. Mayerhoff disputed the authenticity of Colossians—mainly because of its alleged dependence on Ephesians, which he accepted as genuine. But the relationship of Ephesians and Colossians does not warrant this conclusion. Indeed, a few years after Mayerhoff's work appeared, W.M.L. DeWette reversed this argument, defending the authenticity of Colossians and rejecting Ephesians as the work of a later writer who drew on the former Epistle. F.C. Baur and his pupils denied the Pauline authorship of both Ephesians and Colossians because they thought both Epistles reflected second-century Gnosticism. But it is no longer widely held that the heresy opposed in Colossians is to be identified with the fully developed gnostic systems of the second century. Fresh knowledge of the bewildering variety of syncretistic religious movements of the Graeco-Roman world of the first century has been gained, and arguments such as Baur advanced have in recent years been largely abandoned. H.J. Holtzmann advanced the theory that there was a shortened Pauline Colossians written at the same time as Philemon, but that it was interpolated by a later writer to give it its present form. Holtzmann's theory is not taken seriously today, though C. Masson (*L'Epitre de Saint Paul aux Colossians*, 1950) and P.N. Harrison (*Paulines and Pastorals*, 1964) both adhere to the interpolation theory.

In recent years doubts concerning the authenticity of Colossians have focused on vocabulary (more than fifty words not found elsewhere in Paul's writings and other distinctive Pauline terms not found in Colossians), style (said to be unlike that of the recognized Pauline Epistles, being cumbersome, wordy, and marked by a multiplicity of genitival constructions, participles, and prepositional phrases), and doctrine. Vocabulary is not a great problem, however, for the distinctive vocabulary is most apparent where Paul is dealing with the Colossian problem. Therefore, it is not unlikely that at least some of these words were borrowed from the errorists for purposes of refutation; naturally, then, they would not be used in other totally different contexts. Paul had new things to say in this Epistle and found new ways of saying them. Moreover, the absence of familiar Pauline words such as *justify, believe,* and *salvation* seems less significant when we remember that equally familiar Pauline words are missing from letters such as Galatians. Caird calls the argument from style the "only valid argument against the Pauline authorship of Colossians."[2] Yet the weakness of the argument lies in its failure to apply equally to all of Colossians; parts of the Epistle are generally conceded to have the authentic ring of Paul's style. Moreover, some of the generally accepted letters of

---

[2]G.B. Caird, *Paul's Letters From Prison* in The New Clarendon Bible, gen. ed. H.F.G. Sparks (Oxford: Oxford University Press, 1976), p. 156.

Paul (Romans, 1 Corinthians, and Philippians) have passages that exhibit the same features of style found in Colossians. Bruce feels that the stylistic distinctiveness of Colossians is bound up with the sustained note of thanksgiving that runs through the Epistle, especially through chapter one. He further thinks that the creedal affirmations of 1:12–17 "probably echo the language of primitive Christian confessions of faith."[3] The doctrinal argument is that the Epistle's teachings about Christ—especially the cosmic aspects of his redemptive work—are more fully developed than in other Pauline Epistles. The overall Christology of Colossians, it is sometimes argued, shows such a pronounced similarity to the Logos doctrine of John (John 1:1–18) that it betrays a post-Pauline date. But why could not two apostles share this exalted view of Christ's person and work? Moreover, this doctrine was not entirely new to Paul (cf. Rom 8:19–22; 1 Cor 8:6); it was only given greater prominence and a more systematic exposition in Colossians.

Others argue that such christological passages as 1:15–20 and 2:9ff. reflect an un-Pauline manner of combating false teaching. The terminology of the errorists, for example, is said to be only Christianized, not repudiated. Furthermore, their Gnostic Christology is simply countered by a *radicalized* Gnostic Christology; their Gnostic soteriology, by a *radicalized* Gnostic soteriology. Reference is especially made to the cosmic character of the Christology in the representation of Christ as "the head of the body, the church" (1:18; cf. 2:19). Kümmel answers that "although in comparison with the recognized Pauline letters the idea of Christ as 'the head of the body, the church' ... is new, it is really not surprising in the framework of Pauline ecclesiology if one notes that in the acknowledged letters ... Paul knows the concept of Christ's identity with the ἐκκλησία as his 'body'" (1 Cor 1:13; 12:12c; Gal 3:28).[4]

A strong argument for Pauline authorship is the relation of Colossians to Philemon. Both of these books, sent to the same town and in all likelihood conveyed by the same messenger, contain the names of Paul, Timothy, Onesimus, Archippus, Epaphras, Mark, Aristarchus, Demas, and Luke. The consensus of scholarly opinion is that Philemon is incontestably Pauline, and it is the feeling of many NT scholars that this carries over to Colossians. Kümmel sums up his discussion by affirming that "all the evidence points to the conclusion that Colossians ... is to be regarded as Pauline."[5]

3. Place of Origin

Colossians was obviously written during an imprisonment of Paul (4:10, 18), but the Epistle contains no indication as to the place of imprisonment. Caesarea has from time to time had its advocates, and a few present-day scholars (e.g., E. Lohmeyer, W.G. Kümmel, B. Reicke, J.A.T. Robinson) support the Caesarean hypothesis. It is unlikely that so small a city as Caesarea would have been the center of such vigorous missionary activity as Colossians 4:3, 4, 10–14 seems to suggest. Furthermore, if Colossians was written from Caesarea, how are we to account for Paul's silence about Philip the evangelist, in whose home Paul had been a guest shortly before his arrest (Acts 21:8)? Others (e.g., G.S. Duncan and Ralph P. Martin) argue for Ephesus as the place of origin. But this view has not gained wide acceptance. One of the chief points against it is the lack of

---

[3]E.K. Simpson and F.F. Bruce, *The Epistles of Paul to the Ephesians and to the Colossians*, NIC, p. 171.

[4]Werner G. Kümmel, *Introduction to the New Testament*. Rev. Eng. ed., trans. Howard C. Key (Nashville: Abingdon, 1975), p. 344.

[5]Ibid., p. 346.

clear and certain evidence that Paul was ever a prisoner in Ephesus. Moreover, though Luke was with Paul when Colossians was written (4:14), he was not with the apostle during the Ephesian ministry (note the absence of "we"/"us" at this point in the Acts narrative). The traditional theory, and the one still most generally held, is that Paul was in Rome when Colossians was written.[6] The Epistle should therefore be dated about A.D. 62, during Paul's first Roman imprisonment (cf. Acts 28:30, 31). Perhaps it was written before Ephesians, but surely not much time separated the two Epistles.

4. Occasion

The immediate occasion for the writing of Colossians was the arrival of Epaphras (1:8) in Rome with disturbing news about the presence of heretical teaching at Colosse that was threatening the well-being of the church. The Epistle gives no direct account of the tenets of this strange teaching, and for that reason it is difficult to obtain a clear and consistent understanding of it. Yet from the many allusions to the heresy, we are able to sketch its leading features: (1) It professed to be a "philosophy," but Paul, refusing to recognize it as genuine, called it a "hollow and deceptive philosophy" (2:8). Moulton characterizes it as a "dabbling in the occult."[7] (2) It placed much emphasis on ritual circumcision, dietary laws, and the observance of holy days (2:11, 14, 16, 17). (3) Affirming the mediation of various supernatural powers in the creation of the world and the whole process of salvation, the false teaching insisted that these mysterious powers be placated and worshiped (2:15, 18, 19). As a result of this, Christ was relegated to a relatively minor place in the Colossian system. "One thing is certain as to the 'Colossian Heresy,'" writes H.C.G. Moule. "It was a doctrine of God and of salvation that cast a cloud over the glory of Jesus Christ."[8] (4) Some of the errorists were ascetic (2:20–23), teaching that the body is evil and must be treated as an enemy. (5) The advocates of this system claimed to be Christian teachers (cf. 2:3–10).

From these considerations we may conclude that the Colossian heresy was a syncretistic movement combining at least three separate elements. First, the insistence on legalism, ritualism, and the observance of holy days points to a *Jewish element*. It seems not, however, to have been the Pharisaic Judaism Paul combated in Galatians. Bruce calls it a "native Phrygian variety," something "worse than the simple Jewish legalism" that earlier threatened the Galatian churches.[9]

Second, the system's "philosophical" character, angelolatry, and perhaps ascetic tendencies point to a *pagan element*. This was probably an incipient form of what later became known as Gnosticism, a very complex system that reached its zenith in the second century. This incipient Gnosticism—some use the expression proto-Gnosticism—was essentially a religio-philosophical attitude, not a well-defined system. R.E.O. White speaks of it as "a climate of thought as widespread as evolutionary theory is today."[10] It sought by its oriental myths and Greek philosophy to absorb the various religions with

---

[6]For an able defense of this position see C.H. Dodd, "The Mind of Paul: II," in *New Testament Essays* (Manchester: University Press, 1953).

[7]Harold K. Moulton, *Colossians, Philemon and Ephesians* (Naperville, Ill.: Allenson, 1963).

[8]Handley C.G. Moule, *Colossian Studies* (New York: Hodder & Stoughton, 1898), p. 9.

[9]Simpson and Bruce, *Ephesians and Colossians*, pp. 166, 168.

[10]Reginald E.O. White, *Colossians* in *The Broadman Commentary*, vol. 11 (Nashville: Broadman, 1969), p. 219.

which it came into contact. It lent itself to an air of exclusiveness, cultivating an "enlightened" elite for whom alone salvation was possible. Gnosticism, in all its forms, was characterized by belief in the evil of matter, in mediating beings, and in salvation through knowledge. Beginning with the assumption that all matter is evil, the Gnostics argued that God and matter were therefore antagonistic. Indeed, they contended that God didn't create this world and that he has absolutely no contact with it. However, intellectual necessity did not permit them to break completely the bond between divinity and the material world. They therefore taught that God put forth from himself a series of "aeons" or emanations, each a little more distant from him and each having a little less of deity. At the end of this chain of intermediate beings there is an emanation possessing enough of deity to make a world but removed far enough from God that his creative activities could not compromise the perfect purity of God. The world, they argued, was the creation of this lesser power, who being so far removed from God was both ignorant of and hostile to him. These "aeons"—"offshoots of deity" Martin calls them[11]—were thought to inhabit the stars and rule man's destiny. They therefore were to be placated and worshiped. Paul's references to "thrones ... powers ... rulers ... authorities" (1:16), "power and authority" (2:9), "powers and authorities" (2:15), and "worship of angels" (2:18) are allusions to these supposed intermediate beings.

Belief in the inherent evil of matter made it impossible for the Gnostics to accept the real incarnation of God in Christ. Some of them explained it away by denying the actual humanity of Jesus, holding that he only seemed to be human. The body of Jesus, they taught, was an illusion, a phantom, only apparently real. In their view, Christ was only one of many intermediaries between God and the world, but he was sufficiently related to God to share his abhorrence of any direct contact with matter. The advent of Christ "was a piece of play-acting when God wore a mask of humanity on the stage of human history, giving the appearance of being a man but really being still God-in-disguise."[12] Other Gnostics explained away the incarnation by denying the real deity of Jesus. That is, they stopped short of making a complete identification of the man Jesus with the aeon Christ. Both of these tendencies were perhaps present at Colosse in embryo form and both may be alluded to in the Epistle—for example, in the affirmation that "in Christ all the fullness of the Deity lives in bodily form" (2:9).

Belief that matter is evil also led to a distorted view of the Christian life. Some Gnostics turned to asceticism, others to libertinism. The ascetics felt that they had to free themselves from the influence of matter (the body) by inflicting punishment on their bodies. Those who gave in to license assumed an attitude of indifference to things physical and material, the idea being that only the soul is important and therefore the body may do what it pleases. Indications of both tendencies may be found in the Colossian letter, the former being opposed in 2:20ff. and the latter in 3:5ff.

As its name would indicate, Gnosticism—the word is related to *gnosis*, "knowledge"— taught that salvation is obtained not through faith but through knowledge. The knowledge of which the Gnostics spoke, however, was knowledge acquired through mystical experience, not by intellectual apprehension. It was an occult knowledge, pervaded by the superstitions of astrology and magic. Moreover, it was an esoteric knowledge, open only to those who had been initiated into the mysteries of the gnostic system.

Third, there was a *"Christian" element* in the Colossian error. While at its heart it was

---

[11]Ralph P. Martin, *The Church's Lord and the Christian's Liberty* (Grand Rapids: Zondervan, 1973), p. 5.
[12]Ibid., p. 7.

a combination of Judaism and paganism, it wore the mask of Christianity. It did not *deny* Christ, but it did *dethrone* him. It gave Christ a place, but not the supreme place. This Christian façade made the Colossian error all the more dangerous.

That Paul found it necessary to write this letter to the community of Christians at Colosse is evidence that the false teachers had made a strong impression on them and that the threat to the well-being of the church was real. There are indications, however, that the errorists had not achieved complete success (cf. 2:4, 8, 20). Paul therefore can express gratitude for the Colossian Christians and rejoice over the order within their ranks and in their continued fidelity to Christ (cf. 1:3ff.; 2:5).

5. Purpose

Paul's purpose in writing Colossians was threefold: (1) to express his personal interest in the church, (2) to warn them against reverting to their old pagan vices (cf. 3:5ff.), and (3) to refute the false teaching that was threatening the Colossian church. The last named was undoubtedly Paul's major concern. He met the Colossian false knowledge, not by appealing to ignorance and obscurantism, but by making a plea for the fuller knowledge found in Christ. He confronted the false representation by a positive setting forth of the exalted nature and unmatched glory of Christ.

6. Theme

Colossians proclaims the absolute supremacy and sole sufficiency of Jesus Christ (cf. esp. 1:18; 2:9; 3:11). It is, as Robertson says, Paul's "full-length portrait of Christ."[13] He is God's Son (1:14), the object of the Christian's faith (1:4), the Redeemer (1:14), the image of God (1:15), Lord of creation (1:15), head of the church (1:18), reconciler of the universe (1:20). In him dwells the fullness of the Godhead (2:9), and under him every power and authority in the universe is subjected (2:10). He is the essence of the mystery of God (2:3), and in him all God's treasures of wisdom and knowledge lie hidden (2:3). He is the standard by which all religious teaching is to be measured (2:8) and the reality of the truth foreshadowed by the regulations and rituals of the old covenant (2:17). By his cross he conquered the cosmic powers of evil (2:15), and following his resurrection he was enthroned at the right hand of God (3:1). Our life now lies hidden with God in Christ, but one day both he and we will be gloriously manifested (3:3, 4). In short, the central thought of the Epistle is summed up in the lines of Charles Wesley's hymn:

> Thou, O Christ, art all I want,
> More than all in Thee I find.

7. Relation to Ephesians

From even a casual reading of Ephesians and Colossians one must conclude that they are kindred Epistles. Both the Epistles were written by Paul out of an experience of imprisonment. Both were sent originally to believers in Asia. Both were entrusted to Tychicus, the messenger who was to bear them to their respective destinations (cf. Eph

---

13A.T. Robertson, *Paul and the Intellectuals*, rev. and ed. W.C. Strickland (Nashville: Broadman, 1959), p. 12.

6:21; Col 4:7). Moreover, many of the topics treated are common to both (the person of Christ, the church as Christ's body, ethical duties, relationships within the family, etc.). Even the language of the two Epistles is strikingly similar. Wisdom, knowledge, fullness, mystery, principalities, powers—these are just a few of the terms common to the two Epistles. Moulton points out that in Colossians the margin of the English Revised Version has seventy-two references to Ephesians but only eighty-eight to all of the other Pauline Epistles. Goodspeed writes that "three-fifths of Colossians is reflected in Ephesians."[14] We can best account for the similarities of the epistles on the supposition that Ephesians is an expansion by Paul of ideas presented in compact form in Colossians.

There are also significant differences between the Epistles. For instance, there is a difference in emphasis. Both Epistles are concerned with the lordship of Christ and the unity of his body, the church. However, in Ephesians the stress is on the church as the body of Christ; in Colossians the emphasis is on Christ as the head of the church. There is also a difference of style. Colossians is terse and abrupt; Ephesians is diffuse and flowing. Colossians is specific, concrete, and elliptical; Ephesians is abstract, didactic, and general. Finally, there is a difference in mood. Colossians, argumentative and polemical, is a letter of discussion; Ephesians, calm and irenical, is a letter of reflection.

8. Bibliography

Books

Abbott, T.K. *The Epistles to the Ephesians and to the Colossians.* ICC. Edited by S.R. Driver; Alfred Plummer; and C.A. Briggs. Edinburgh: T. & T. Clark, 1897.

Barclay, William. *The Letters to the Philippians, Colossians, and Thessalonians.* The Daily Study Bible. Philadelphia: Westminster, 1959.

Beare, F.W. *The Epistle to the Colossians.* IB. New York: Abingdon, 1955.

Caird, G.B. *Paul's Letters From Prison.* The New Clarendon Bible. Edited by H.F.D. Sparks. Oxford: Oxford University Press, 1976.

Calvin, John. *The Epistles of Paul the Apostle to the Galatians, Ephesians, Philippians and Colossians.* Translated by T.H.L. Parker. Edited by David W. and Thomas F. Torrence. Grand Rapids: Eerdmans, 1965.

Carson, H.M. *The Epistles of Paul to the Colossians and Philemon.* TNTC. Edited by R.V.G. Tasker. Grand Rapids: Eerdmans.

Eadie, John. *Commentary on the Epistle of Paul to the Colossians.* Classic Commentary Library. Grand Rapids: Zondervan, 1957.

Grant, R.M. *Gnosticism and Early Christianity.* 2nd ed. New York: Columbia University Press, 1966.

Kümmel, Werner G. *Introduction to the New Testament.* Rev. Engl. Ed. Translated by Howard C. Key. Nashville: Abingdon, 1975.

Lightfoot, J.B. *St. Paul's Epistles to the Colossians and to Philemon.* London: Macmillan, 1879.

Maclaren, Alexander. *The Epistles of St. Paul to the Colossians and Philemon.* The Expositor's Bible. Edited by W. Robertson Nicoll. New York: Hodder and Stoughton, n.d.

Macphail, S.R. *The Epistle of Paul to the Colossians.* Edinburgh: T. & T. Clark, 1911.

Martin, Ralph P. *Colossians: The Church's Lord and the Christian's Liberty.* Grand Rapids: Zondervan, 1973.

Meyer, H.A.W. *Critical and Exegetical Hand-Book to the Epistles to the Philippians and Colossians and to Philemon.* Meyer's Commentary on the NT. New York: Funk & Wagnalls, 1885.

14Edgar J. Goodspeed, *The Key to Ephesians* (Chicago: University of Chicago Press, 1956), p. 8.

Moule, C.F.D. *The Epistles of Paul the Apostle to the Colossians and to Philemon.* CGT. Edited by C.F.D. Moule, Cambridge: Cambridge University Press, 1957.

Moule, Handley C.G. *Colossian Studies.* New York: Hodder and Stoughton, 1898.

Moulton, Harold K. *Colossians, Philemon and Ephesians.* Epworth Preacher's Commentaries. London: Epworth, 1963.

Nicholson, W.R. *Oneness with Christ.* Edited by James M. Gray. Grand Rapids: Kregel, 1951.

Peake, A.S. *The Epistle to the Colossians.* EGT. Edited by W. Robertson Nicoll. Vol. 3. London: Hodder and Stoughton, 1903.

Radford, Lewis B. *The Epistle to the Colossians.* WC. London: Methuen, 1931.

Robertson, A.T. *Paul and the Intellectuals.* Revised and edited by W.C. Strickland. Nashville: Broadman, 1959.

Scott, E.F. *The Epistles of Paul to the Colossians, to Philemon and to the Ephesians.* MNT. Edited by James Moffatt. London: Hodder and Stoughton, 1930.

Simpson, E.K., and Bruce, F.F. *Commentary on the Epistles to the Ephesians and the Colossians.* NIC. Grand Rapids: Eerdmans, 1957.

White, R.E.O. *Colossians.* Broadman Bible Commentary. Edited by Clifton J. Allen, Vol. 11. Nashville: Broadman, 1971.

Wilson, R. McL. *Gnosis and the New Testament.* Philadelphia: Fortress, 1968.

Yamauchi, E.M. *Pre-Christian Gnosticism: A Survey of the Proposed Evidences.* Grand Rapids: Eerdmans, 1973.

Articles

Brandenburger, E. "Cross." *The New International Dictionary of NT Theology.* Edited by Colin Brown. Vol. 1. Grand Rapids: Zondervan, (1976), pp. 398–405.

Casey, R.P. "Gnosis, Gnosticism and the NT." *The Background of the NT and its Eschatology.* (In honor of Charles Harold Dodd). Edited by W.D. Davies and D. Daube. Cambridge: Cambridge University Press, (1956), pp. 52–80.

Eicken, E. von; Lidner, H.; Müller, D.; Brown, C., "Apostle." *New International Dictionary of NT Theology.* Edited by Colin Brown. Vol. 1. Grand Rapids: Zondervan, (1976), pp. 127–137.

Schippers, R. "Fullness." *The New International Dictionary of NT Theology.* Edited by Colin Brown. Vol. 1. Grand Rapids: Zondervan, (1976), pp. 728–744.

Schmitz, E.D. "Knowledge." *The New International Dictionary of NT Theology.* Edited by Colin Brown. Vol. 1. Grand Rapids: Zondervan, (1976), pp. 390–406.

Walls, A.F. "Gnosticism." *The Zondervan Pictorial Encyclopedia of the Bible.* Edited by Merrill C. Tenney. Vol. 2. Grand Rapids: Zondervan, (1975), pp. 736–739.

9. Outline

I. Introduction (1:1–14)
  A. Salutation (1:1, 2)
  B. Prayer of Thanksgiving (1:3–8)
  C. Prayer of Petition (1:9–14)
II. The Supremacy of Christ (1:15–23)
  A. The Scope of Christ's Supremacy (1:15–18)
  B. The Basis for Christ's Supremacy (1:19–23)
    1. The fullness of God in Christ (1:19)
    2. The reconciling work of Christ (1:20–23)
III. The Ministry of Paul (1:24–2:7)
  A. A Ministry of Suffering (1:24)

Text and Exposition

I. Introduction (1:1–14)

A. *Salutation*

1:1, 2

¹Paul, an apostle of Christ Jesus by the will of God, and Timothy our brother,

²To the holy and faithful brothers in Christ at Colosse:

Grace and peace to you from God our Father.

Paul follows the standard form of greeting of first century letters but puts a distinctly Christian content into it. He names himself, with appropriate Christian expressions, as the author of the Epistle (v.1), identifies the readers (v.2a), and then expresses the characteristic greeting of grace and peace (v.2b).

1 In designating himself as "an apostle of Christ Jesus," Paul gives his authority for writing. The literal meaning of *apostolos* is "one sent"; but at its deepest level it denotes an authorized spokesman for God, one commissioned and empowered to act as his representative. Such is the meaning of the word when applied to the Twelve (e.g., Luke 6:13), to Barnabas (Acts 14:14), and to Paul. The word is occasionally used in the NT in the weakened sense of "messenger" (e.g., John 13:16; 2 Cor 8:23; Phil 2:25). Here, however, the term is used to designate Paul as a commissioned ambassador for Christ.

Timothy, who was with Paul at the time of writing and is here identified as a "brother" (*adelphos*; i.e., fellow Christian) of Paul, was named as a matter of courtesy. He appears to have had no part in the actual writing of the book (cf. 4:18). (It is true that the first person plural pronoun is occasionally used [1:3, 4, 9], but ordinarily the singular form is found [1:24, 25, 29; 2:1–5; 4:7–18].)

2 In the OT, holiness is ascribed not only to persons (Lev 20:7; Deut 7:6; 2 Kings 4:9, et al.), but also to places (Exod 29:31; Lev 6:16, 26; Deut 23:14; Ps 65:4, et al.) and things (Exod 28:2; 29:6; 30:25; Num 5:17, et al.). This suggests that the root idea in "holy" (*hagios*) is not excellence of character but dedication, the state of being set apart for the work and worship of God. Here the word may mark the Colossian Christians as a part of the people of God, the new Israel (cf. NEB, TCNT, TEV), though NIV does not bring out that idea. NIV, however, is truer to the Greek in retaining the adjectival force of both *hagios* ("holy") and *pistos* ("faithful").

Most commentators think "faithful" (*pistois*) should be interpreted in the sense of believing. It may, however, also imply the secondary sense of loyalty to Christ, a quality especially appropriate for a church under fire.

"Brothers" (*adelphois*), a term of affection used of Christians in every letter of Paul, calls attention to the intimacy of the fellowship of the Christian community. Despite their differences of culture, social status, and racial background, the Colossian believers were bound together by a common bond of love and thus constituted one spiritual family. The word points also to oneness of parentage. Christians are "brothers" because they are spiritually begotten by one Father.

"In Christ," a phrase used by Paul more than 160 times in various forms ("in the Lord," "in him," "in whom," etc.), emphasizes the spiritual position of believers. They are "in Christ" in the sense that they are united with Christ, joined to him as closely as limbs are joined to the body of which they are a part.

The greeting takes the form of a prayer for "grace and peace" to be given the readers. The Greek word for "grace" (*charis*), which here denotes the favor of God, is built on a root that was used of things that produce well-being. *Charis* appears 155 times in the NT, mostly in the writings of Paul. For him it expresses the essence of God's saving activity in Christ, and is not, even in a greeting such as this, to be interpreted as merely a polite cliché.

In our thinking, "peace" usually suggests, as it did for the early Greeks, the opposite of war or the absence of conflict. The NT concept, however, is richer and broader. Among the Jews the word denoted wholeness or soundness and included such ideas as prosperity, contentedness, good relations with others. In this passage spiritual prosperity is perhaps the leading thought of *eirēnē*.

Notes

1 Ἀπόστολος (*apostolos*), built on a root meaning "to send," was first used of a cargo ship or a fleet of ships. Later it denoted the commander of a naval expedition or leader of a band of colonists sent overseas. The LXX employs the word only in 1 Kings 14:6, where it is used of the commissioning and empowering of Ahijah as a messenger of God. In the NT, where the word occurs at least seventy-nine times, it regularly denotes an authorized spokesman—one clothed with the power of the one sending him and serving as his personal representative.
2 Ἅγιος (*hagios*, "holy"), though not primarily an ethical term, does (in the NT) imply a relationship with God and demands conduct that expresses and corresponds to that relationship. Persons consecrated to a God of absolute moral purity must of necessity take on something of his character.

B. *Prayer of Thanksgiving*

1:3–8

> [3]We always thank God, the Father of our Lord Jesus Christ, when we pray for you, [4]because we have heard of your faith in Christ Jesus and of the love you have for all the saints—[5]the faith and love that spring from the hope stored up for you in heaven, and which you have already heard about in the word of truth, the gospel [6]that has come to you. All over the world this gospel is producing fruit and growing, just as it has been doing among you since the day you heard it and understood God's grace in all its truth. [7]You learned it from Epaphras, our dear fellow servant, who is a faithful minister of Christ on our behalf, [8]and who also told us of your love in the Spirit.

The content of this thanksgiving is determined by the condition of the church, and by Paul's relation to it through Epaphras. In these verses we may observe the circumstances and character of the apostle's thanksgiving (v.3) as well as the grounds and occasion for it (vv.4–8). (Appeals for thanksgiving run through Colossians like the refrain of a song [cf. 1:12; 2:7; 3:15, 17; 4:2]. This passage, which expresses the apostle's own gratitude, shows that what he enjoined upon others he himself practiced.)

3 Paul addresses his thanksgiving to God, thus recognizing that he is the one responsible for the virtues and graces of his people and for the ultimate success of the gospel—both of which items are mentioned in the verses that follow.

God is identified as "the Father of our Lord Jesus Christ." At this point the Greek MSS exhibit some variety in wording, but the essential meaning is not radically affected. The suggestion in all the readings is that the God to whom we pray is the God whom Jesus Christ made known to us in his character as Father.

4,5 Verses 4–8 express the grounds and occasion of Paul's thanksgiving. The apostle specifically mentions three things, the first being the good report that had come to him of the well-being of the Colossian Christians. His reference to "hearing" of their spiritual condition is in keeping with the fact that he had not personally visited Colosse (cf. 1:9; 2:1). The source of this information was probably Epaphras (cf. v.8), though we must not rule out the possibility that Paul's reference includes other previous reports of the faith of the Colossians.

The NIV rendering of the first part of v.5 is quite free. A more literal translation is "on account of the hope ..." (*dia tēn elpida ...*). It is a question whether these words are to be construed with "We ... thank God" (v.3), with "your faith ... and ... love" (v.4), or only with "love" (v.4). In the first construction the Colossians' hope (along with their faith and love) is taken as expressing a reason for Paul's gratitude. This is the interpretation found, with some variation, in both Moffatt and Goodspeed. In the second construction, hope is interpreted as a ground for, or an incentive to, faith and love—or, as H.C.G. Moule puts it, "a grand *occasion* to develop them, and call them out into action" (p. 41). This is the interpretation expressed essentially by NIV, though it represents hope as the *source* of the Colossians' faith and love. The third construction, which is only slightly different from the second, is reflected in Weymouth. Grammatically, one can make a case for any one of these, but our preference is for the first. Whatever construction one chooses, however, it is valid to see hope as a part of the total experience of the Colossians that Paul is thanking God for.

The triad of "faith" (v.4a), "love" (v.4b), and "hope" (v.5a) appears with some degree of frequency in Paul's writings (e.g., Rom 5:2–5; 1 Cor 13:13; 1 Thess 1:3; 5:8). "Faith" (*pistis*), which is commitment to, or trust in, another person, is here defined as being "in Jesus Christ." This English phrase sometimes translates a Greek construction (*eis* with an accusative) that denotes Christ as the object on whom faith rests or toward whom it is directed. In this passage the Greek is different (*en* with a locative), pointing to Christ as *the sphere* in which faith operates. As H.C.G. Moule puts it, the phrase speaks of the Colossians' faith as "anchored" in Christ, "resting" in him (p. 37). Ellicott calls it "Christ-centered faith" (p. 112).

"Love" (*agapē*) is the fruit of faith and the proof of its genuineness (cf. Gal 5:6; James 2:14ff.; 1 John 3:14). The Greek word denotes caring love, the love that counts no sacrifice too great for the one loved. (The verb built on the same root is used in John 3:16.) The Colossians' love was expressed toward "all the saints," that is, all the people of God. Such love bespoke the warmth of their fellowship and the depth and breadth of their brotherly concern. Perhaps the apostle was contrasting the broad good will of the Colossians with the narrow exclusiveness of the heretical teachers.

"Hope" (*elpis*) may be either subjective or objective, depending on the context in which the word is found. In the former sense it indicates the emotion or the faculty of hope (e.g., Rom 5:2, 1 Cor 13:13) and suggests joyful expectancy, a sense of certainty and confidence. In its objective sense, which is its use in the present passage, "hope" denotes the thing hoped for (cf. Gal 5:5; 1 Peter 1:3). The reference then is to the glorious reward, that is, the future heavenly blessedness of the people of God.

Paul affirms two things about the hope of the Colossians. First, it is securely "stored up" for them in heaven, like a treasure. Second, the Colossians' knowledge of hope came from hearing "the word of truth," which is here defined as the gospel that had come to them. The reference is to the original proclamation of the gospel message that resulted in the Colossians' conversion. That message, preached by Epaphras, seems to be contrasted tacitly with the more recent and heretical preaching of the Colossian errorists.

6 Having mentioned the gospel as the source from which the Colossians had heard of the Christian hope, Paul is now led to develop the thought of the progress of the gospel in the world. This is brought out in such a way as to suggest that this, as well as the report of the Colossians' welfare, was for Paul a basis for thankfulness. Two ideas are stressed: First, the gospel is a fruit-bearing power wherever it is preached. Perhaps Paul means that the ever-widening scope and deepening influence of the gospel on its recipients is a mark of its authenticity. "All over the world" is not to be taken in strict literalness, as if Paul were saying that the gospel has been preached in every single place. He uses a deliberate exaggeration. Actually the gospel had spread amazingly in the years between Pentecost and the time when Paul wrote this letter and his language, though an overstatement, dramatically calls attention to this. "Producing fruit," which translates a middle voice (*karpophoroumenon*), probably points to "the inward energy of the gospel . . . in its adherents" (Peake, p. 498). Lightfoot sees in this word the suggestion that "the Gospel is essentially a reproductive organism, a plant whose seed is in itself" (p. 135). The term is interpreted by TEV in the very general sense of "bringing blessings." "Growing" (*auxanomenon*) denotes the rapid spread of the gospel. Thus the two terms— "producing fruit" and "growing"—speak respectively of the inner working and the outward extension of the gospel. Nicholson, commenting on this, remarks that the gospel "is not like corn, which having borne fruit, dies, even to its roots, but like a tree, which bears fruit and at the same time continues to grow" (p. 35). The tense of both verbs is present, suggesting constant and continuing action.

Second, the gospel conveys the knowledge of "God's grace in all its truth." The phrase "in all its truth" may be intended to suggest that the "gospel" that had been recently introduced to the Colossians by the heretical teachers was a travesty. Their so-called "gospel" was not a message of divine grace; it was a system of legal bondage and human traditions.

7,8 A third item in Paul's expression of thankfulness concerns the work of Epaphras, through whom the Colossians had been instructed in the gospel. We know very little about this man. Outside of the references in this passage (vv.4, 7, 9), his name, which is a shortened form of Epaphroditus, appears only in Colossians 4:12, 13 and Philemon 23. In the former passage we learn that he was a native of Colosse and that he had ministered not only in that city but also in Laodicea and Hierapolis. In Philemon he is described by Paul as his "fellow-prisoner in the cause of Christ Jesus" (Wms). (The Epaphroditus of Philippians 2:25 and 4:18 is not to be identified with the Epaphras of Colossians. The former was a resident of the province of Macedonia; this Epaphras was a resident of the province of Asia.)

Three things are told us in this passage about Epaphras. First, he was Paul's "dear fellow servant" (v.7a). This means that he was, like Paul, a bondslave of Jesus Christ and that Paul looked upon him as a valued comrade in the work. Second, he was "a faithful minister of Christ on our [Paul's] behalf " (v.7b). The thought seems to be that Epaphras had represented Paul, that is, had preached in his stead, in establishing the work at Colosse. There is perhaps the suggestion that Epaphras was himself a convert of Paul (perhaps during the Ephesian ministry) and that Paul had delegated him to take the gospel to the Colossians. Yet as a "minister of Christ," Epaphras had acted not so much under the authority of Paul but under that of Paul's Lord. The Greek word for "minister," rendered "deacon" in Philippians 1:1 and 1 Timothy 3:8, is used here simply in the sense of "one who serves." NEB translates it "a trusted worker." Third, as a messenger from Colosse, Epaphras had communicated to Paul the fact of the Colossians' love (v.8). The reference may be to the love they had for all the people of God (cf. v.4) or to the love they had for Paul. "In the Spirit" means that it was the Spirit of God who had awakened this love in Paul's readers. (This is the only reference to the Holy Spirit in Colossians.)

There were other matters not so favorable that Epaphras must have told Paul about the Colossians, but for the moment the apostle is concerned only with "the bright features in the report" (Scott, p. 16).

Notes

7 NIV translates $\dot{v}\pi\grave{\epsilon}\rho$ $\dot{\eta}\mu\hat{\omega}\nu$ (hyper hēmōn, "on our behalf "), the reading supported by P^{46} and early Alexandrian and Western authorities. This is also the text followed by ASV, RSV, NEB, NAB, et al. The editors of the UBS text, however, prefer $\dot{v}\pi\grave{\epsilon}\rho$ $\dot{v}\mu\hat{\omega}\nu$ (hyper hymōn, "on your behalf "). The former reading has superior Greek evidence but the UBS editors were impressed by "the widespread currency of $\dot{v}\mu\hat{\omega}\nu$ in versional and patristic witnesses" (B.M. Metzger, A Textual Commentary on the Greek New Testament [New York: United Bible Societies, 1972]). KJV, Mof, and BV represent this reading.

C. Prayer of Petition

1:9-14

> 9For this reason, since the day we heard about you, we have not stopped praying for you and asking God to fill you with the knowledge of his will through all spiritual wisdom and understanding. 10And we pray this in order that you may live a life worthy of the Lord and may please him in every way: bearing fruit in every good work, growing in the knowledge of God, 11being strengthened with all power according to his glorious might so that you may have great endurance and patience, and joyfully 12giving thanks to the Father, who has qualified you to share in the inheritance of the saints in the kingdom of light. 13For he has rescued us from the dominion of darkness and brought us into the kingdom of the Son he loves, 14in whom we have redemption, the forgiveness of sins.

To the thanksgiving of verses 3-8, the apostle adds a fervent petition. He prays that the Colossians may be so filled with the knowledge of God's will (v.9) that they may be enabled to live worthily of the Lord, pleasing him in everything (v.10a). This worthy life involves fruitfulness in every good work (v.10b), growth in (or by) the knowledge of God (v.10c), patience and long-suffering (v.11), and gratitude to God for the blessings of redemption (vv.12-14).

9 The words "for this reason" (*dia touto*), referring back to the entire discussion of vv.3–8, show that the petitionary prayer is Paul's response to the news that had come to him of the Colossians' experience in Christ. He was grateful for what had already happened to them. He prays now for the further enrichment of their lives.

The Greek word (*kai*) in the opening part of v.9 is not expressed in NIV. C.F.D. Moule construes it with the phrase "for this reason" and interprets the entire construction to mean "that is *precisely* why" or "that, in fact, is why" (p. 52). On the other hand, H.C.G. Moule connects *kai* with the pronoun "we," rendering it "we also." The meaning then is "we on our part, meeting your love with a love-prompted prayer" (p. 48). Either way, the word shows that v.9 stands in close connection with the preceding paragraph.

Paul's prayer contains two requests. The first, and the one on which the rest of the prayer is based, is that God might fill the readers with the knowledge of his will through all spiritual wisdom and understanding. Scott thinks that the apostle here "begins to touch gently on his complaint against the Colossians," namely, that with all their devotion they had failed to attain true knowledge, "mistaking windy speculations for a deeper wisdom" (p. 17).

The Greek word for "knowledge" (*epignōsis*), a compound form used in the NT only of moral and religious knowledge, has engendered considerable debate. Armitage Robinson, for instance, concludes that the simple, uncompounded form (*gnōsis*) is the wider word and denotes knowledge in "the fullest sense." The compound form used here he takes to be "knowledge directed toward a particular object" (*Epistle to the Ephesians*, p. 254). Earlier scholars, on the other hand, are inclined to see *epignōsis* as the larger and stronger word. Meyer, for example, defines it as "the knowledge which *grasps and penetrates into* the object" (p. 215). Lightfoot remarks that "it was used especially of the knowledge of God and of Christ as being the perfection of knowledge" (p. 138). The older interpreters who understand the word as denoting thorough knowledge, that is, a deep and accurate comprehension, are probably correct. Such knowledge of God's will is the foundation of all Christian character and conduct.

The will of God in its broadest and most inclusive sense is the whole purpose of God as revealed in Christ. In this passage the term perhaps has special reference to God's intention for the conduct of the Christian life.

To be "filled" with the knowledge of the divine will suggests that such knowledge is to pervade all of one's being—thoughts, affections, purposes, and plans. (The reader should be alert to the unusual emphasis on "fullness" in this Epistle. The recurrence of this idea suggests that the Colossian errorists claimed to offer a "fullness" of blessing and truth not found, they said, in the preaching of Epaphras. Paul answers by stressing the true fullness available in Christ.)

The phrase containing the words "all spiritual wisdom and understanding" is taken by some interpreters as a fuller explanation of "knowledge of his [God's] will" (cf. TEV). The thought then is that knowledge of the divine will consists or takes the form of spiritual wisdom and understanding. NIV interprets the phrase to denote the means by which we acquire knowledge of the will of God (cf. Ph, TCNT, NEB).

"Wisdom" and "understanding" probably should not be treated separately but should be looked on as expressing a single thought, something like practical wisdom or clear discernment. The use of the two words simply gives a certain fullness to the statement and thus deepens its impression on the reader.

10 Paul's second petition, that the Colossians might "live a life worthy of the Lord," is built on, and grows out of, the request for knowledge of the divine will; living a worthy life is thus represented as a result (or purpose) of knowing God's desire for one's life. This suggests that knowledge of God's will is not imparted as an end in itself; it is given with a practical intent. "The end of all knowledge, the Apostle would say, is conduct" (Lightfoot, p. 139).

"Live a life" translates a single word (*peripatēsai*) that literally means "to walk." But it is often used in Scripture to depict life in its outward expression (cf. Col 2:6; 3:7; 4:4, et al.).

To live a life "worthy of the Lord" (*axiōs tou kyriou*) probably means to live a life that is commensurate with what the Lord has done for us and is to us. It may also suggest acting in conformity with our union with Christ and with his purpose for our lives.

The ultimate aim of knowing the will of God and living a worthy life is that the readers "may please him [God] in every way" (lit., "unto all pleasing"). The Greek word for "please" (*areskō*) suggests an attitude of mind that anticipates every wish. In classical Greek it had a bad connotation, denoting, as H.C.G. Moule observes,

> a cringing and subservient habit, ready to do anything to please a patron; not only to meet but to anticipate his most trivial wishes. But when transferred to . . . the believer's relations to his Lord, the word at once rises by its associations. To do anything to meet, to anticipate His wishes is not only the most absolutely right thing we could do. It is His eternal due; it is at the same time the surest path to our own highest development and gain (*Cambridge Bible for Schools*, p. 72).

Verses 10b-14 underline some of the elements in, or constituent parts of, the kind of life that is pleasing to the Lord. The leading ideas, expressed in Greek by four participles, are rendered in English by "bearing fruit" (v.10b), "growing" (v.10c), "being strengthened" (v.11a), and "giving thanks" (v.12). Grammatically, they all modify, and express attendant circumstances of, *peripatēsai*—the word translated "live a life."

"Bearing fruit" renders a present tense (*karpophorountes*), the meaning being that the Christian life is to exhibit continual fruitfulness. The fruit itself consists in "every good work"—or, as NEB puts it, "active goodness of every kind." (Paul lays great stress on good works in his letters [cf. Eph 2:10; Gal 5:5; Titus 1:16; 2:7, 14; 3:8, 15, et al.]. But he represents them as the fruit, not the root, of a right relationship with God.)

The Christian should not only bear the fruit of good works in his life; he should at the same time experience personal spiritual enlargement. This idea is expressed in the words "growing in the knowledge of God." "Growing" (*auxanomenoi*), like "bearing fruit," represents a present tense and puts emphasis on habitual action. The preposition *in* represents the knowledge of God as the sphere or realm in which spiritual growth takes place. It is possible, however, to translate the phrase as "growing *by* the knowledge of God." When rendered like this, the text affirms that the knowledge of God is the means by which the Christian grows. What rain and sunshine are to the nurture of plants, the knowledge of God is to the growth and maturing of the spiritual life.

11 "Being strengthened with all power" expresses a third element in the life pleasing to God. Christians are engaged in moral conflict with the cosmic powers of a darkened world (cf. Eph 6:12), and nothing short of divine empowerment can enable them to stand. "Strengthened," which speaks of continuous empowerment, translates the same root word used in Philippians 4:13: "I can do everything through him who gives me strength."

This empowerment is "according to his [God's] glorious might." That is to say, it is not proportioned simply to our need, but to God's abundant supply. The Greek behind the phrase "his glorious might" (*to kratos tēs doxēs autou*) is more literally rendered "the might of his glory." Though NIV represents a legitimate interpretation, possibly we should retain the literal rendering and understand the thought to be *the might of God's own manifested nature*. In this interpretation "glory" (*doxēs*) stands for the revealed splendor or majesty of God—the sum total of his divine perfections. (Paul uses the word *glory* more than seventy times in his Epistles. Its basic meaning is physical brightness or radiance, but its exact meaning must be determined by its various contexts. In Romans 6:4 Christ is said to have been "raised from the dead through the glory of the Father.")

The twofold issue of such empowerment is "endurance and patience." The first term renders a Greek word (*hypomonēn*) denoting the opposite of cowardice and despondency. Beare defines it as "the capacity to see things through" (p. 158). The second term (*makrothymian*), translated "longsuffering" in KJV, is the opposite of wrath or a spirit of revenge. It speaks of even-temperedness, the attitude that in spite of injury or insult does not retaliate.

It is debatable whether "joyfully" (*meta charas*; lit., "with joy") should be construed with "endurance and patience" (KJV, ASV, RSV, NEB) or with "giving thanks" (NIV.) In the former construction, joy is seen as the pervading element of endurance and patience. Goodspeed renders it "the cheerful exercise of endurance and forbearance." A distinctively Christian quality (cf. Gal 5:22; Phil 1:18; 2:17; 3:1, et al.), joy is often associated in the NT with hardship and suffering.

12 The fourth ingredient, and the crowning virtue, of the worthy Christian life is gratitude. One reason for giving thanks to God is that he has "qualified" believers "to share in the inheritance of the saints." The Greek word for "qualified" (*hikanōsanti*), which basically has in it the thought of making sufficient or competent, may shade into the sense of empowering or authorizing. From its use in this passage we may conclude that in themselves believers have no fitness for sharing in the heritage of God's people. They can experience this only as God qualifies them for such a privilege. The tense of the word is aorist, pointing to the time of the Colossians' conversion. The suggestion is that the qualifying is not a process but an instantaneous act.

To "share in" the inheritance of the saints is to have a portion of the heritage belonging to God's people. There is an obvious allusion to the inheritance of ancient Israel in the Land of Promise and the share of the inheritance each Israelite had. Christians, as the new people of God, also have an inheritance, and each believer has a share allotted to him.

"In the kingdom of light" appears at first to mark the inheritance as future and heavenly (cf. TCNT). But the following verse affirms that Christians have already been rescued from the dominion of darkness and are even now in the kingdom of God's Son. H.C.G. Moule therefore rightly argues that the reference is "properly to the believer's position and possession even now. This Canaan," he explains, "is not in the distance, beyond death; it is about us today, in our home, in our family, in our business, . . . in all that makes up mortal life" (pp. 65, 66).

13 The proof that God has qualified us for a share of the inheritance of the saints is that he has "rescued us from the dominion of darkness and brought us into the kingdom of the Son he loves." "Rescued" translates *errusato*, a word that means to liberate, save, or deliver someone from something or someone; that from which Christians have been rescued is a "dominion of darkness." Luke (22:53) reports Jesus' use of the same phrase at the time of his arrest in Gethsemane. "Darkness" in Scripture is symbolic of ignorance, falsehood, and sin (cf. John 3:19; Rom 13:12). But Paul probably had the Colossian heresy in mind, because the principalities and powers to which the false teachers urged Christians to pay homage are designated by him "the powers of this dark world" (Eph 6:12).

God's action in behalf of his people does not stop with deliverance from the authority of darkness. He has also "brought" them "into the kingdom of the Son he loves." "Brought" translates *metestēsen*, a word that was used in secular literature in reference to removing persons from one country and settling them as colonists and citizens in another country. It might be rendered "reestablished." The tense of the verb points to the time of conversion. The "kingdom" (rule) is not to be interpreted eschatologically. It was for the Colossians a present reality (cf. John 3:3-5). Nor is the kingdom to be interpreted in a territorial sense. That is to say, it is not an area that may be designated on a map; it is the sovereign rule of the Lord Christ over human hearts.

"The Son he loves" translates a phrase (*tou huiou tēs agapēs autou*) that literally reads "the Son of his love." It is a Hebraic way of saying "God's dear Son." The expression is reminiscent of the words of the Father at the baptism and the transfiguration of Jesus.

14 "In whom," which has its antecedent in "the Son" (v.13), affirms that redemption and forgiveness are ours by virtue of union with Christ. "Redemption" (*apolytrōsin*), a term that speaks of a release brought about by the payment of a price, was used of the deliverance of slaves from bondage or of prisoners of war from captivity. "Emancipation" expresses the idea. "We have" teaches that the believer's redemption is a present possession.

Aphesis ("forgiveness") literally means "a sending away." It thus speaks of the removal of our sins from us, so that they are no longer barriers that separate us from God. Redemption and forgiveness are not exactly parallel or identical concepts, but by putting the two terms in apposition to each other, the apostle teaches that the central feature of redemption is the forgiveness of sins.

Notes

13 The "for" of NIV has no exact equivalent in the Gr. text. However, ὅς (*hos*, "who") in this context has a semi-argumentative—almost causal—force, and in light of this the NIV rendering is justified (cf. RHG, pp. 960-62).

14 Between ἀπολύτρωσιν (*apolytrōsin*, "redemption") and τὴν ἄφεσιν (*tēn aphesin*, "the forgiveness") the TR inserts διά τοῦ αἵματος αὐτοῦ (*dia tou haimatos autou*, "through his blood"). Support for this reading is quite weak, and this explains the omission of the English equivalent from versions such as ASV, RSV, and NIV. The words are genuine in Eph 1:7, where there is a thought very similar to the one expressed here.

II. The Supremacy of Christ (1:15-23)

The most dangerous aspect of the Colossian heresy was its depreciation of the person of Jesus Christ. To the errorists of Colosse, Christ was not the triumphant Redeemer to whom all authority in heaven and on earth had been committed. At best he was only one of many spirit beings who bridged the space between God and men.

This passage is a part of Paul's answer to this heretical teaching. One of several great Christological declarations in Paul (cf. 2:9-15; Eph 1:20-23; Phil 2:5-11), it proclaims the unqualified supremacy of our Redeemer. Scott says it "represents a loftier conception of Christ's person than is found anywhere else in the writings of Paul" (p. 20). The affirmations of the passage are all the more remarkable when we remember that they were written of One who only thirty years earlier had died on a Roman cross.

It is somewhat arbitrary to separate this passage from what precedes it. So imperceptibly does Paul move from prayer (vv.3-14) to exposition that it is difficult to know exactly where one leaves off and the other begins. In KJV, for instance, everything from v.9 through v.18 is treated as a single sentence. ASV places a period at the end of v.17. NIV, RSV, JB, and NAB, which begin a new sentence (and a new paragraph) with v.15, seem to represent the best construction of the passage.

A. *The Scope of Christ's Supremacy*

1:15-18

> ¹⁵He is the image of the invisible God, the firstborn over all creation. ¹⁶For by him all things were created: things in heaven and on earth, visible and invisible, whether thrones or powers or rulers or authorities; all things were created by him and for him. ¹⁷He is before all things, and in him all things hold together. ¹⁸And he is the head of the body, the church; he is the beginning and the firstborn from among the dead, so that in everything he might have the supremacy.

Three profound and sweeping statements concerning Christ are made. These show his relation to deity (v.15a), to creation (vv.15b-17), and to the church (v.18). In making these assertions, Paul refuted the Colossian errorists, in whose system angelic mediators usurped the place and function of Christ. His task in earlier correspondence (such as Galatians and Romans) had been to expound the importance of Christ for salvation; in the face of this new teaching at Colosse, he found it necessary to affirm Christ's cosmic significance.

15 In regard to deity, Christ is "the image of the invisible God" (cf. 2 Cor 4:4). In interpreting this statement, we must not understand the apostle to be teaching that Christ is the image of God in a material or physical sense. The true meaning must be sought on a level deeper than this. Nor should we limit the concept to one stage or period of Christ's existence. Some interpreters think Paul's primary reference is to the preincarnate Christ, and the statements of vv.15b, 16, which speak of Christ's relation to creation, do lend some support to this view. Others prefer to think the apostle had in mind the incarnate Christ in his glorified state. Peake, a proponent of this view, says the passage assumes the preexistence of the Son, but its assertions are of the exalted Christ (p. 502). In view of the uncertainty of the matter, it seems best not to limit the concept at all. Christ always has been, is, and always will be the image of God. His incarnation did not make him the image of God, but it did bring him, "as being that Image, within our grasp" (Nicholson, p. 75).

Eikōn, the Greek word for "image," expresses two ideas. One is *likeness*, a thought brought out in some of the versions (e.g., Moff., Am. Trans., Wms., and Knox). Christ is the image of God in the sense that he is the exact likeness of God, like the image on a coin or the reflection in a mirror (cf. Heb 1:3). The other idea in the word is *manifesta-*

tion. That is, Christ is the image of God in the sense that the nature and being of God are perfectly revealed in him (cf. John 1:18). Therefore Paul can boldly say that we have "the light of the knowledge of the glory of God in the face of Christ" (2 Cor 4:6) and that believers, reflecting the Lord's glory, "are being transformed into his likeness with ever-increasing glory" (2 Cor 3:18). Paul's statement leaves no place for the vague emanations and shadowy abstractions so prominent in the gnostic system.

In relation to the universe, Christ is "the firstborn over all creation." Each word of this phrase must be interpreted cautiously. "Firstborn" (*prōtotokos*) is used of Christ, in addition to the passage under study, in Colossians 1:18; Romans 8:29; Hebrews 1:6; and Revelation 1:15. (It is used also in Luke 2:7, but in a different setting.) It may denote either priority in time (cf. Moff., Am. Trans.) or supremacy in rank (NIV). In the present passage perhaps we should see both meanings. Christ is *before* all creation in time; he is also *over* it in rank and dignity. The major stress, however, seems to be on the idea of supremacy.

Some see in the word an allusion to the ancient custom whereby the firstborn in a family was accorded rights and privileges not shared by the other offspring. He was his father's representative and heir, and to him the management of the household was committed. Following this line of interpretation, we may understand the passage to teach that Christ is his Father's representative and heir and has the management of the divine household (all creation) committed to him. He is thus Lord over all God's creation.

16,17 The apostle now states the ground for Christ's dominion over creation: he is firstborn (Lord) over creation *because he made it.* To him it owes its unity, its meaning, indeed its very existence.

Three prepositional phrases define the creative activity of Christ: All things came to be "in [NIV, by] him" (v.16a), "through [NIV, by] him" (v.16b) and "for him" (v.16c). Creation was "in [*en*] him" in the sense that it occurred within the sphere of his person and power. He was its conditioning cause, its originating center, its spiritual locality. The act of creation rested, as it were, in him. Creation is "through" (*dia*) Christ in the sense that he was the mediating Agent through whom it actually came into being. The preposition is frequently used of Christ's redemptive mediation between God and men (cf. Eph 2:18; 1 Thess 5:9, et al.), but the thought here is that the entire life of the universe is mediated from God through Christ (cf. John 1:3, 10). Creation is "for" (*eis*) Christ in the sense that he is the end for which all things exist, the goal toward whom all things were intended to move. They are meant "to serve His will, to contribute to His glory. . . . Their whole being, willingly or unwillingly, moves . . . to Him; whether, as His blissful servants, they shall be as it were His throne; or as His stricken enemies, 'His footstool' " (H.C.G. Moule, p. 78).

"All things," used twice in the verse, translates an expression (*ta panta*) that was sometimes used in the sense of our word "universe." It denoted the totality of things in heaven and on earth, visible and invisible. The reference to "thrones," "powers," "rulers," and "authorities" is perhaps an allusion to the angelic hierarchy that figured so prominently in the Colossian heresy. Paul's mention of these things does not, of course, mean that he recognized the existence of a hierarchy of spirit beings. His words do suggest, however, that whatever supernatural powers there may be, Christ is the One who made them and he is their Lord.

17 Verse 16 has stated the essential reason for Christ's lordship over creation, namely, that he is its creator. Verse 17 is a sort of summing up of the thought of vv.15, 16. But in addition, it rounds out and completes the statement of Christ's relation to creation. "He is before all things, and in him all things hold together." That Christ is "before" all things means primarily that he is before all *in time;* however, the statement is general enough to include also the notion that he is above all in rank. The thought is similar to that of the earlier expression, "firstborn over all creation" (v.15b).

That all things "hold together" in Christ means that he is both the unifying principle and the personal sustainer of all creation. It springs from him and finds in him its common bond and center. He is, to use the words of Lightfoot, "the principle of cohesion" who makes the universe "a cosmos instead of a chaos" (p. 156; cf. Heb 1:3).

18 Paul's third affirmation concerning Christ's supremacy relates to the new creation: "And he is the head of the body, the church" (v.18a; cf. 2:19; Eph 1:22, 23; 4:15). To be the "head" of the church is to be its sovereign. In the figure there may also be the suggestion that Christ is the source of the church's life, but this is not its primary significance. Christ, as Head of the church, is its Chief, its Leader. It is he who guides and governs it. "He" is emphatic, the meaning being that Christ alone—Christ and no other—is Head of the church.

"Church" (*ekklēsia*), which means "assembly" or "congregation," is best interpreted here as a term embracing all the redeemed people of God. The mention of the church as "the body" of Christ suggests at least three things: (1) that the church is a living organism, composed of members joined vitally to one another, (2) that the church is the means by which Christ carries out his purposes and performs his work, and (3) that the union that exists between Christ and his people is most intimate and real. Together they constitute one living unit, each, in a sense, being incomplete without the other.

Verse 18b gives one ground of Christ's headship over the church: "He is the beginning and the firstborn from among the dead." In the Greek the first word is a relative pronoun (*hos*), and in this context is almost equivalent to "because he is" (cf. Moff., and see notes on v.13). The word *beginning* may be interpreted in any one of three ways: as referring to (1) supremacy in rank, (2) precedence in time, or (3) creative initiative. There is, of course, truth in each of these, but it seems best to see in Paul's word the idea of creative initiative. The meaning then is that Christ is the origin and source of the life of the church, the fount of its being (cf. NEB).

"Firstborn" (*prōtotokos*), which in the Greek text is in apposition with "beginning," defines more precisely what Paul means. This term was used earlier (v.15) to point up Christ's relation to creation, and we concluded that it suggested both precedence in time and supremacy in rank. In the present passage the idea of precedence is the more prominent. Thus, the meaning is that Christ was the first to come from the dead in true resurrection life (i.e., never to die again, cf. 1 Cor 15:20). And because he was the first to be born from the dead, he possesses in himself the new and higher life that his people, by virtue of their union with him, now share. Thus, his being the firstborn from the dead is that which establishes his place as the beginning, the origin of the church's life.

The idea of sovereignty, however, is not entirely absent from this passage. Because Christ was the first to be born from the dead, he has the dignity and sovereignty belonging to the Firstborn. Peake, who is a proponent of this view, interprets the passage to mean that "from among the dead [Christ] has passed to his throne, where he reigns as the living Lord" (p. 507).

"So that in everything he might have the supremacy" in one sense is a summary of all that Paul has affirmed from v.15 to this point, but syntactically it must be seen as expressing the purpose of the immediately preceding statement about Christ's being the beginning, the firstborn from the dead. He rose from the dead in order that his preeminence might become universal, extending both to the old creation and to the new. He had always been first, but by his resurrection he entered upon an even wider and more significant sovereignty (cf. Acts 2:26; Rom 1:4).

The word for "he" (*autos*) is normally not expressed in Greek because it is implied in the personal ending of the verb. Here, however, it is expressed, suggesting that preeminence is the exclusive right of Christ. "He himself" or "he alone" is the idea. "Have supremacy" literally means "have the first place"; or perhaps better still, "become first." C.F.D. Moule takes the whole phrase to mean: " 'that he might be alone supreme among all'—sole head of all things" (p. 70).

Notes

15–20 Much scholarly debate has centered on these verses, and it is often asserted that they contain material not composed by the author of Colossians. The discussions offer a bewildering variety of theories, among which are those that see in the passage a formula emanating from the Hellenistic Jewish synagogue and praising the divine Word or Wisdom, those that claim it was a Gnostic hymn celebrating the authority of the World Ruler over the powers of the cosmos, and those that view it as a pre-Pauline Christian hymn incorporated by the apostle into Colossians. My position is that the passage is genuinely Pauline and, whether hymnic or not, presents a true and exalted view of Christ. Brief but helpful critiques of the various theories may be found in Caird (pp. 174–78) and Martin (pp. 40–55).

15 A superficial reading of the KJV ("of all creation") might lead one to conclude that Christ is a part of creation, the first of God's created beings. Such a reading of the phrase, however, is not in keeping with the context, which in the sharpest manner distinguishes Christ from creation. Nor is that understanding of the phrase demanded by the grammar. κτίσεως (*ktiseōs*, "creation") might be construed either as an ablative of comparison ("before creation") or as a genitive. In the latter case, it is either a genitive of reference ("with reference to creation") or an objective genitive ("over creation"), which is the NIV interpretation. Peake points out that in LXX πρωτότοκος (*prōtotokos*, "firstborn") in some instances had altogether lost its temporal significance. He questions whether the word retains any of its temporal sense in this passage.

16 Ἐν (*en*) may here have in it both the ideas of sphere ("in," ASV) and of agency ("by," NIV), but the former is perhaps the more prominent in this verse. The notion of agency is expressed by διά (*dia*) in the latter part of the verse.

The tenses of the verbs are significant: ἐκτίσθη (*ektisthē*, "were created"), an aorist, points to a particular time and views creation as a definite act; ἔκτισται (*ektistai*, "have been created"; NIV, "were created"), a perfect tense, represents creation as a resultant state. "Stand created" might be an apt rendering for the latter form.

17, 18 The contrast in verbs must not be overlooked. Christ *is* (ἐστιν [*estin*], present tense) first in reference to all creation; his resurrection made it possible for him to *become* (γένηται [*genētai*], aorist tense) first with respect to the church (cf. Phil 2:9–11).

B. *The Basis for Christ's Supremacy*

1:19–23

> ¹⁹For God was pleased to have all his fullness dwell in him, ²⁰and through him to reconcile to himself all things, whether things on earth or things in heaven, by making peace through his blood, shed on the cross.

²¹Once you were alienated from God and were enemies in your minds because of your evil behavior. ²²But now he has reconciled you by Christ's physical body through death to present you holy in his sight, without blemish and free from accusation— ²³if you continue in your faith, established and firm, not moved from the hope held out in the gospel. This is the gospel that you heard and that has been proclaimed to every creature under heaven, and of which I, Paul, have become a servant.

Paul has ascribed unique supremacy to Jesus Christ. He has affirmed him to be Image of God, Lord over creation, Head of the church—indeed, preeminent in all things. Verses 19–23 state the grounds—observe the first word of v.19—on which such supremacy is affirmed.

The last phrase of v.18 implies that Christ has unshared supremacy because God has decreed it. "It was," as Calvin says, "so arranged in the providence of God" (p. 154). The present passage states this in different terms, but still puts it within the context of the divine will. Two things that God willed are specifically set forth, one having to do with the fullness of God in Christ (v.19), the other with the reconciling work of Christ (vv.20–23).

1. The fullness of God in Christ (1:19)

19 The subject of the verb translated "was pleased" is uncertain. Some take it to be "Christ." Lightfoot calls this view "grammatically possible" but thinks "it confuses the theology of the passage hopelessly" (p. 159). Others construe the subject to be "fullness" (cf. Moff., Am. Trans., RSV, PH). The NIV understands the passage as affirming an action of God. *God willed* that in Christ all fullness should dwell.

The word for "fullness" (*plērōma*), which Scott calls "perhaps the most difficult" in the Epistle (p. 25), is the focal point of much discussion. The term is found about seventeen times in the NT, but there are only four places in which the meaning is parallel to that of the present passage (Eph 1:23; 3:19; 4:13; Col 2:9). The word seems to have been in current use by the false teachers, and was possibly, though not certainly, employed by them of the totality of supernatural powers ("aeons") that they believed were in control of men's lives. Calvin understands Paul to use it of "fulness of righteousness, wisdom, power, and every blessing," explaining that "whatever God has he has conferred upon his Son" (p. 154). Peake, following Meyer, Eadie, Alford, and others, interprets "fullness" to mean "the fulness of grace, 'the whole charismatic riches of God'" (p. 508; cf. John 1:14). He understands the whole statement "as having reference to the sending of the Son in the incarnation. The Father was pleased that He should come 'with the whole treasure of Divine grace'" (p. 508).

Others interpret "fullness" as a reference to Deity. C.F.D. Moule, for instance, explains it to mean "God in all his fullness," that is, "all that God is" (p. 70). Phillips renders it "the full nature of God"; NEB, "the complete being of God." Lightfoot paraphrases it, "the totality of Divine powers and attributes" (p. 159), the suggestion being that nothing of deity is lacking in Christ. The similar expression found in Colossians 2:9 lends support to this view.

It is significant that Paul says "all" the fullness dwells in Christ. The Colossian errorists perhaps looked upon the many spirit beings they thought of as filling the space between God and the world as intermediaries and taught that any communication between God and the world had to pass through them. They probably included Christ among these supernatural powers, admitting that he was of heavenly origin and that God was in some sense present in him. He was, however, only one aspect of the divine nature and in himself was not sufficient for all the needs of men. Paul, in contrast, declares that Christ is not just one of many divine beings. He is the one Mediator between God and the world, and all, not part, of the attributes and activities of God are centered in him.

"Dwell" translates *katoikēsai*, a verb that suggests permanent residence as opposed to temporary sojourn. Lightfoot thinks Paul was refuting a Colossian notion that the divine fullness had only a transient and incidental association with Christ. In distinction from this, the apostle asserts that it abides in him permanently.

2. The reconciling work of Christ (1:20–23)

20 The Father was pleased "to reconcile to himself all things" through Christ. This statement sustains a close connection with v.19. For one thing, the Greek word for "to reconcile" (*apokatallaxai*) is parallel with the word for "dwell" (v.19), both terms being grammatically dependent on the verb rendered "was pleased" (*eudokēsen*) (v.19). The Father willed that all fullness should dwell in Christ; he also willed to reconcile all things to himself through Christ. "Reconcile," the essential meaning of which is "to change" (from enmity to friendship), suggests the effecting in man of a condition of submission to, and harmony with, God (cf. Rom 5:10, 11; 2 Cor 5:18–20; Eph 2:14, 15). The Greek verb, a double compound form, probably has intensive force: to change completely, to change so as to remove all enmity.

This work of reconciliation is on the widest possible scale, having to do with "all things." Calvin limits "things in heaven" to angels. H.C.G. Moule interprets it similarly but admits that reconciliation affects the angelic world "in a sense as yet known only to the Lord" (p. 88). It is perhaps better to understand the word *heaven* as an inclusive term taking in everything not belonging to the "earth"—perhaps what is sometimes called the "starry heavens." "Things on earth ... things in heaven" thus denotes everything in God's universe.

One must be careful not to interpret this in such a way as to make it contradict the clear teaching of other Scriptures. Admittedly, the statement might appear, on its surface, to indicate that eventually everything will be brought into a saving relationship with God. Such universalism, however, is contrary to those passages that affirm that apart from personal trust in Christ there is no salvation. Our Lord, in fact, spoke of the impenitent as going away into "eternal punishment" (Matt 25:46). We should therefore understand this statement to be a reference to the cosmic significance of Christ's work, the thought being similar to, but not identical with, that of Romans 8:19–22. There the general sense is that the disorder that has characterized creation will be done away and divine harmony restored. Here perhaps the main idea is that all things eventually are to be decisively subdued to God's will and made to serve his purposes.

21 Verse 20 has presented the general aspect of the reconciling work of Christ ("all things ..."). Verses 21–23 show how this applies personally and specifically to the Colossians. Prior to their conversion to Christianity they had been "alienated from God," "enemies" in their minds. The former word (*apēllotriōmenous*), which literally means "transferred to another owner," speaks of estrangement from God. The perfect tense of the Greek word denotes a fixed state or condition. The latter word ("enemies" [*echthrous*]) affirms the Colossians' hostility to God. This hostility, Paul explains, affected their "minds" (*dianoia*; lit., "thought," "disposition," "attitude") and was outwardly expressed in their "evil behavior" (*ergois tois ponērois*; lit., "wicked deeds").

22 God reconciled the Colossians "by Christ's physical body through death." "Physical body" renders *sōmati tēs sarkos* (lit., "body of flesh"). Perhaps Paul deliberately used this rather redundant expression to emphasize (in contradiction to the views of the heretics) the reality of Christ's body. Peake understands Paul to be alluding to and answering "the false spiritualism" of the Colossian heretics. Asserting that reconciliation could be accomplished only by spiritual (angelic) beings, they attached little or no value to the work of Christ in a physical body. In opposition to this, Paul stressed the importance of Christ's physical body.

The result of Christ's reconciling work is the presentation of the Colossians "holy in his sight, without blemish and free from accusation." Some interpreters, perhaps most, take these words as a description of a yet-future presentation to God (at the Judgment Day). And this is the view this passage seems naturally to suggest. There are, however, a number of scholars (e.g., Lightfoot and Beare) who see it as a statement of what God through Christ had already done for the Colossians. In reconciling them, he brought them into his presence, no longer as unhallowed, stained by sin, and bearing the burden of guilt; but "holy" and "without blemish and free from accusation." So the reference is to the standing effected for the believer at the time of and by the death of Christ.

Bruce presents a view in which there is a balance between the present and the future: "The sentence of justification passed upon the believer here and now anticipates the pronouncement of the judgment day; the holiness which is progressively wrought in his life by the Spirit of God here and now is to issue in perfection of glory on the day of Christ's parousia" (p. 213).

"Holy" suggests consecration and dedication (see the discussion of v.2). "Without blemish," which translates a technical sacrificial term (*amōmous*), was used of animals that were without flaw and therefore worthy of being offered to God. The use of this word gives support to the view that in this statement Paul was not thinking about our personal conduct but about our position in Christ. There has never been, nor will there ever be, a Christian life that is without blemish in actual conduct. But Christians' identification with Christ is such that his righteousness and his standing before God are theirs (2 Cor 5:21; 1 John 4:17).

"Free from accusation," like the other two terms, expresses a condition possible only because men are in Christ, covered by and sharing in the benefits of his death for them.

23 Some interpreters, especially some of those who understand the foregoing words as a description of the believers' presentation before God at the time of judgment, explain v.23 as a warning against indolence and complacency. The Colossians, they understand Paul to say, will be thus presented to God only "if [they] continue in [their] faith, established and firm," and so forth. Bruce comments, "If the Bible teaches the final perseverance of the saints, it also teaches that the saints are those who finally persevere —in Christ. Continuance is the test of reality" (p. 213).

Those who take v.22 to be a statement of accomplished fact contend that the words of v.23 are *proof* of a past (and continuing) experience, not a condition of what is future. "No reference," affirms Nicholson, "is here made to the future, no doubt of any kind is insinuated, no threatening danger is implied. The apostle's purpose is simply to state the absolute accomplishment of salvation in the past sufferings of Christ, and the demonstration of it which is furnished to an individual soul in the present existence of his faith" (p. 122).

It is significant for both interpretations that the condition is stated in such a way as to express the apostle's confidence in his readers. "The Greek," writes Radford, "indicates not an uncertain prospect but a necessary condition and an almost certain assumption. . . . Paul is at once insistent and confident; they must [continue], and he is sure that they will" (p. 194).

"Faith" may denote a body of doctrine, but perhaps here, as usual in the NT, it means personal faith, that is, reliance on Christ. Therefore, instead of "the faith" (KJV, ASV, RSV), it should read "your faith" (NIV, NEB). The words that follow "faith" explain what is involved in continuance in faith, namely, being "established and firm, not moved from the hope held out in the gospel." "Established" suggests being founded securely, as on a rock. "Firm" (lit., "settled") depicts a steady and firm resolve.

The "hope held out in the gospel" is in its fullest sense the expectation of ultimate, complete salvation that will belong to believers upon the return of their Lord. There may be an implicit contrast between the certainty of the gospel and the delusive promises offered by the Colossian errorists.

In the closing words of v.23 three statements are made to stress the importance of remaining true to the apostolic gospel: (1) It is the message "that you heard." The reference is to the gospel that had been initially preached to them by Epaphras (cf. 1:7) and was the instrument of their conversion. (2) It has been "proclaimed to every creature under heaven." Its universality is a mark of its authenticity. C.F.D. Moule suggests that the statement does not mean that the gospel had been preached to every individual, but that it had been "heard in all the great centers of the Empire (cf. Rom 15:19–23)" (p. 73). Bruce suggests that Paul was "perhaps indulging in a prophetic prolepsis" (p. 213). Obviously there is an element of hyperbole in the statement. (3) Paul closes with the affirmation that he himself had "become a servant" of the gospel. Paul does not designate himself in this fashion for the purpose of magnifying his office, but to impress on the Colossians that the gospel heard by them from Epaphras and proclaimed in all the world, was the same gospel he preached.

Notes

19 Πλήρωμα (*plērōma*, "fullness") was a technical term used by second-century Gnostics of the hierarchy of the supernatural beings lying between God and the world. Many present-day scholars think it likely that the word was employed in this sense during Paul's lifetime. We cannot deny that the Colossian errorists made use of the term or that it bore some relation to gnosticism, but only with great caution can we assert that at this early time it contained the connotations of later fully developed Gnostic systems.

The tense of κατοικῆσαι (*katoikēsai*; NIV, "dwell") is aorist, perhaps having ingressive force and meaning "take up lasting abode." Whether the reference to "taking up" abode marks an action belonging to eternity or to time has been debated. For instance, Findlay argues for the resurrection-ascension of Jesus as the event when the fullness came to reside in the Son. Eph 1:20–23 and 4:8–10 are cited as confirmation of this interpretation. H.C.G. Moule feels that the context points to a time-act, but he adds that in a very real sense the fullness "is eternally in the Son; it does not take up its abode in Him as if it had to begin" (p. 87). Macphail, on the other hand, thinks that the grand sweep of the passage is an argument for taking the term in its widest possible range and understanding an eternal residence of the divine fullness to be meant. This is the view to be preferred. In it the aorist tense may be interpreted not as ingressive but as constative, serving to sum up in a single point the whole action.

22 There is considerable uncertainty about v.22—both the text and the punctuation. Most MSS read ἀποκατήλλαξεν (apokatēllaxen, "he reconciled"), though a few have ἀποκατηλλάγητε (apokatēllagēte, "you were reconciled"). The passive was preferred by the editors of UBS text (2nd ed.), but the third edition has the active.

Lightfoot makes v.22a (νυνὶ ... θανάτου, nuni ... thanatou, "now ... death") a parenthesis and understands παραστῆσαι (parastēsai, "to present," v.22b) to be dependent on εὐδόκησεν (eudokēsen, "was pleased," v.19). Peake puts a comma at the end of v.20, a period at the end of v.21; ὑμᾶς (hymas, "you," v.21) is then the object of ἀποκαταλλάξαι (apokatallaxai, "to reconcile," v.20).

III. The Ministry of Paul (1:24–2:7)

This passage, which is somewhat parallel to Ephesians 3:1ff., comes as a sort of digression. Though decidedly autobiographical, it is not so much concerned with Paul the man as with the office he filled. In the course of his discussion, Paul mentions his suffering and its bearing on the Colossians (1:24), his commission to preach and its implications for them (1:25–29), and his personal interest in and concern for them (2:1–5). The passage closes with a direct appeal to the Colossians (2:6, 7).

A. A Ministry of Suffering

1:24

24Now I rejoice in what was suffered for you, and I fill up in my flesh what is still lacking in regard to Christ's afflictions, for the sake of his body, which is the church.

24 This is a much-disputed verse, but the general sense of it is clear. In it the apostle teaches that the sufferings he endured in the course of his work were in the interest of the Colossians, indeed, of the whole church, and in the knowledge of that, he is able to rejoice (cf. Eph 3:13).

"Now" may possibly be both temporal and transitional in force. In its temporal sense, the word indicates that Paul's joy and his suffering were both realities at the time of writing this letter. There may be a note of emphasis in the word (nun), viz., "just now, at this very moment." In its transitional sense "now" shows that this paragraph is closely related to the thought of the preceding section, in which Christ's unique supremacy has been expounded. Looked at in this manner, the term is almost equivalent to "therefore" and shows that the thought of Christ's supremacy is a factor in Paul's ability to rejoice in the midst of suffering.

Three things are said in the verse about the sufferings of Paul: First, they are for the sake of other people. The apostle speaks of suffering "for you" and "for the sake of his [Christ's] body." In both phrases the preposition means not "in place of " but "in the interest of." The first phrase alludes to the fact that Paul's bonds and imprisonment had been incurred in the course of bringing the gospel to the Gentiles, to which class the Colossians belonged. The sufferings, therefore, were for their sake in the sense that they shared in the benefit of the ministry that brought on those sufferings. The second phrase affirms that the benefit of Paul's sufferings extends not simply to the Colossians, nor to the Gentile portion of the church only; they in some sense have a bearing on the whole body of Christ. Indeed, the apostle's sufferings contribute even to our well-being, for had he not suffered imprisonment, this letter might never have been written, and we would have been deprived of its message.

97

Second, Paul's sufferings are identified with the afflictions of Christ. "I fill up in my flesh what is still lacking in regard to Christ's afflictions." These words have evoked a great amount of discussion. Many Roman Catholics, for instance, interpreting the "afflictions" of Christ as Christ's redemptive sufferings, have used this verse as grounds for asserting that Christ's atonement is defective and that the sufferings of the saints are needed to supplement his work on our behalf. But whatever is meant by "what is still lacking in regard to Christ's afflictions," we may be sure that Paul did not regard the death of Jesus as lacking in efficacy (cf. Col 2:11-15). That death was complete, once for all, and wholly adequate to meet man's need. The Roman doctrine, as Lightfoot says, can be imported into this passage only "at the cost of a contradiction to the Pauline doctrine" of the satisfaction of Christ's sacrifice (p. 167).

In Lightfoot's interpretation, the afflictions of Christ are those endured personally by him on earth, but he insists that the reference is to Christ's ministerial afflictions, not his mediatorial redemptive sufferings. The word "afflictions" (*thlipseōn*), he explains, is never employed elsewhere in the NT of the sufferings of Christ on the cross; the reference, then, is to the tribulations our Lord endured in the course of his life and ministry. The sufferings his people endure are a continuation of what he endured, and in that sense they complete his afflictions. "It is a simple matter of fact," writes Lightfoot, "that the afflictions of every saint and martyr do supplement the afflictions of Christ. The Church is built up by repeated acts of self-denial in successive individuals and successive generations. They continue the work which Christ began" (p. 166).

The underlying principle is the believer's union with Christ. That union is so intimate —Christ the Head, his people the body—that he suffers when they suffer (cf. Isa 63:9). His personal sufferings are over, but his sufferings in his people continue (cf. 2 Cor 1:5; Phil 3:10). Perhaps Paul was thinking of Christ's words to him on the Damascus road (Acts 9:4, 5).

"What is still lacking" is not an intimation of deficiency in Christ's own sufferings but a reference to what is yet lacking in Christ's suffering *in Paul*. In his experience as a prisoner the apostle was filling up the sum or quota of suffering yet remaining for him to endure.

Third, they are the sphere of Paul's joy. The sufferings Paul endured for the gospel seem never to have been to him a source of perplexity or of sadness. "You may," writes MacPhail, "occasionally hear the clang of the Roman chain, but you never hear a groan from the brave prisoner" (p. 49).

Paul's attitude had nothing in common with those ascetics of a later time who inflicted torture on themselves in the belief that they would thereby gain merit with God. Paul's joy was not in suffering as such, but in "what was suffered *for you*." That is to say, it was the distinctive character and circumstances of his sufferings that enabled him to find joy in the midst of them. He saw them as a necessary part of his ministry and knew that they were incurred in the line of duty. (For other NT references to the theme of joy in the face of suffering, see Matthew 5:12; Acts 5:41; Hebrews 10:34.)

B. *A Ministry of Preaching*

1:25-29

25I have become its servant by the commission God gave me to present to you the word of God in its fullness— 26the mystery that has been kept hidden for ages and generations, but is now disclosed to the saints. 27To them God has chosen

to make known among the Gentiles the glorious riches of this mystery, which is Christ in you, the hope of glory.
[28]We proclaim him, counseling and teaching everyone with all wisdom, so that we may present everyone perfect in Christ. [29]To this end I labor, struggling with all the energy he so powerfully works in me.

A second feature of Paul's ministry was the proclamation of God's message. His statement concerning this is of great value to all who wish a better understanding of preaching. The thought revolves around four conceptions: Paul's appointment to the office of preacher (v.25), the message he preached (vv.25b–28a), the method he employed (v.28b), and his ultimate aim (vv.28c–29).

25 Elsewhere Paul speaks of himself as a minister of the gospel (v.23; Eph 3:7), of God (2 Cor 6:4), of Christ (2 Cor 11:23), of a new covenant (2 Cor 3:6). Here he is the church's minister, and as such is bound to toil and suffer in whatever way the church's welfare requires. Suffering is not, then, simply a matter of joy (v.24) but of duty as well. "I" (*egō*), expressed in Greek for emphasis, suggests that Paul was thinking of a ministry peculiar to himself. The word for "minister" (*diakonos*), the same as that used earlier of Epaphras (1:7) and of Paul (1:23), simply means "one who serves."

Paul's appointment to his office was "by the commission God gave" him—literally, "according to the dispensation [arrangement] of God." "Commission" is a free rendering of the word *oikonomian*, which has a rather wide range of meanings. "Plan," "arrangement," "stewardship," "management," "administration,"—these are all possible meanings. The KJV and ASV here translate it "dispensation"; Am. Trans. has "divine appointment"; RSV, "divine office." "Dispensation" ("arrangement") suggests that Paul looked upon his call to the ministry as part of the divine plan for the evangelization of the world; *oikonomia* is in fact sometimes used in Scripture for the plan by which God has ordered the course of history (cf. Eph 1:10, RSV). But *oikonomia*, related to our words "economy" and "economics," is perhaps best rendered here by "stewardship" (cf. Luke 16:2–4). This rendering suggests that Paul conceived of the work to which God appointed him as both a high privilege and a sacred trust (cf. Williams, TCNT, JB). He was a servant of the church, but in the deepest sense he was a steward of God.

The purpose of the apostle's stewardship was "to present the word of God in all its fullness." Some understand this to refer to the geographical extension of the gospel (cf. Rom 15:19). But Paul probably means that his special ministry was to make clear the true nature of the gospel as a divine provision intended for all people.

26 The preceding verse has spoken of Paul's message as "the word of God," a general term that sums up the oral proclamation of the apostles. Verses 26, 27 define the word of God more specifically in terms of a "mystery." A word borrowed from the religious vocabulary of the day, "mystery" (*mystērion*) is used in the NT of truth undiscoverable except by divine revelation (cf. 1 Cor 2:6ff.; 14:51). In Ephesians it is used six times— more often than in any other book of the NT. In 1:9 the term is used of the mystery of God's dealing with the world; in 3:3–9, where it occurs three times, the word has special reference to the inclusion of Gentiles in the privileges and blessings of the messianic salvation; in 5:22 it speaks of the spiritual union of Christ and his church; and in 6:19 it is practically equated with the gospel. In Colossians the word occurs four times (1:26, 27; 2:2; 4:3). Coming from a root that means to initiate, *mystērion* in a general sense denotes a secret. In its various contexts in the NT, however, it ordinarily speaks of an "open secret"; that is, it denotes something that, though once a secret, has now been fully revealed in the gospel.

This mystery, Paul explains, "has been kept hidden for ages and generations, but is now disclosed to his saints." The words express the two characteristics of a mystery in the NT: "hidden for ages and generations . . . now disclosed."

Some interpreters understand "ages" to refer to the ages before the creation of the world; "generations," to the generations of human history. The whole expression is thus equivalent to a declaration that the mystery had been previously concealed from both angels and men. NIV suggests that "ages" and "generations" are used generally to refer to people living in former times. This is perhaps the better interpretation.

To the people of God ("the saints") the truth that was once hidden is now "disclosed." The Greek construction is grammatically irregular, involving a change from a participle ("has been kept hidden," first part of v.26) to an indicative verb ("disclosed," last part of the verse). The sudden shift from participle to indicative may be a reflection of "Paul's intense joy that the long silence has been broken; he is content with nothing short of a definite statement of the glorious fact" (Peake, p. 516).

27 The thought is that God was pleased to reveal to his people how great is the glorious character of the gospel mystery (lit., "the riches of the glory of this mystery"). Paul's frequent use of "riches" suggests that Christ had "opened the door for him to an inexhaustible treasure of goodness (Rom 2:4), glory (Rom 9:23; Eph 1:18; 3:16; Phil 4:19), wisdom (Rom 11:33), and grace (Eph 1:7; 2:7), and every time he explores it he finds something new to take his breath away" (Caird, p. 186). Scott, observing that "glory" in Paul's writings "carries with it the idea of something divine," thinks the whole phrase suggests "richness in divine significance" (p. 33). "Among [lit., in] the Gentiles" defines the sphere in which the wealth of glory has been especially displayed. Paul seems to have been thinking of the wonder of the unfolding of the divine mystery in the conversion of pagan people and in their being drawn into the one body of Christ.

The inner content of the mystery is defined as "Christ in you." (Cf. vv.25, 26, where the mystery is defined as the gospel.) Some scholars read "Christ among you," that is, among you Gentiles (cf. Lightfoot). If the words are understood in this fashion, the mystery consists in the offer of redemption to the Gentiles. They had appeared to be forever excluded from God's favor, but it had been a part of God's secret plan from the beginning that they should be included in the messianic salvation. There is much to be said for this interpretation, but the context requires that we understand the phrase as referring to an inner, subjective experience. The mystery, therefore, long hidden but now revealed is not the diffusion of the gospel among the Gentiles but the indwelling of Christ in his people, whether Jews or Gentiles.

Christ in you is now declared to be "the hope of glory." "Hope" is joyous expectation or anticipation. "Glory" is that which will belong to the Christian in the heavenly state (cf. 3:4; Rom 5:2; 8:17). The general truth is that Christ dwelling in the believer is the ground for certainty of complete salvation. A kindred notion is found in Ephesians 1:13, 14, where the Spirit is designated as "the earnest of our inheritance." In this letter "Christ himself occupies the sphere that Paul elsewhere assigns to the Spirit" (Beare, p. 181).

28 In v.25 Paul has defined his message as "the word of God." In vv.26, 27 he has used the term *mystery*. Here his message is shown to center in the Christ who indwells believers. At the deepest level, therefore, the apostle conceived of his message not as a system or as a collection of rules and regulations, but as a living and glorious Person who is the fulfillment of the deepest hopes of mankind and the source of new life for all his people. "We" is emphatic (like "I" in vv.23, 25) and distinguishes Paul (and his fellow preachers) from the Colossian errorists. "Proclaim" translates *katangellomen*, a word suggesting a solemn or public proclamation. Scholars of an earlier period (e.g., Westcott, Vincent) thought there was in it the notion of proclaiming with authority. Schniewind, who speaks of it as belonging to the "language of mission," asserts that the term includes the idea of "instruction, admonition and tradition" (TDNT, 1:71, 72). It perhaps has a wider significance than the more common word for "preach" (*kērusso*) in Paul's writings (cf. v.23).

"Counseling" (*nouthetountes*) and "teaching" (*didaskontes*) describe two attendant circumstances of Paul's preaching. The former word, used in the Pauline Epistles eight times and only once elsewhere in the NT (Acts 20:31), has to do with the will and emotions and connotes warning. Here it relates to non-Christians, the thought probably being that the apostle sought to awaken each of them to his need of Christ. Some interpreters think the word corresponds to the demand for repentance in the Gospels. "Teaching," which probably refers to a ministry for converts, stresses the importance of instruction in proclaiming the Word. "With all wisdom" seems to express the way the teaching was done.

"Everyone," stated twice in v.28 for emphasis (three times in the Greek text), shows that Paul's gospel was not marred by the exclusiveness that characterized the false teachers. They believed the way of salvation to be so involved that it could be understood only by a select few who made up a sort of spiritual aristocracy. Unlike the errorists, Paul slighted no one. Every person was the object of his direct concern.

The aim of Paul's proclaiming, admonishing, and teaching was to "present everyone perfect in Christ." "Present" (*paristēmi*) refers to the bringing into God's presence at the return of Christ (cf. 1 Thess 2:19–20; 5:23). Only then will God's work in the believer be complete. "Perfect" suggests attainment of the proper end of one's existence. Other versions use such terms as "complete" (NAB), "full grown" (Montgomery), "mature" (RSV). The reference is to maturity in faith and character (cf. Eph 4:13), and it is a prospect held out for "everyone." Such maturity is possible "in Christ," that is, by virtue of the believer's union with Christ.

29 To accomplishing this end Paul gave himself unstintedly. "I labor" translates *kopiō*, a word denoting wearisome toil. Weymouth expresses it, "I exert all my strength." "Struggling" renders the word *agōnizomenos*, which our familiar English "agonize" transliterates. A term from the athletic arena, it signifies intense exertion. This struggle, Paul affirms, is "according to his [God's] working" (*kata tēn energeian autou*). That is to say, the struggle is carried on, not through Paul's own natural powers, but by the supernatural power at work in him. "Working" is the rendering of a Greek term (*energeian*) from which we get the word "energy." It is an energy that "powerfully works" (lit., "energizes") in the apostle. The entire statement shows that through faith in Christ we can link our life with a source of strength that enables us to rise above our natural limitations.

C. A Ministry of Intercession

2:1–5

¹I want you to know how strenuously I am exerting myself for you and for those at Laodicea, and for all who have not met me personally. ²My purpose is that they

may be encouraged in heart and united in love, so that they may have the full riches of complete understanding, in order that they may know the mystery of God, namely, Christ, ³in whom are hidden all the treasures of wisdom and knowledge. ⁴I tell you this so that no one may deceive you by fine-sounding arguments. ⁵For though I am absent from you in body, I am present with you in spirit and delight to see how orderly you are and how firm your faith in Christ is.

A third feature of Paul's ministry was his pastoral concern for those he served. The concern expressed in these verses arose from Paul's anxiety about the response of the Colossian Christians to the error being propagated by the false teachers. Such an expression of concern is what we would expect from the man who wrote Philippians 3:18. Anyone who shares Paul's exalted concept of Christ (cf. Col 1:15ff.), we may add, can never be indifferent to the inroads of error.

1 The metaphor of the arena is implicit in this verse, the Greek word translated "exerting" (agōna) being built on the same root as the word rendered "struggling" in 1:29 (agōnizomenos). "How strenuously I am exerting myself" freely renders words that literally mean, "how great a struggle I have." "Struggle" (agōna), which denotes strenuous activity, here speaks of deep and earnest solicitude. The powers that wrestled with Paul for the ruin of his work were real and resolute; he therefore had to "meet them, foot to foot, force to force, in Christ" (H.C.G. Moule, p. 118).

The particular struggle Paul had in mind appears to have been that of prayer. At the time he wrote these words he could not move beyond the walls of his "rented house" (Acts 28:30), being continuously held by the chain linking him to a Roman soldier. But even under these circumstances he could engage in the combat of prayer and so exert himself strenuously in behalf of his readers.

This brings before us an aspect of Paul's prayers that we often overlook—namely, that they sometimes involved him in a truly awesome conflict, an intense struggle of the soul. (Cf. the Gethsemane experience of our Lord.)

Paul's agony in prayer was "for," that is, in behalf of, the Colossians. But it was also in behalf of "those at Laodicea and for all who have not met me personally" (lit., "have not seen my face in the flesh"). Laodicea (cf. Introduction, 1) was an important banking center in ancient times. It is mentioned elsewhere in the NT only in Colossians 4:13, 15, 16 and in Revelation 3:14. The wording of v.1, though capable of being interpreted otherwise, seems to suggest that the Colossians and the Laodiceans were among those who had not met Paul personally.

2 Paul's concern for his readers was that "they may be encouraged in heart and united in love." The Greek word for "encouraged" (paraklēthōsin), which literally means "to call to one's side," signifies such ideas as comfort, encouragement, and exhortation, depending on the context in which it is found. Here perhaps it means being strengthened against the onslaught of error.

"United" suggests being "compacted, welded into genuine unity" (H.C.G. Moule, p. 126). The NIV places "united in love" in a coordinate relation to "encouraged in heart." The Greek text, however, employs a participle for "united" (symbibasthentes) and thereby implies that the means by which the strengthening (encouraging) takes place is the readers' being knit together in love (cf. RSV). But NIV does no violence to the essential meaning of the passage.

One consequence of being "encouraged" and "united" is attaining "the full riches of complete understanding." The idea is that heart encouragement and being united in love bring an inward wealth that consists in full or assured understanding. This in turn brings knowledge of "the mystery of God." The word for "knowledge" (*epignōsin*) indicates a depth of full knowledge, perhaps a true knowledge (cf. 1:9). On "mystery," see 1:26.

There is considerable variation in the last part of the Greek text of v.2. Our own preference is to accept the shorter reading (*tou theou, Christou*) and to understand "Christ" to be an appositive defining the mystery. This is the interpretation preferred by most modern scholars and is represented among the versions by ASV, TCNT, NASB, NAB, NIV, etc. The great truth taught is that all that is deepest in God is summed up in Christ.

3 This Christ who is the essence of the mystery of God is described as the One "in whom are hidden all the treasures of wisdom and knowledge." Two thoughts are contained in this statement: First, all the treasures of wisdom and knowledge are in Christ. The false teachers claimed to have, through their relation with a supposed hierarchy of supernatural beings, a higher knowledge than that possessed by ordinary believers. Against this, Paul argues that all wisdom and knowledge are in Christ and that their treasures are accessible to every believer. Second, the treasures of wisdom are in Christ in a hidden way. "Hidden" does not, however, mean that they are concealed but rather that they are laid up or stored away as a treasure.

4 Paul now expresses the reason for his anxious concern: "I tell you this so that no one may deceive you by fine-sounding arguments." The pronoun "this" refers to the utterances of vv.1-3, containing the declaration that all knowledge is stored up in Christ and also Paul's own expression of anxiety about the Colossians. The Greek word for "deceive" (*paralogizētai*) implies leading astray by false reasoning. "Fine-sounding arguments" (*pithanologia*), translated as "persuasive rhetoric" by Lightfoot, has something of the same meaning. It implies the attempt to convince someone by "fast talk" or, to put it colloquially, by handing him "a smooth line." Paul was obviously thinking of the attempt of the errorists to lead the Colossians away from their convictions about Christ.

5 Paul was no indifferent spectator of his readers' problems but had a sincere interest in them. Though not physically with them, he felt his spiritual oneness with them and rejoiced in their orderliness and in the firmness of their faith. "How orderly you are" (lit., "your order") contains a military term (*taxin*) connoting the orderly array of a band of disciplined soldiers. "Firm" translates *stereōma*, a word meaning solidity and compactness. In applying it to the faith of the Colossians, Paul emphasizes the unyielding nature of their faith or, as Eadie puts it, "the stiffness of its adherence to its one object—Christ" (p. 123). Like the word for "orderly," "firm" belonged to military parlance. It may therefore mean something like "solid front" (Lightfoot, p. 176). If this is the imagery Paul intended, he sees the situation of the Colossians as being like that of an army under attack and affirms that their lines were unbroken, their discipline intact, and their "faith in [reliance on] Christ" unshaken.

Notes

---

2 Another possible meaning for συμβιβάζω (*symbibazō*, "unite") is "instruct"; it is, in fact, always used in LXX in this sense. Compare Moff.: "May they learn the meaning of love."

D. *A Ministry of Exhortation*
2:6, 7

> 6So then, just as you received Christ Jesus as Lord, continue to live in him, 7rooted and built up in him, strengthened in the faith as you were taught, and overflowing with thankfulness.

NIV represents the two verses comprising this section as introducing the warnings of 2:8ff. rather than as closing out the section on Paul's ministry (begun at 1:24). NEB and JB, as well as the UBS text, support this arrangement. Although it is not a matter of great importance, it would seem best to take these verses as a kind of summary appeal made in light of the preceding discussion—an appeal for the readers to remain true to Christ as Lord. This is the arrangement of ASV and RSV.

6 "So then" (*oun*) shows that Paul makes his appeal in light of the foregoing discussion. The Colossians had received Christ in a certain manner: as the Anointed of God ("Christ"), as the historic Savior ("Jesus"), and as the sovereign ("Lord"). Paul's appeal is that they "continue to live [lit., walk] in him" in the same manner. That is to say, he wants their present and continuous conduct to conform to the doctrine taught them at the beginning, the doctrine they had committed themselves to at conversion.

7 In this verse four participles describe the walk in Christ. The first two, translated "rooted and built up in him," go together. "Rooted" (*errizōmenoi*) is in the perfect tense, suggesting a once-for-all experience, that is, a being permanently rooted. "Built up" (*epoikodomoumenoi*), a present tense, indicates a continual process. "Strengthened" (*bebaioumenoi*), the third participle, is also a present tense. "In the faith" conceives of faith as the body of truth (the faith system) and looks on this as the sphere within which the being "strengthened" takes place. Some versions render it "your faith," suggesting faith in its more usual sense of trust in, and reliance on, Christ. The whole appeal was to be carried out in accordance with what had been taught the Colossians in their initial experience—"as you were taught." The final phrase, "overflowing with thankfulness," uses *perisseuontes*, a favorite word Paul uses more than twenty-six times. Often translated "abound" in KJV, its literal meaning is expressed in NIV—viz., "overflowing" (like a river overflowing its banks). The tense is present, meaning that for believers thanksgiving is to be a continual, habitual thing.

Gratitude, which Lightfoot calls "the end of all human conduct" (p. 177), receives great emphasis in Paul's Epistles. The present passage may imply that those who lack a deep sense of thankfulness to God are especially vulnerable to doubt and spiritual delusion.

Notes

---

7 KJV reads "abounding therein [i.e., in faith] with thanksgiving," but this rendering is based on an inferior text. NIV follows UBS, which is supported by very strong evidence.

IV. Warning Against Error (2:8–23)

The apostle now makes his most direct attack against "the Colossian heresy." The entire passage bristles with exegetical difficulties, and calls for closer attention to its wording and argument than any other part of the Epistle.

The tone of the passage is both admonitory and affirmative, but admonition is the prevailing note sounded throughout. The affirmations, which mainly concern Christ and his sufficiency (cf. vv.9–15), form the basis on which the warnings are issued and give point and power to them.

It is characteristic of Paul in Colossians to use the vocabulary of his opponents, though, as H. Chadwick has well stated it, "in a different and disinfected sense" (NTS, 1:272). Instances of this in the present passage may be "philosophy" (2:8), "fullness" (2:9), "Deity" (2:9), "powers and authorities" (2:15), "humility" (2:18), "disqualify" (2:18), "self-imposed worship" (2:23).

A. *The Error of False Philosophy*

2:8–15

⁸See to it that no one takes you captive through hollow and deceptive philosophy, which depends on human tradition and the basic principles of this world rather than on Christ.

⁹For in Christ all the fullness of the Deity lives in bodily form, ¹⁰and you have this fullness in Christ, who is the head over every power and authority. ¹¹In him you were also circumcised, in the putting off of your sinful nature, not with a circumcision done by the hands of men but with the circumcision done by Christ. ¹²In baptism you were buried with him and raised with him through your faith in the power of God, who raised him from the dead.

¹³When you were dead in your sins and in the uncircumcision of your sinful nature, God made you alive with Christ. He forgave us all our sins, ¹⁴having canceled the written code, with its regulations, that was against us and that stood opposed to us; he took it away, nailing it to the cross. ¹⁵And having disarmed the powers and authorities, he made a public spectacle of them, triumphing over them by the cross.

1. *The warning stated* (2:8)

8 Paul first warns against being taken captive through a false philosophy. "See to it" alerts the readers to the danger. NEB has "Be on your guard." The singular "no one" leads some interpreters to conclude that Paul had in mind a particular person, perhaps the leader, among the heretical teachers. The words translated "that no one takes you captive" (*mē tis hymas estai sylagōgōn*) use an indicative verb and point to a real, not merely a supposable, danger. The word translated "takes captive" (*sylagōgōn*), which was regularly used of taking captives in war and leading them away as booty, depicts

the false teachers as "men-stealers" wishing to entrap the Colossians and drag them away into spiritual enslavement.

"Through hollow and deceptive philosophy" expresses the means by which the errorists attempted to do this. This is the only occurrence of the word *philosophy* in the NT. It would, of course, be a mistake to conclude that Paul intended his statement to be a condemnation of all philosophy. The word (*philosophia*) is a noble one, literally meaning "love of wisdom." Here, however, because the reference is to the Colossian error, it has a derogatory connotation.

Paul uses three descriptive phrases to characterize this "hollow and deceptive" system, and each constitutes a reason for its rejection. First, it is "after [according to] the tradition of men" (NIV, "depends on human tradition"). By "tradition" (*paradosin*) Paul may mean the mass of oral tradition the Jews had engrafted on the written law. It is more likely, however, that the term refers to various pagan theories current in that day. The apostle asserts that these, not divine revelation, were the bases of the "philosophy" of the Colossian errorists. Second, it was a philosophy that "depends on ... the basic principles of this world." "Basic principles" translates (*stoicheia*), a word of multiple meanings. Originally it denoted the letters of the alphabet, its root meaning being "things in a row." The term then came to be used of the elements ("ABC's") of learning (cf. Gal 4:3, ASV, NASB, NIV; Heb 5:12, ASV, TCNT, NASB, NIV), of the physical elements of the world (cf. 2 Peter 3:10), of the stars and other heavenly bodies (cf. 2 Peter 3:10, Moff., Am. Trans.), and of the elemental spirits, that is, the supernatural powers believed by many ancients to preside over and direct the heavenly bodies (cf. Gal 4:3, RSV, NEB). The sense in the present passage may be either the elements of learning (NIV, "basic principles") or the elemental spirits (RSV).

If the former sense is intended, the whole statement means that the Colossian system, though represented by its proponents as advanced "philosophy," was really only rudimentary instruction, the ABC's of the world—that is to say, it was elementary rather than advanced, earthly rather than heavenly. The rendering "elemental spirits" (cf. RSV, Moff.) is, however, to be preferred. Understood in this manner, the passage means either (1) that the "philosophy" of the errorists was a system instigated by the elemental spirits (perhaps thought of as the powers of evil) or (2) that it was a system having the elemental spirits as its subject matter. The second meaning is more likely the one intended by Paul, for we know from 2:18 that the Colossian heresy made much of the "worship of angels."

Third, it was a system "not after [according to] Christ" (lit. translation). This is Paul's most telling criticism of the teaching at Colosse. The meaning is that the "philosophy" of the heretics did not accord with the truth as it is revealed in Christ. He is the standard by which all doctrine is to be measured, and any system, whatever its claims, must be rejected if it fails to conform to the revelation God has given us in him.

2. The warning justified (2:9–15)

Paul's warning rests on the fact of Christ's unshared supremacy (v.9) and his complete adequacy to meet human need (vv.10–15). Because of who he is and what we find in him, any system "not after Christ" must be wrong. The passage takes up the central phrase of 1:19 ("fullness") and draws out its consequences in relation to the Colossian heresy. Bruce gives his discussion of it the heading "Christ is all—and all you need" (p. 228).

a. *The full deity of Christ* (2:9a)

9a Nearly every word in this statement is significant. "For," linking this and the following verses to v.8, shows that the warning there rests on what is said here about Christ and his fullness. The phrase "in Christ" (see comment at 1:2), by its position within the sentence, is emphatic, the thought being that in Christ alone the fullness of deity dwells. "Lives" (lit., "dwells") translates *katoikei*, a verb that suggests taking up permanent residence. The tense is present, stating a general truth and denoting continuous action. The full thought, then, is that in Christ the fullness of deity permanently resides, finding in him "a settled and congenial home" (H.C.G. Moule, p. 144). The context suggests that the primary reference is to Christ in his present glorified state. As Robertson puts it, "The fulness of the Godhead . . . dwells 'in the once mortal, now glorified body of Christ' (Ellicott), now 'the body of his glory' (Phil 3:21)" (p. 81).

"Fullness" translates *plērōma*, a word used earlier in 1:19 (see comment there). Here it is defined by the addition of *tēs theotētos* ("of the Deity"). The word *theotētos* is found only here in the NT, though a similar but weaker word (*theiotēs*, denoting divine nature) is found in Romans 1:20. *Theotētos* is an abstract term, meaning not just divine qualities and attributes but the very essence of God—"the whole glorious total of what God is, the supreme Nature in its infinite entirety" (H.C.G. Moule, p. 144).

b. *The real humanity of Christ* (2:9b)

9b The preceding statement (v.9a) corresponds to John 1:1, "the Word was God"; v.9b corresponds to John 1:14, "the Word became flesh." The fullness of deity dwells in Christ "in bodily form," that is, in incarnate fashion. This fullness, to be sure, resided in the preincarnate Word (cf. John 1.1ff.), but not in bodily fashion.

c. *The complete adequacy of Christ* (2:10–15)

10 This statement crowns Paul's argument. Because Christ is fully God and really man, believers, in union with him, "are made full" (ASV), that is, share in his fullness. "In Christ" (lit., "in him"), a phrase denoting vital union with the Savior, is by its position in Greek emphatic.

" 'Ye are made full,' " writes Calvin, "does not mean that the perfection of Christ is transfused into us, but that there are in him resources from which we may be filled, that nothing be wanting in us" (p. 183). Thus, in union with Christ our every spiritual need is fully met. Possessing him, we possess all. There was no need, therefore, for the Colossians to turn to the "philosophy" of the errorists, the ritual of the Mosaic law, or to the spirit-beings worshiped by the pagan world. All they needed was in Jesus Christ. As Charles Wesley put it, "Thou, O Christ, art all I want, / More than all in Thee I find."

Paul goes on to affirm the all-sufficiency of Christ by stating that he is "the head over every power and authority." He is "the head" in the sense that he is the source of life for all that exists and sovereign Lord over it all. Whatever powers there are in the universe, whatever ranks and orders of authority and government, they all owe their being to Christ and are under his lordship. It is important to observe that though Christ is here described as Head, the powers and authorities are not called his body. That distinction is reserved for Christ's people.

11–15 The thought of Christ's sufficiency, expounded in detail in vv.11–15, is now stressed by the mention of three things Christ (or God in Christ) has done for us. These have to do with spiritual circumcision (vv.11, 12), forgiveness of sins (vv.13, 14), and victory over the forces of evil (v.15).

11 In union with Christ, believers have true circumcision, that is, they have found in him the reality symbolized by Mosaic circumcision. The Christian's "circumcision" is defined as "the putting off" of one's "sinful nature" (lit., "the body of the flesh"). The Greek word for "putting off" (*apekdusei*), a double compound, denotes both stripping off and casting away. The imagery is that of discarding—or being divested of—a piece of filthy clothing. "The body of the flesh" has been variously explained, but of the many explanations proposed only two seem worthy of consideration. One understands "body" to be a reference to the physical body, "flesh" to be a descriptive genitive marking the body as conditioned by our fallen nature. Compare TEV: "freed from the power of this sinful body." The other takes "body" to denote something like "mass" or sum total, "flesh" to denote evil nature. Calvin, a proponent of this view, interprets the phrase to mean "accumulation of corruptions" (p. 184). Scott, in similar fashion, defines it as meaning "the whole carnal nature" (p. 44); Beare uses the expression "the whole of our lower nature" (p. 197). NIV seems to reflect this interpretation, and it is to be preferred.

The description of Christian circumcision as "not ... done by the hands of men" is obviously intended to contrast the Christian's "circumcision" with that required by the Mosaic law (and advocated also by the errorists of Colosse). That (Mosaic) circumcision, which represented the cutting away of man's uncleanness and was the outward sign of one's participation in Israel's covenant with God, was made with hands (i.e., was physical) and affected an external organ of the body. The circumcision that the believer experiences in Christ is spiritual, not physical, and relates not to an external organ but to one's inward being. In short, it is what elsewhere in Scripture is called "circumcision of the heart" (Rom 2:28 cf. Phil 3:3). The tense of the verb ("were ... circumcised") points to the time of conversion.

12 Here Paul gives a further explanation of the spiritual circumcision he affirmed in the preceding verse. The context suggests that Christian baptism is the outward counterpart to that experience and as such is the means by which it is openly declared. The emphasis of the verse, however, is not on the analogy between circumcision and baptism; that concept, though implied, is soon dismissed, and the thought shifts to that of baptism as symbolizing the believer's participation in the burial and resurrection of Christ (cf. Rom 6:3ff.).

Being "buried" and "raised" with Christ conveys the thought not simply of burying an old way of life and rising to a new kind of life but of sharing in the experience of Christ's own death and resurrection. That Paul did not think of baptism as actually effecting participation in that experience is made clear when he adds that the Colossians were raised through their "faith in the power of God." Baptism, then, is not a magic rite, but an act of obedience in which we confess our faith and symbolize the essence of our spiritual experience. Faith is the instrumental cause of that experience and, apart from real faith, baptism is an empty, meaningless ceremony.

13,14 In the closing words of v.12 Paul has mentioned God's raising Christ from the dead. Now he assures his readers that in Christ they share the resurrection experience. In Christ's case it was a literal bodily resurrection from the dead. In their case, the death was spiritual ("dead in your sins," "uncircumcision," etc.), and the being made alive is also spiritual. (Eventually, of course, believers will experience a bodily resurrection. The resurrection of Christ, who is "the firstfruits" of those who sleep in death, is God's pledge of that.)

The NIV translation "dead in your sins and . . . and in the uncircumcision of your sinful nature" suggests that "sins" and "uncircumcision" are the sphere in which death was manifested. It is perhaps better to follow ASV and understand the Greek to mean dead *through* or *by reason of* trespasses and an uncircumcised (unregenerate or pagan) nature. (The figurative use of the term *uncircumcision* in this passage is quite legitimate and readily understood. Compare Acts 7:51, where it is said of Jews that they were "uncircumcised in heart and ears.")

The first part of v.13 affirms the readers' deadness through trespasses and their being made alive in union with Christ. The last part of the verse (which NIV translates as the beginning of a new sentence) indicates that their being made alive involved the forgiveness of everything that had once alienated them from God. Forgiveness and making alive are in fact "the same act of divine grace viewed under a different but complementary aspect" (Beare, p. 198). The Greek participle translated "forgave" (*charisamenos*), built on the root of the word for "grace," means literally "to grant as a favor." It was sometimes used for the cancellation of a debt (Luke 7:42, 43). Its use here simply points to divine grace as the root principle in forgiveness.

Verse 14 vividly describes the attendant circumstances of forgiveness in Christ. One is the cancellation of "the written code . . . that was against us." The NIV translation "having canceled" suggests that this act is the ground for forgiveness. Perhaps it would be better to translate it "canceling out" and understand the phrase as specifying the act by which the forgiveness was carried out. At any rate, the word expresses one feature of the forgiveness believers experience. The strict meaning of the Greek term is "to wipe out" or "wipe away" (cf. Acts 3:19; Rev 3:5; 7:17; 21:4). In secular literature it was used of blotting out a writing or of abolishing a law.

What is canceled is called "the written code" (*chairographon;* lit., "handwriting," so KJV), an expression used of any document written by hand. Exactly how Paul uses the term is not certain. Scott, for example, points to its use in ancient times for an indictment drawn up against a prisoner, and understands the apostle to be employing the word similarly (cf. Phillips). Barclay calls it "a self-confessed indictment," "a charge-list which, as it were, they themselves had signed and had admitted was accurate" (p. 170). Others point to the use of the word for a note of hand, an IOU. Bruce, for instance, calls it a "signed confession of indebtedness" (p. 238). Either way, the reference is to the Mosaic law; and whether it is interpreted as an official indictment or as a bond of indebtedness, the thought is that God has blotted it out so that it no longer stands against us.

Paul uses three expressions to describe the law: (1) It was "written in ordinances" (lit.). That is to say, it contained "regulations" (NIV) and "legal demands" (RSV; cf. Eph 2:15). (2) It was "against us." That is to say, God's law had a valid claim on us. It was (if we follow the imagery of a "bond") like a promissory note having our signature attached as evidence that we acknowledged its claim and our debt. (3) It "stood opposed to us." This probably suggests that because we could not meet the claims of the law, it was hostile toward us or that it stood as an obstacle in our way.

Verse 14a has asserted that this bond or indictment has been "canceled out"; v.14b now adds that God (or Christ) "took it away, nailing it to the cross." "Took . . . away," the rendering of *ērken,* a perfect indicative, emphasizes abiding results. The bond (the Mosaic law) has been removed permanently, that is, removed so that its claims against us can never again alienate us from God.

Paul's vivid metaphor of nailing the law to the cross has been variously explained. Some think it alludes to an ancient custom dictating that when decrees were nullified, a copy of the text should be nailed up in a public place. On the other hand, Scott, who interprets the "written code" as an indictment, sees here an allusion to the custom of hanging over the head of an executed person a copy of the charge on which he was condemned. When Jesus was crucified, the superscription nailed to his cross contained the words "The King of the Jews." Paul "boldly ignores the real superscription, and imagines the Law as nailed above the cross. This, on the deeper view," explains Scott, "was the charge on which Christ was put to death. He suffered in order to satisfy in our stead 'the indictment which was against us' and has thus set it aside" (p. 47). Others understand the idea to be that the indictment was itself crucified.

To sum up, the great principle asserted in v.14 is the destruction of the law in and by the cross of Christ. The law, however, is viewed in a certain character (i.e., as a bond of indebtedness or as an instrument of condemnation, something that "stood opposed to us").

15 The meaning of nearly every word of this verse is disputed. One of the key issues concerns the interpretation of "powers and authorities." The interpretation preferred here is that which sees these as hostile supernatural powers, the hierarchy of evil. The words include all the spiritual forces of this world that are in rebellion against God, designated elsewhere as "the world-rulers of this darkness" (Eph 6:12, ASV; cf. Col 1:16; 2:8, 19, RSV).

Paul affirms that Christ has "disarmed" these forces of evil. The Greek verb (*apekdusamenos*), which is in the middle voice, is interpreted by some in the sense of stripping off *from himself*, as though the powers and authorities had attached themselves to the Son of God in determination to bring about his destruction. Christ strips them from himself like a wrestler casting from himself a disabled antagonist. Perhaps it is better to construe the middle as intensive. The meaning then is simply "having stripped," and the object of the action is not "himself" but the powers and authorities. In this interpretation the imagery is that of a conquered antagonist being stripped of his weapons and armor and put to public shame. (A Greek word built on the same root as the word employed here is used in LXX of the "stripping" of enemies in war.) NIV expresses this meaning.

Paul goes on to say that Christ, having thus disarmed the powers and authorities, "made a public spectacle of them." That is to say, he exposed them to public disgrace by exhibiting them to the universe as his captives. The added words, "triumphing over them by the cross," expand this idea. The picture, quite familiar in the Roman world, is that of a triumphant general leading a parade of victory. The conqueror, riding at the front in his chariot, leads his troops through the streets of the city. Behind them trails a wretched company of vanquished kings, officers, and soldiers—the spoils of battle. Christ, in this picture, is the conquering general; the powers and authorities are the vanquished enemy displayed as the spoils of battle before the entire universe. To the casual observer the cross appears to be only an instrument of death, the symbol of Christ's defeat; Paul represents it as Christ's chariot of victory.

Notes

8 "Through hollow and deceptive philosophy" translates Διὰ τῆς φιλοσοφίας καὶ κενῆς ἀπάτης (*dia tēs philosophias kai kenēs apatēs*). The use of a single article and a single preposition with the two nouns suggests that Paul intended his readers to understand the second term ("empty deceit") as explanatory of the first ("philosophy"). That is to say, the so-called "philosophy" of the Colossian heretics is more aptly and precisely described as an empty delusion. NIV's "hollow and deceptive philosophy" expresses this accurately. Phillips paraphrases it "high-sounding nonsense." Moffatt, avoiding the use of the word *philosophy*, renders the phrase "a theosophy which is specious make-believe."

9 Lightfoot, Abbott, and others think the interpretation of σωματικῶς (*sōmatikōs*, "in bodily form") given above is the only tenable one. There are, however, other views. Calvin, followed by Scott and Beare, takes the word to mean something like "substantially," "really," or "genuinely." Peake, following Haupt, interprets it to mean "as a complete and organic whole." Others have suggested "embodied," that is, in the corporate life of the church. Each of these alternatives puts an unnatural strain on the Greek term.

13 Scholars debate whether God or Christ is to be thought of as the subject of συνεζωοποίησιν (*synezōopoiēsin*, "made alive"). Chrysostom, Ellicott, and others argue for Christ as subject; most modern interpreters take God to be the subject. Likewise, they consider God to be the subject of the verbs "forgave" and "having canceled."

B. *The Error of Legalism*

2:16, 17

16Therefore do not let anyone judge you by what you eat or drink, or with regard to a religious festival, a New Moon celebration, or a Sabbath day. 17These are a shadow of the things that were to come; the reality, however, is found in Christ.

16,17 The false teachers at Colosse laid down rigid restrictions with regard to eating and drinking and with regard to the observance of the religious calendar. "Therefore" shows that this and the following warnings grow out of what Paul says of Christ's complete sufficiency in the preceding verses. There is perhaps a special reference to his removal of the law and his triumph over the forces of evil (vv.14, 15). In light of what Christ did, the Colossians were to let no one "judge" their standing before God on the basis of their observance or nonobservance of the regulations of the Mosaic law. In such matters the principle of Christian liberty comes into play (cf. Gal 5:1). Elsewhere Paul insists that under some circumstances Christian freedom should be voluntarily limited by one's respect for the tender conscience of a weaker brother (cf. Rom 14:1ff.; 1 Cor 8:1ff.). This caution is necessary for those inclined to assert their liberty regardless of the damage their actions might bring to another person. But "at Colosse it is precisely Christian liberty that requires to be asserted in the face of specious attempts to undermine it" (Bruce, p. 243). "What you eat or drink" (lit., "eating and ... drinking") is probably a reference to the dietary rules in the Mosaic law about clean and unclean food. It is possible, however, that Paul was not thinking of Jewish law at all, but simply of the peculiar ascetic tendencies of the Colossian heresy. If this line of interpretation is followed, the question is not one of lawful and unlawful foods but of eating and drinking as opposed to abstinence from such things as animal flesh and wine and strong drink. Caird speaks of it as "an asceticism" that was "the product of an exaggerated and puritanical form of Judaism," but he thinks some "allowance must be made for pagan influence" (p. 197). Then he adds that "Paul treats it as an offshoot of Judaism, but it was probably put together by Gentile Christians who looked to the Old Testament to provide the justification for their ascetic principles" (p. 198).

"Religious festival," "New Moon celebration," and "Sabbath day" probably refer to various holy days of the Jewish calendar—annual, monthly, and weekly. The reference to "Sabbath day" points clearly to the Jewish calendar, for only Jews kept the Sabbath. That being the case, "religious festival" and "New Moon celebration" must point primarily to the ritual calendar of the Jews. Paul's thought is that the Christian is freed from obligations of this kind (cf. v.14; Gal 4:9–11; 5:1). No one, therefore, should be permitted to make such things a test of piety or fellowship (cf. Rom 14:1ff.). Christianity, as Eadie explains, "is too free and exuberant to be trained down to 'times and seasons'.... Its feast is daily, for every day is holy; its moon never wanes, and its serene tranquillity is an unbroken Sabbath" (p. 177). Moulton's caution, however, is apropos today. He writes, "In past generations this verse might ... have been gently shown to Sabbatarians. Now they are harder to find. It is not that we have learnt its lesson, but that we care less about worship" (p. 40).

17 All such legal stipulations were but "a shadow [i.e., an anticipation] of the things that were to come." Therefore to cling to the prophetic shadow is to obscure the spiritual reality of which those things were a prefigurement. "The reality" (substance) belongs to Christ. In him, the things to come have come. (The concept of shadow and substance is found also in Hebrews 8:5; 10:1.)

These two verses, writes H.C.G. Moule, are

> an appeal for "Christian liberty," as earnest ... as [Paul's] appeal to the Galatians "not to be entangled again in the yoke of bondage." But let us note well that the "liberty" he means is the very opposite of licence and has nothing in the world akin to the miserable individualism whose highest ambition is to do just what it likes. The whole aim of St. Paul is for the fullest, deepest and most watchful holiness. He wants his Colossian converts above all things to be holy; that is, to live a life yielded all through to their Redeemer, who is also their Master (p. 171).

Notes

16 Σάββατα (*sabbata*), though plural, is regularly used in the NT in a singular sense—thus "sabbath day" (NIV), not "sabbath days" (KJV).

C. *The Error of Angel Worship*

2:18, 19

18Do not let anyone who delights in false humility and the worship of angels disqualify you for the prize. Such a person goes into great detail about what he has seen, and his unspiritual mind puffs him up with idle notions. 19He has lost connection with the Head, from whom the whole body, supported and held together by its ligaments and sinews, grows as God causes it to grow.

18 Paul's third warning brings before us two of the most puzzling verses in the NT. The Greek expression for "disqualify you" (*hymas katabrabeuetō*) has been rendered in many different ways: KJV, "beguile you of your reward"; Knox, "cheat you"; ASV, "rob you of your prize"; BV, "defraud you of salvation's prize," etc. The literal meaning of the clause is "let no one act as umpire against you," that is, give an adverse decision against you. Perhaps it is only a stronger and more picturesque way of saying, "Let no one judge you" (cf. v.16). The essential meaning is, "Let no one deny your claim to be Christians."

The person attempting to make such judgment is described as one "who delights in false humility and the worship of angels." The context suggests that he seeks to impose these things on the Colossians and that this is the means by which he attempts to disqualify them for their prize. "Delights in" translates a Hebraism not uncommon in LXX, but found nowhere else in the NT. "False humility," translated "self-abasement" in RSV, is thought by some to be a technical term for fasting, since in the OT this was the usual way for one to humble himself before God. Whether this be so or not, the word in this context appears to denote a mock humility. The same word is used in 3:12 in a list of virtues. "Worship of angels" is an allusion to the deference the heretical teachers paid to the hierarchy of spirit-beings who, in their system, filled the whole universe. Perhaps the "humility" and the "worship of angels" were closely related. (In Greek the word for "false humility" and the expression for "worship of angels" are governed by the same preposition.) That is to say, the heretics probably insisted that their worship of angels rather than the supreme God was an expression of humility on their part. Lightfoot writes that "there was an officious parade of humility in selecting these lower beings as intercessors, rather than appealing directly to the throne of grace" (p. 196).

We see a further indication of the method of the false teachers in the words "goes into great detail about what he has seen." The meaning, according to some, is that the heretical teacher *takes his stand* on his (imaginary or alleged) visions (cf. RSV). He "harps" on his visions, claiming more than he can prove. NIV reflects this interpretation. Others think there is an allusion to the initiatory rites of the mystery cults and that Paul is scornfully quoting some of the jargon ("entering in," "what he has seen") used by the heretical teachers. The meaning of the Greek construction is so obscure that many interpreters have resorted to conjectural emendation.

Paul depicts the heretical teacher as inflated with conceit. "His unspiritual mind puffs him up with idle notions." The "unspiritual" (*tēs sarkos;* lit., "of the flesh") mind is a mind dominated by the unrenewed nature, a mind lacking spiritual enlightenment.

19 The false teacher lacks vital contact with Jesus Christ. This is profoundly serious because it is from Christ as Head that "the whole body [the church], supported and held together by its ligaments and sinews, grows." Each believer is thought of as forming a vital connection with Christ the Head. Thus joined to him, they all become the joints and ligaments by which the church is supplied with energy and life. The heretical teacher, without this contact with Christ, cuts himself off from the source of spiritual vitality for God's people and cannot possibly contribute to their growth.

Notes

---

18 Θέλων ἐν ταπεινοφροσύνῃ (*thelōn en tapeinophrosynē*, "who delights in false humility") is a particularly difficult expression. The noun (*tapeinophrosynē*) must here mean something like "mock humility" (cf. NIV, "false humility"). Θέλων (*thelōn*), a participle, may mean something like "self-imposed" (cf. KJV and ASV, "voluntary"). Its literal meaning is "willing" (cf. NIV, "delighting in"; RSV, "insisting on"). NEB takes the whole phrase to mean "people who go in for self-mortification." NIV is perhaps to be preferred. KJV translates a text that employs a negative and thus changes the meaning entirely: "intruding into those things which he hath not seen." The thought expressed by this reading is that the false teacher deals with mysteries he has no immediate knowledge of. Lightfoot suspects that the Greek text may be corrupted here and proposes that the reading might originally have been a construction that he translates as "treading the void" (p. 197).

D. *The Error of Asceticism*

2:20–23

> 20If you died with Christ to the basic principles of this world, why, as though you still belonged to it, do you submit to its rules: 21"Do not handle! Do not taste! Do not touch!"? 22These are all destined to perish with use, because they are based on human commands and teachings. 23Such regulations indeed have an appearance of wisdom, with their self-imposed worship, their false humility and their harsh treatment of the body, but they lack any value in restraining sensual indulgence.

Paul's fourth and final warning is against asceticism—the imposition of man-made rules as a means of gaining favor with God. For ascetics the body is a thing to be buffeted and punished, a thing to be treated like an enemy. They see the body as evil and conclude that the way to holiness is to deny all the body's desires, refuse its appetites, and cut its needs down to an irreducible minimum. Asceticism was apparently a prominent feature of the Colossian heresy, and in various periods of history it has appealed strongly to misguided people. It was the ascetic spirit that led to the deprecation of marriage, the exaltation of virginity and monasticism, and the devising of endless means of self-torture. Paul condemns asceticism and urges the Colossians to reject it as a way of life.

1. *The Christian's death to the world* (2:20–22a)

20 When one becomes a Christian, his connection with the world of legal and ascetic ordinances is severed. Asceticism, then, is not in keeping with the nature and circumstances of the new life in Christ. For the Christian, all the rules and requirements of asceticism are a kind of anachronism.

The "if" clause is not intended to express doubt or uncertainty. Its force is argumentative, and the meaning is: "Since [because] you died. . . ." The use of this type of conditional clause is Paul's emphatic way of stating something that is unquestionable (cf. 3:1; Phil 2:1, et al.).

"Died" translates an aorist, pointing to the time of the believer's conversion. In the mention of dying and rising (3:1) with Christ, there may be an allusion to Christian baptism (see comments on 2:12); however, baptism only *pictures* the believer's death to

114

an old way of life and his rising to a new life. The actual change is effected when he is joined to Christ by faith. So he enters into fellowship with Christ, and in dying with him is delivered from "the basic principles of this world."

"Basic principles" (*stoicheiōn*) has the same ambiguity that marks it elsewhere (cf. discussion at 2:8). Perhaps it should be understood as a reference to the supernatural powers of evil (cf. RSV), but the passage also yields an acceptable meaning if *stoicheiōn* is interpreted as in the NIV. At any rate, to order life by ascetic rules is to revert to an inferior state supposedly abandoned at the time of conversion. To die to "the basic principles of this world" (or "the elemental spirits of the universe," RSV) is to have all connections with them severed, to be done with them, to be liberated from their authority once for all. (The Greek preposition *apo* ("to") ordinarily means "from," and here perhaps expresses something like "out of the control of.")

"Submit to its rules," which translates a single Greek word (*dogmatizesthe*), recalls v.14, where reference was made to the canceling out of the bond of ordinances (*dogmata*) against us. To permit oneself to be "dogmatized" is to permit life to become a round of rules again.

21 The "rules" Paul had in mind are such decrees as "Do not handle! Do not taste! Do not touch!" The reference is to the dietary restrictions the errorists imposed as a means of attaining salvation. (Caird thinks it more probable that "Paul is ridiculing his opponents by attributing to them a total withdrawal from all worldly contacts: 'Don't handle that, don't taste this, don't touch anything!' If you pursue to its logical conclusion the notion that holiness consists in avoiding contamination, you can only end in avoiding everything.") Some may have been reenactments of the Mosaic law; others were doubtless prohibitions stemming from pagan asceticism. There is a descending order in the terms, the climax being reached in the last word—i.e., "Don't even touch."

22a Parenthetically (cf. RSV) Paul adds that all such things are "destined to perish with use." Dietary restrictions have to do with things made to be used; and with their use they perish, for food ceases to be food once it is eaten. The underlying thought, then, is that the restrictive regulations of the Colossian heresy deal with matters that are temporary and unimportant. Christ, in fact, has made all food clean (Mark 7:19). (NIV seems to represent a different interpretation, the things destined to perish being the rules themselves, not the things forbidden by the rules. But the words "with use" militate against this view.)

2. *The human origin of ascetic restrictions* (2:22b)

22b Such regulative prohibitions as "Do not handle! Do not taste! Do not touch!" are "based on human commands and teachings." The thought is that the rules of the ascetic are, both in origin and in medium of communication, strictly human.

3. *The ineffectiveness of ascetic restrictions* (2:23)

23 Ascetic rules masquerade as wisdom. They seem, on the surface, to be reasonable and wise. But what seems to be wisdom is only an appearance of, or pretension to, wisdom. In reality these rules are expressions of "self-imposed worship" and spurious "humility." The RSV renders the first expression "rigor of devotion," but the stress is not on rigor but on the voluntary nature of the act. Calvin defines it as "voluntary service, which men

115

choose for themselves at their own option, without authority from God" (p. 202). The NIV rendering is in line with this thought. The context suggests that the errorists engaged in such "worship" in the hope that they would thereby acquire superior merit before God. The Greek word (*ethelothrēskia*), a rare compound that has not been found in extrabiblical writings and is used in the NT only here, calls to mind the reference to "worship of angels" in v.18.

"Humility" (*tapeinophrosynē*) must in this context refer to a mock humility (cf. v.18). The idea is that asceticism, while parading under the guise of humility, actually panders to human pride. "Harsh treatment of the body" (lit., "unsparingness") is a reference to ascetic torturings of the body. "Lack any value in restraining sensual indulgence" translates a very difficult Greek construction—*ouk en timē tini pros plēsmonēn tēs sarkos*—which has given rise to many different interpretations. The two that have the most to commend them are those expressed in NIV and in Moff.; the latter reads: "but they are of no value, they only pamper the flesh!" (cf. RSV margin). The Greek behind "sensual indulgence" may be more literally translated "indulgence of the flesh," and by "flesh" Paul probably means more than sensuality. See Galatians 5:19–21, where such sins of disposition as arrogance and pride are listed as works of the flesh.

To sum up, v.23 teaches that ascetic rules have the appearance of wisdom for many people in that they seem to be expressions of devotion to God, of humility, and of a commendable discipline of the body. Paul, however, declares that these regulations have nothing to do with real wisdom, and the worship and humility they seem to express are both spurious. His final appraisal is that asceticism is a dismal failure. On the surface it may appear to be the way to spiritual victory, but it actually is not. Christianity is not a religion of prescriptions but of a living relationship with Jesus Christ. This, of course, does not mean that once we are in Christ everything is permissible. That would amount to moral and spiritual anarchy, a thing contrary to the very nature of the new life in Christ. It does mean that the controls of the Christian life spring from within, that genuine piety grows out of inward conviction generated by a consciousness of union with Christ. Indwelt by the Spirit, we walk by the Spirit and thus avoid carrying out the desires of the lower nature (Gal 5:16). Maclaren says it with characteristic force: "There is only one thing that will put the collar on the neck of the animal within us, and that is the power of the indwelling Christ" (p. 255).

V. Appeal for Christian Living (3:1–4:6)

The apostle has refuted both the doctrinal and practical errors of the false teachers and, in the course of doing this, has given a profound exposition of the cosmic significance of Jesus Christ. In the present section, which is practical and ethical in its emphasis, he exhorts his readers to give outward expression in daily living to the deep experience that is theirs in Christ. The Christian life is a life "hidden with Christ in God," but it is still, Paul explains, a life lived out on earth. The Christian must therefore give attention not only to his inward experience with God but also to his outward relations with his fellowman.

A. The Root Principle of the Christian Life

3:1–4

¹Since, then, you have been raised with Christ, set your hearts on things above, where Christ is seated at the right hand of God. ²Set your minds on things above,

not on earthly things. ³For you died, and your life is now hidden with Christ in God. ⁴When Christ, who is your life, appears, then you also will appear with him in glory.

The opening verses of chapter 3 sustain the closest connection with the closing verses of chapter 2. There the apostle reminds the Colossians that ascetic regulations are of no real value in restraining indulgence of the flesh. The only remedy for sinful passions is found in the believers' experience of union with Christ—a union by virtue of which the Christian dies to sin and to the world's way of thinking and doing. The opening verses of the third chapter, representing the positive counterpart of those verses, teach that this death with Christ involves also participation in his resurrection life. This releases into the believer's life a power that is more than adequate as a check against the appetites and attitudes of the lower nature. These four verses, then, point to the believer's union with Christ as the root principle of the whole Christian life. It is the point of departure and the source of power for all that he does.

On the basis of this mystical but real experience with Christ, the Colossians are urged to seek heavenly things (v.1) and set their minds on them (v.2). As a further incentive to doing this, they are reminded that their lives are now securely hidden with Christ in God and thus belong to the invisible realm. Their sphere of being, action, and enjoyment is therefore now totally different from that of their former situation (v.3). Believers' lives, however, will not always be hidden in this way. Now there is concealment, but when Christ appears, there will be a glorious manifestation of who they truly are (v.4).

1. Seeking the things above (3:1)

1 To set the heart on (*zēteite*; lit., "seek") things above is to desire and to strive for those things. It is to see to it that one's interests are centered in Christ, that one's attitudes, ambitions, and whole outlook on life are molded by Christ's relation to the believer, and that one's allegiance to him takes precedence over all earthly allegiances. The verb is a present imperative, suggesting a continuing action: "Keep on seeking."

The description of Christ as "seated at the right hand of God" is another implied rejoinder to those who were seeking to diminish Christ's role as mediator, inasmuch as the right hand of God is a metaphor for the place of supreme privilege and divine authority.

2. Setting the mind on things above (3:2)

2 NIV interprets the commands of vv.1, 2 as essentially the same. There may, however, be a slight difference. Setting the heart on things above (v.1) is descriptive of the aim, the practical pursuit of the Christian life. Setting the mind (v.2) on things above refers more to inner disposition. Lightfoot comments, "You must not only *seek* heaven; you must also *think* heaven" (p. 209). There is, of course, an intimate connection between the two.

To set the mind on (lit., "think on") things above has, among other connotations, that of giving such things a large place in one's thought life—seeing to it that the bent of the inner nature, the governing tendency of thought and will is toward God. This, of course, does not mean withdrawal from all the activities of this world to engage only in contemplation of eternity and heaven. The verses that follow make it quite clear that Paul expected Christians to maintain normal relationships in this world. "But," as Barclay explains, "there will be this difference—from now on the Christian will see everything

117

in the light and against the background of eternity. . . . He will no longer live as if this world was all that mattered; he will see this world against the background of the large world of eternity" (p. 177).

"Earthly things" are not all evil, but some of them are. Even things harmless in themselves become harmful if permitted to take the place that should be reserved for the things above. In the present passage "earthly things" may be understood to include wealth, worldly honor, power, pleasures, and the like. To make such things the goal of life and the subject of preoccupation is unworthy of those who have been raised with Christ and look forward to sharing in his eternal glory.

3. *The motivations for these actions* (3:3, 4)

3 One motive for seeking and setting the mind on the things above is the believer's union with Christ in death and in resurrection (2:20; 3:1). Verse 3 in a sense repeats and summarizes this. Paul is implying that since Christians have died with Christ, all that is alien to him should be alien to them.

Death with Christ (2:20) was followed by resurrection with Christ (3:1), and so our lives are indeed "hidden with Christ in God." This suggests not only that the believer's life is secure, but also that it belongs in a very real and profound sense to the invisible spiritual realm. At the present time his connection with God and Christ is a matter of inner experience; one day it will come into full and open manifestation.

4 Another motivation to seeking and setting the mind on the things above is the prospect of the believer's future manifestation with Christ in glory. Christ is called the believer's "life" because he is, quite literally, the essence of his life. It is he who gives him life and nurtures it by his own continuing presence (cf. Rom 8:10).

"Appears," a reference to the return of Christ, translates one of several Greek terms used in the NT for this event: *parousia* (often rendered "coming") speaks specifically of Christ's (future) presence with his people; *epiphaneia* ("manifestation," "appearance"; cf. "epiphany") relates to the visibility and splendor of his coming; *apokalypsis* ("revelation") denotes the inner meaning of the event. *Phaneroō*, the word Paul uses here, emphasizes the open display of Christ at his coming. Paul's teaching is that when Christ is thus manifested, believers also "will appear with him in glory." "The veil which now shrouds your higher life from others, and even partly from yourselves, will be withdrawn. The world which persecutes, despises, ignores now, will then be blinded with the dazzling glory of the revelation" (Lightfoot, p. 210).

Notes

1 NIV takes οὗ ὁ Χριστός ἐστιν ἐν δεξιᾷ τοῦ Θεοῦ καθήμενος (*hou ho Christos estin en dexia tou theou kathēmenos*, "where Christ is seated on the right hand of God") as a single thought. It is possible that the participle (καθήμενος, *kathēmenos*, "sitting") should be understood as expressing a separate idea. The things above are "where Christ is," and he is there as One "seated [*kathēmenos*] at the right hand of God."

B. *Guidelines for the Christian Life* (3:5–4:6)

Paul has reminded his readers of their vital union with Christ and the power and encouragement this gives to holy living. The present passage (3:5–4:6) shows in a practical way how this principle of union with Christ is to be applied in daily life. In short, the apostle teaches that the Christian's experience in Christ calls not simply for regulating the old earthbound life but for digging out its roots and utterly destroying it. In this way the new life in Christ will have full control over the believer. The underlying thought is: Let the life that is in you by virtue of your union with Christ work itself out and express itself in all your thoughts, actions, and relationships. Union with Christ, explains Caird, is "the supreme reality," but it is "a reality of status not yet fully worked out in experience. Believers [are] like immigrants to a new country, not yet completely habituated to its ways of life. They [have] accepted citizenship in a new world and must learn to live in it" (p. 204).

1. *Sins of the old life to be abandoned*

3:5–11

> [5]Put to death, therefore, whatever belongs to your earthly nature: sexual immorality, impurity, lust, evil desires and greed, which is idolatry. [6]Because of these, the wrath of God is coming. [7]You used to walk in these ways, in the life you once lived. [8]But now you must rid yourselves of all such things as these: anger, rage, malice, slander, filthy language. [9]Do not lie to each other, since you have taken off your old self with its practices [10]and have put on the new self, which is being renewed in knowledge in the image of its Creator. [11]Here there is no Greek or Jew, circumcised or uncircumcised, barbarian, Scythian, slave or free, but Christ is all, and is in all.

Paul speaks forthrightly about the demands of the new life and our urgent need to repress all the degrading tendencies of the old nature. The three imperatives of the paragraph ("put to death," v.5; "rid yourselves," v.8; and "do not lie," v.9) are the pegs on which the thought hangs.

a. *Sins to be put to death* (3:5–7)

5 In principle the Colossians had, in becoming Christians, died with Christ (cf. 2:20;3:3). Now they are charged to make this death to the old life real in everyday practice. As Caird puts it, "The old life is dead; they must let it die. The indicative of faith must be matched by the imperative of ethics" (p. 203). The verb *nekrōsate*, meaning literally "to make dead," is very strong. It suggests that we are not simply to suppress or control evil acts and attitudes. We are to wipe them out, completely exterminate the old way of life. "Slay utterly" may express its force. The form of the verb (aorist imperative) makes clear that the action is to be undertaken decisively, with a sense of urgency. Both the meaning of the verb and the force of the tense suggest a vigorous, painful act of personal determination. Maclaren likens it to a man who while working at a machine gets his fingers drawn between rollers or caught in the belting. "Another minute and he will be flattened to a shapeless bloody mass. He catches up an axe lying by and with his own arm hacks off his own hand at the wrist. . . . It is not easy nor pleasant, but it is the only alternative to a horrible death" (p. 275).

"Whatever belongs to your earthly nature" is defined by the list of sins placed in apposition with it in this verse. Paul is calling, then, not for the maiming of the physical body, but for the slaying of the evil passions, desires, and practices that root themselves in our bodies, make use of them, and attack us through them.

His catalog of sins is a grim one, and all of the sins, with the possible exception of the last, have to do with sexual vice. "Sexual immorality" translates *porneia*, the most general Greek word for illicit sexual intercourse. Originally it denoted the practice of consorting with prostitutes; eventually it came to mean "habitual immorality."

"Impurity" (*akatharsia*), though sometimes used of physical impurity (Matt 23:27), here has a moral connotation. Including uncleanness in thought, word, and act, it has a wider reference than "sexual immorality" (*porneia*).

The word for "lust" (*pathos*), which essentially means "feeling" or "experience," was used by classical Greek writers to refer to any passive emotion, whether good or bad. Later it came to be specially used of violent emotions. In the NT, where it *always* has a bad sense, it means uncontrolled desire. The phrase following (*epithymian kakēn*, "evil desires") is similar but perhaps more general in meaning.

The Greek word for "greed" (*pleonexian*) is a compound form whose root meaning suggests a desire to have more. It has a much wider significance than its English equivalent. Souter's *Lexicon*, calling it "a word active in meaning and wide in scope," defines it as "greediness, rapacity, entire disregard of the rights of others." Caird sees it as "the arrogant and ruthless assumption that all other persons and things exist for one's own benefit" (p. 205). Some interpreters think the context supports the view that greed for sex is the meaning here. But it may be better to retain the more usual meaning and understand it as a ruthless desire for, and a seeking after, material things. This attitude is identified with "idolatry" because it puts self-interest and *things* in the place of God. (Cf. Romans 1:18ff., where the visible degradation of pagan life is represented as proof that the wrath of God is being poured out upon those who have rebelled against his rule in their lives.)

6,7 Paul now mentions two factors that point to the impropriety of the sins listed in v.5 existing in the lives of the Colossian believers. First, they are sins that incur "the wrath of God." Some understand the "wrath of God" (*orgē tou Θεου*) as referring to a general principle in life—that is, we reap what we sow and can never escape the consequences of our sin. It is better, however, to interpret Paul's term as meaning the eschatological wrath of God. "Is coming," a present tense, may represent God's judgment upon sin as already on the way, but more likely the present tense depicts more vividly the certainty with which God's judgment will fall on the disobedient. Second, the sins mentioned in v.5 are those that characterized the pre-Christian experience of the Colossian believers: "You used to walk in these ways, in the life you once lived" (v.7). The two verbs—"used to walk" and "lived," both past tenses—emphasize that this kind of life belongs to the past and that the Christian should be done with it. "Used to walk" (*periepatēsate*), an aorist tense in Greek, has summary force—i.e., it gathers up their whole life as pagans and focuses it in a point; "lived" (*ezēte*), an imperfect tense, stresses the course and habit of their existence. "Walk" calls attention to outward conduct; "live," to the attitudes and feelings from which that conduct flows.

b. Sins to be put away (3:8)

8 Whereas the sins of v.5 had to do with impurity and covetousness, the catalog of v.8 concerns sins of attitude and speech. "But now" marks an emphatic contrast. The imagery in "rid yourselves" is that of putting off clothes—like stripping off from oneself a filthy garment. Perhaps the term has both a forward and a backward reference, but it seems mainly to point forward (note NIV punctuation).

The first three terms—"anger," "rage," "malice"—speak of sins of disposition. Scholars are not in agreement on the distinction, if any, between the words for "anger" (*orgē*) and "rage" (*thymos*). The view perhaps most widely held looks upon *orgē* as the settled feeling of anger, and *thymos* as the sudden and passionate outburst of that feeling. Others, however, take the opposite view. In the LXX the terms are virtually synonymous. "Malice" (*kakia*), a general term for badness, seems here to denote a vicious disposition, the spirit that prompts one to injure his neighbor. "Slander" (KJV, "blasphemy") renders a word (*blasphēmia*) that denotes insulting and slanderous talk—here, against one's fellowman.

The Greek for "filthy language" (*aischrologia*) may denote either filthy or abusive speech, and the authorities are divided as to its meaning here. Weymouth, following Lightfoot, combines both ideas: "foul-mouthed abuse."

c. *A sin to be discontinued* (3:9a)

9a Some think the sin of falsehood is singled out for special mention because in it more frequently than in anything else we manifest ill-will toward our fellowmen. At any rate, the fact that the sin of lying is given separate treatment makes the condemnation of it more emphatic. The verb (*pseudesthe*), unlike those in vv.5, 8, is present imperative, which with the negative forbids the continuance of the act. It might therefore be rendered, "Stop lying."

d. *The reason: the new self* (3:9b–11)

9b,10 Grammatically there is a strict connection between these verses and the prohibition against lying; probably, however, there is a sense connection with the total thought of vv.5–9a. The essence of it is that the Christian has had a radical, life-changing experience in which he has put off the old self with its practices (i.e., habits or characteristic actions) and has put on the new self. The metaphor again is one of clothing. The "old self" (i.e., the old, unregenerate self; RSV, "old nature") is like a dirty, worn-out garment that is stripped from the body and thrown away. The "new self" (i.e., the new, regenerate self; RSV, "new nature") is like a new suit of clothing that one puts on and wears. The picturesque language gives vivid expression to a great truth, but one must be careful not to press the imagery too far, for we are painfully aware that the old nature is ever with us.

The new self is described as "being renewed in knowledge." The essential thought is that the new self (new nature) does not decay or grow old but by constant renewal takes on more and more of the image of its Creator. "Being renewed" (*anakainoumenon*) is present tense, expressing a continuous process of renewal. "Knowledge," which is represented either as the goal (object of *eis*) or as the sphere (NIV) of this process, denotes true knowledge (cf. 1:9).

11 The various groups mentioned reflect distinctions of national privilege ("Greek or Jew"), legal or ceremonial standing ("circumcised or uncircumcised"), culture ("barbarian, Scythian," the former denoting persons who did not speak Greek [that is, foreigners], the latter thought of as the lowest of the barbarians), and social caste ("slave or free"). In the realm of the new self—that is, where the image of God is truly reflected—these distinctions have no real significance (cf. Gal 3:28). Differences, to be sure, remain in the Christian community, but not in such a way as to be barriers to fellowship. To the extent that Christians do permit them to be barriers, they are acting out of character.

"Christ is all, and is in all" suggests that Christ is *the* great principle of unity. In him all differences merge, all distinctions are done away. C.F.D. Moule, who thinks the phrase ought not to be too precisely analyzed, looks on it as "a vigorous and emphatic way of saying that Christ is 'absolutely everything.' " Loyalty to him must therefore take precedence over all earthly ties (p. 121).

Notes

---

9 For the idea of renewal see Rom 12:2; 1 Cor 4:16. For the thought of creation in the "image" of God see Gen 1:26–28.

---

2. *Virtues of the new life to be cultivated*

3:12–17

12Therefore, as God's chosen people, holy and dearly loved, clothe yourselves with compassion, kindness, humility, gentleness and patience. 13Bear with each other and forgive whatever grievances you may have against one another. Forgive as the Lord forgave you. 14And over all these virtues put on love, which binds them all together in perfect unity.

15Let the peace of Christ rule in your hearts, since, as members of one body, you were called to peace. And be thankful. 16Let the word of Christ dwell in you richly as you teach and counsel one another with all wisdom, and as you sing psalms, hymns and spiritual songs with gratitude in your hearts to God. 17And whatever you do, whether in word or deed, do it all in the name of the Lord Jesus, giving thanks to God the Father through him.

a. *Expressions of love* (3:12–14)

12 The Christian has already put on the new self (the regenerate nature, v.10). Now he must clothe himself with the garments that befit the new self. "Clothe yourselves" (*endysasthe*) should be compared with "put to death" (*nekrōsate*, v.5) and "rid yourselves" (*apothesthe*, v.8). Those terms express the negative, this verse the positive aspects of the Christian's reformation of character. The tense of *endysasthe*, an aorist imperative, speaks of an action to be undertaken with a sense of urgency.

Paul's appeal is based on this threefold fact: Christians are chosen of God, set apart by and for God, and loved by God. The three terms—*chosen, holy* and *dearly loved*—signify essentially the same great fact, but under different aspects. Used in the OT of Israel, they emphasize the favored position now enjoyed by Christians as the heirs of Israel's privileges.

Verse 12b contains a pentad of great Christian virtues: "compassion, kindness, humility, gentleness and patience." They point to those qualities of life which, if present in the community of believers, will eliminate, or at least reduce, frictions. All of them are manifestations of love, which is mentioned in v.14 as the crowning virtue. "Compassion" (*splanchna oiktirmou*) betokens pity and tenderness expressed toward the suffering and

122

miserable. The word for "kindness" (*chrēstotēs*) combines the ideas of goodness, kindliness, and graciousness. Ellicott defines it as "sweetness of disposition" (p. 181). In Romans 11:22 it is contrasted with "severity," and in Galatians 5:22 it is listed as a fruit of the Spirit. "Humility" and "gentleness," which are related terms, were not considered virtues by the pagan world. The NT, however, deepened and enriched their meanings and made them two of the noblest of Christian graces. Humility (*tapeinophrosynē*), which originally meant servility, came to denote a humble disposition—"the thinking lowly of ourselves because we are so" (Ellicott, p. 182). "Gentleness" (*prautēs*), the opposite of arrogance and self-assertiveness, is the special mark of the man who has a delicate consideration for the rights and feelings of others. C.F.D. Moule aptly defines it as "willingness to make concessions" (p. 123). It is mentioned in the NT as a characteristic of Christ (Matt 11:29), a fruit of the Spirit (Gal 5:23), a distinctive trait of those who belong to Christ (Matt 5:5), and so on. "Patience" (*makrothymia*; lit., "longsuffering") denotes the self-restraint that enables one to bear injury and insult without resorting to hasty retaliation. It is an attribute of God (Rom 2:4) and a fruit of the Spirit (Gal 5:22).

13 Two Greek participles (*anechomenoi*, "bear with" and *charizomenoi*, "forgive") expand the thought of patience. Paul uses them to show that Christians who are truly patient will manifest this attitude by (1) a willingness to bear with those whose faults or unpleasant traits are an irritant to them and (2) a willingness to forgive those they have grievances against. "Bear with" suggests the thought of putting up with things we dislike in others. "Forgive," a word used in 2:13 of God's action toward us, has the sense of forgiving freely.

14 The final article in this description of Christian attire is "love" (*agapē*, the distinctive Christian term for caring love; cf. commentary on 1 Cor 13). All the virtues listed in vv.12, 13 are, on the highest level, manifestations of love; but love is larger than any one of them, indeed, larger than all of them combined. The mention of love as a separate "article of clothing" is therefore not superfluous.

b. *The rule of peace* (3:15)

15 Those who see this verse as a continuation of the appeal for loving concern (v.14) among Christians are inclined to interpret "peace" to mean peace among the members of the Christian community. Those who understand it as introducing a new idea interpret "peace" as inward "heart" peace. Eadie defines it as "that calm of mind which is not ruffled by adversity, overclouded by sin or a remorseful conscience, or disturbed by the fear and the approach of death" (p. 247). Perhaps we should not limit the word but should understand it as including peace in the largest sense. It is the peace "of Christ" because it is the peace he gives—peace that comes by way of obedience to him (cf. John 14:27).

The word for "rule" (*brabeuō*), an expressive term used only here in the NT, originally meant "to act as umpire." Scholars are not agreed whether in Paul's time the word retained the connotation of a contest or simply had the general sense of administering, ruling, or deciding. In 2:18 Paul used a compound form of it. Here it means that in all inner conflicts as well as in all disputes and differences among Christians, Christ's peace must give the final decision. We are to do nothing that would violate that peace.

"And be thankful" (*kai eucharistoi ginesthe*) is added not as an afterthought but because gratitude is intimately associated with peace. The meaning probably is that we are to be grateful for the peace Christ bestows on us (which is the main idea of the verse). Thankfulness for this peace becomes an incentive for preserving it. It may be that the injunction should be taken in its broadest sense: Be thankful—both to God and to men. Such gratitude surely promotes peace and harmony within a fellowship. The verb *ginesthe* ("be") may be rendered "become," the implication being that it is a habit (present tense) that must be acquired. Knox: "Learn, too, to be grateful."

c. The indwelling of Christ's word (3:16)

16 All the preceding appeals (with the possible exception of that in v.15) have to do largely with duties Christians owe one another. Verses 16, 17 focus attention on matters that have to do more directly with the personal life. Even here, however, the thought of our duty to others is not entirely absent.

"The word of Christ" (*ho logos tou Christou*) probably refers to the gospel, that is, the message *about* Christ. It may, however, refer to Christ's teaching—a message *from* Christ—recorded or remembered by his apostles. To "let the word of Christ dwell in you richly" is to let it "have ample room" (BV) or "remain as a rich treasure" (Wey.) in the heart. Thus we are to submit to the demands of the Christian message and let it become so deeply implanted within us as to control all our thinking.

The correct punctuation of the remainder of v.16 is uncertain. NIV (along with most other modern versions) construes "with all wisdom" with "teach" and "counsel." The thought is that under the influence of the word of Christ Christians are to do two things: (1) Making use of every kind of wisdom, they are to teach and admonish one another. (2) Using psalms, hymns, and spiritual songs, they are to sing with gratitude in their hearts to God.

No rigid distinctions should be made between "psalms," "hymns," and "spiritual songs." Paul is simply emphasizing the rich variety in Christian song. Essentially the three terms heighten the idea of joyousness called for in the passage. If any differences are made, "psalms" may be taken to refer to the OT psalter, "hymns" and "spiritual songs" to distinctly Christian compositions. The great periods of renewal in Christendom have always been accompanied by an outburst of hymnology. Armitage Robinson describes the apostolic age as "characterized by vivid enthusiasm" and as "a period of wonder and delight. The floodgates of emotion were opened: a supernatural dread alternated with an unspeakable joy" (*St. Paul's Epistle to the Ephesians*, p. 168). Robertson writes that Christian hymns "demand two things above all else. They must express real emotion of the heart, adoration and worship. They must do it in a way worthy of our Saviour God" (p. 113).

d. The name of Christ (3:17)

17 Here Paul gives us a kind of summary. There are various ways of interpreting "do it all in the name of the Lord Jesus." Some understand the meaning to be that everything a Christian does is to be undertaken *in dependence on the Lord* (cf. Moff.). Others think it means that everything a Christian does is to be done *in recognition of the authority of Jesus' name*. Still others take "in the name of the Lord Jesus" to mean "as followers of the Lord Jesus" (cf. Am. Transl.). This last interpretation reflects the thought that to act in the name of a person is to act as his representative. The last two interpretations are both acceptable, but the third is the preferred. Bruce appropriately points out that "the NT does not contain a detailed code of rules for the Christian .... Codes of rules, as Paul explains elsewhere, are suited to the period of immaturity when he and his readers were still under guardians.... What the NT does provide is those basic principles of Christian living which may be applied to all situations of life as they arise" (p. 285). The words under consideration enunciate such a principle. Maclaren writes that the name of Christ "hallows and ennobles all work. Nothing can be so small but this will make it great, nor so monotonous and tame but this will make it beautiful and fresh" (p. 333).

"Giving thanks" points to an essential accompaniment of acting in the name of the Lord Jesus—viz., that in everything we do we are to retain a sense of God's goodness and are to be careful to thank him.

Notes

14 Some take τελειότητος (*teleiotētos*, "bond") to be an appositive genitive. The meaning is then "the bond that is [or consists in] perfection." Peake, who adopts this view, says, "When love binds all Christians together the ideal of Christian perfection is attained" (p. 541). Others construe the genitive as attributive. The meaning is then that love is "the bond characterized by perfectness," that is, the perfect bond—in the sense that it embraces and completes all the other virtues.

3. *Family relationships to be strengthened*

3:18–4:1

18Wives, submit to your husbands, as is fitting in the Lord.
19Husbands, love your wives and do not be harsh with them.
20Children, obey your parents in everything, for this pleases the Lord.
21Fathers, do not embitter your children, or they will become discouraged.
22Slaves, obey your masters in everything; and do it, not only when their eye is on you and to win their favor, but with sincerity of heart and reverence for the Lord. 23Whatever you do, work at it with all your heart, as working for the Lord, not for men, 24since you know that you will receive an inheritance from the Lord as a reward. It is the Lord Christ you are serving. 25Anyone who does wrong will be repaid for his wrong, and there is no favoritism. 4:1 Masters, provide your slaves with what is right and fair, because you know that you also have a Master in heaven.

Several observations are in order as we approach this important paragraph. First, we may see it as applying specifically to the general principle Paul set down in v.17. Second, the emphasis of the whole passage is on duties, not rights. (The rights, to be sure, are clearly implied, but the stress does not fall on them.) Third, the duties are reciprocal— that is, not all the rights are on one side and all the duties on the other. Fourth, the entire passage is remarkably similar to Ephesians 5:22–33, though it is much briefer. The chief difference is that in Ephesians, where Paul unfolds the Christian philosophy of marriage, he introduces a rather extended and beautiful statement about the church as the bride of Christ.

a. *The wife's duty to the husband* (3:18)

18 The one duty Paul enjoins on the wife is submission, an attitude that recognizes the rights of authority. His main thought is that the wife is to defer to, that is, be willing to take second place to, her husband. Yet we should never interpret this as if it implies that the husband may be a domestic despot, ruling his family with a rod of iron. It does imply, however, that the husband has an authority the wife must forego exercising. In areas where one must yield—e.g., in the husband's choice of a profession or of a geographical location for doing his work—the primary submission devolves upon the wife.

Three things may be said about a wife's subjection to her husband. First, the context shows that the wife's attitude is prompted and warranted by her husband's unselfish love. Second, the form of the verb (*hypotassesthe*, middle voice) shows that the submission is to be voluntary. The wife's submission is never to be forced on her by a demanding husband; it is the deference that a loving wife, conscious that her home (just as any other institution) must have a head, gladly shows to a worthy and devoted husband. Third, such submission is said to be "fitting in the Lord." The verb has in it the thought of what is becoming and proper. The phrase "in the Lord" indicates that wifely submission is proper not only in the natural order but also in the Christian order. The whole thing, then, is lifted to a new and higher level.

b. *The husband's duties to the wife* (3:19)

19 The ancient world was a man's world, and even among the Jews the wife was often little more than chattel. Paul's counsel in the present passage is in striking contrast to this. Caird's comment is again apropos: "Jew and Gentile alike assumed that the head of a household would wield an authority which others were bound to obey. Paul does not openly challenge this assumption, but he modifies both the authority and its acceptance by the Christian principle of mutual love and deference, so that both are transformed" (p. 208).

Paul speaks of two responsibilities of the husband—one positive and the other negative. Positively, Paul urges husbands to "love [*agapate*] your wives." This of course is their supreme duty. *Agapaō* does not denote affection or romantic attachment; it rather denotes caring love, a deliberate attitude of mind that concerns itself with the well-being of the one loved. Self-devotion, not self-satisfaction, is its dominant trait. Negatively, Paul urges husbands not to be "harsh" with their wives, using a word that suggests a surly, irritable attitude. Perhaps the colloquialism "don't be cross with" best expresses the meaning.

c. *The duty of children to parents* (3:20)

20 The one obligation Paul places on children is obedience to their parents. "Obey" (*hypakouete*) implies a readiness to hear and carry out orders; the child is to listen to and carry out the instructions of his parents. The verb is in the present tense, indicating that such action is to be habitual.

Two things are said about the obedience children owe their parents. First, it is to be complete: "in everything." Paul, of course, sets this in a Christian context. He is dealing with the Christian home and presupposes Christian attitudes on the part of parents. Second, the obedience of children to their parents "pleases the Lord." The meaning is that in the Christian order, just as in the order under the law or in the natural realm, obedience to parents is pleasing to God. The obedience of children is not, therefore, based on accidental factors, nor does it depend essentially on the parents' character. It is an obligation grounded in the very nature of the relationship between parents and children. It is, as the parallel passage in Ephesians (6:1–3) clearly states, a thing that is right in itself. It is therefore especially pleasing to God when believing children are careful to fulfill this duty.

d. The duty of parents to children (3:21)

21 The specific mention of "fathers" suggests that the father as head of the household has a special responsibility for training the children. No slight toward the mother is intended. Paul would surely have recognized her rights and the power of her influence in the home. It is possible that "fathers" as used here has the broad meaning of "parents." (Cf. Heb 11:23, where the same Greek word [*paterōn*] is used of the parents of Moses.)

Fathers are not to "embitter" (*erithizō*) their children. The sense is that they are not to challenge the resistance of their children by their unreasonable exercise of authority. Firm discipline may be necessary, but it must be administered in the right spirit. Parents should not give in to fault-finding, nor always be nagging their children. Wey translates, "Do not fret and harass your children." Ph has "don't over-correct." Knox says, "And you, parents, must not rouse your children to resentment."

Paul gives the reason for this counsel; viz., "or they will become discouraged." Parents can be so exacting, so demanding, or so severe that they create within their children the feeling that it is impossible for them to please. The Greek word (*athymeō*) has in it the idea of "losing heart" and suggests going about in "a listless, moody, sullen frame of mind" (Lightfoot, p. 227). "The twig," writes Eadie, "is to be bent with caution, not broken in the efforts of a rude and hasty zeal" (p. 262). Paul may have had in mind the regimen of "don'ts" that loomed so large in the Colossian heresy.

e. The duty of slaves to masters (3:22–25)

22 Slavery, with all its attendant evils, was not only universally accepted in ancient times but also considered a fundamental institution, indispensable to civilized society. More than half the people seen on the streets of the great cities of the Roman world were slaves. And this was the status of the majority of "professional" people such as teachers and doctors as well as that of menials and craftsmen. Slaves were people with no rights, mere property existing only for the comfort, convenience, and pleasure of their owners. (Cf. vol.1, "The Cultural and Political Setting of the New Testament" by Arthur A. Rupprecht.) Paul deals with the duty of slaves in the context of the family because slaves were considered a part of the household.

It is a matter of concern to some that neither Paul nor the other apostles denounced slavery and demanded its immediate overthrow. The apostles, however, were not social reformers; they were first and foremost heralds of the good news of salvation in Christ. Then again, the church was a very small minority in the Roman world, and there was no hope that its stance on the matter of slavery would influence Roman policies. We should be careful to understand, though, that they did not condone slavery. Indeed, they announced the very principles (such as that of the complete spiritual equality of slave and master) that ultimately destroyed the institution of slavery.

The one duty Paul presses upon slaves is complete obedience—i.e., "in everything." He was obviously thinking of the Christian household and thus did not have in mind orders contrary to the principles of the gospel. They were not, of course, to obey such orders; no matter what their position in life, the Christians' highest duty is to God, and all lesser duties must give way to this. The latter part of the verse insists that obedience of slaves is to be sincere and ungrudging, and rooted in "reverence for the Lord." "Sincerity of heart" (lit., "singleness of heart") translates *en haplotēti kardias*, a phrase that implies the absence of all base and self-seeking motives.

23 Slaves are to see their service as a service rendered not to men but to the Lord. This would transform the most menial responsibilities and give dignity to all of their work.

24 Slaves are reminded of the reward that will be theirs for serving faithfully in Christ's name. "Receive" translates *apolēmpsesthe*, which here combines the ideas of receiving what is due and receiving in full (cf. Rom 1:27, where it is used in the sense of retribution). On "inheritance," see 1:12.

25 This verse, set in contrast to the preceding, shows that wrong will be punished, because "there is no favoritism" with God. Doubtless Paul meant it as a warning to Christian slaves not to presume on their position before God and think that he would overlook their misdeeds. In the parallel passage in Ephesians it is the master who is reminded that there is no partiality with God, while here it is the slave. In Ephesians, masters are not to think that God is influenced by social position; in the present passage, slaves are not to act unscrupulously just because they know men treat them as irresponsible chattel.

The entire passage about the duty of slaves (vv.22–25) may seem completely irrelevant to our day. It contains, however, this enduring principle: Christians, whatever their work, are, like slaves in Paul's day, to see it as a service rendered to the Lord. This is what motivates them to give honest, faithful, ungrudging work in return for the pay they receive. Moreover, it imparts a sense of dignity in work, regardless of how unimportant it may seem.

f. The duty of masters to slaves (4:1)

4:1 Now Paul turns to the duty of masters toward their slaves in terms of dealing justly and equitably with them—"what is right and fair." Though in the Roman world slaves had no rights, Paul does not hesitate to teach that duty is not all on the side of slaves. Masters also have obligations. Maclaren observes that Paul did not counsel masters to give their slaves "what is kind and patronising. He wants a great deal more than that. Charity likes to come in and supply wants which would never have been felt had there been equity. An ounce of justice is sometimes worth a ton of charity" (p. 352).

His reason for their being completely fair with their slaves is a compelling one: "because you know that you also have a Master in heaven." It is to God that Christian masters are accountable for how they treat their slaves. Both bow alike before one Master, with whom there is no "favoritism."

Notes

21 Some manuscripts have παροργίζετε (*parorgizete*, "provoke to anger") instead of ἐρεθίζετε (*erethizete*, "provoke"; NIV, "embitter"). The KJV follows this variant, but it is a patently inferior reading, having probably been inserted from Eph 6:4, where it is genuine.

4. *Religious duties to be faithfully performed*

4:2-6

2Devote yourselves to prayer, being watchful and thankful. 3And pray for us, too, that God may open a door for our message, so that we may proclaim the mystery of Christ, for which I am in chains. 4Pray that I may proclaim it clearly, as I should. 5Be wise in the way you act toward outsiders; make the most of every opportunity. 6Let your conversation be always full of grace, seasoned with salt, so that you may know how to answer everyone.

The immediately preceding paragraph (3:18–4:1) consisted of a series of special appeals based on the several relationships in the Christian household. Now Paul returns to counsel that applies to the entire church. Most of what he says relates to the personal devotional life (vv.2–5), but the section closes with an appeal for wise behavior toward non-Christians (vv.5, 6). Maclaren therefore aptly remarks that the injunctions given in this paragraph touch "the two extremes of life, the first of them having reference to the hidden life of prayer, and the second and third to the outward, busy life of the market place and the street. . . . Continual prayer is to blend with unwearied action" (p. 354, 355).

a. *The duty of prayer* (4:2–4)

2 Here is a general appeal for prayerfulness. The word for "devote yourselves" (*proskartereite*), used ten times in the NT, is translated in a variety of ways in KJV; e.g., "continue," "continue instant," "continue steadfastly." Built on a root meaning "to be strong," it always connotes earnest adherence to a person or thing. In this passage it implies persistence and fervor (cf. Acts 1:14; 2:46; 6:5; Rom 12:12).

"Being watchful" (*grēgorountes*; lit., "keeping awake") suggests constant spiritual alertness. So Christians must be watchful and active in prayer, alive in the fullest sense, never careless or mechanical, dull and heavy (cf. Matt 26:41; Mark 14:38; 1 Thess 5:6; 1 Peter 5:8). "Being thankful" refers to the spirit in which prayers should be offered. "Maintain your zest for prayer by thanksgiving" (Moff.).

3,4 This is Paul's request for prayer for himself while he was imprisoned in Rome. His concern was that he and his associates might have opportunities for witnessing ("that God may open a door for our message") and that Paul might make clear ("proclaim") the great secret ("mystery"; cf. Col 1:26; 2:2 with Eph 1:9; 3:1) of redemption in Christ in a worthy manner. There was no selfish motive behind this prayer; Paul's consuming interest was for the advancement of the gospel, not for his own blessing.

b. *The duty of witnessing* (4:5, 6)

These verses, with their call for discreet behavior in an unbelieving society, may reflect the fact that charges of misconduct on the part of Christians were being circulated. Therefore the Colossian Christians should be all the more cautious, living in so exemplary a way as to give the lie to such slander.

Actually Paul makes two appeals—one having to do with how Christians are to live (v.5), the other relating how they are to speak (v.6). Careful attention to these matters will not only remove unfounded suspicions about Christians but also further the acceptance of the gospel.

5 To "be wise in the way you act toward outsiders" is to show practical Christian wisdom in dealing with secular society. Paul's words imply that believers are to be cautious and tactful so as to avoid needlessly antagonizing or alienating their pagan neighbors. In a positive sense, they also imply that believers should conduct themselves so that the way they live will attract, impress, and convict non-Christians and give the pagan community a favorable impression of the gospel. (See 1 Cor 5:12, 13; 1 Thess 4:12; 1 Tim 3:7 for other passages where unbelievers are designated as "outsiders.")

The verb in the statement "make the most of every opportunity" is a market term that meant "to buy out," "purchase completely" (*exagorazomenoi*). So Christians, as an expression of practical wisdom, must buy up and make the most of every opportunity for witnessing to the faith. (It may be appropriate at this point to recall the parables of the hidden treasure and the pearl of great price in Matthew 13.) The word translated "opportunity" is *kairos*, which essentially denotes a point of time in contrast to duration, which is the idea in *chronos*. *Kairos*, however, is sometimes used for significant time, God's time, or opportunity, and this appears to be the sense to be preferred in the present passage.

6 Like his Lord and also like James the brother of the Lord, Paul knew how important the way Christians speak is (cf. Matt 12:36; Eph 4:24; Titus 2:8; James 3:1–12). Here he may well have had in mind the relation of the right kind of speech to witnessing. So their speech, he reminds the Colossians, must be always full of "grace" and "seasoned with salt." "Grace" (*charis*), which in the NT usually denotes divine favor, seems here to be used in the broader sense of "pleasantness," "attractiveness," "charm," "winsomeness." These ideas are all implicit in the word.

"Seasoned with salt" may mean that Christian conversation is to be marked by purity and wholesomeness. Some, however, understand "salt" in the sense of that which gives taste or flavor (cf. NEB, "never insipid"). Among the ancient Greeks "salt" (*halas*) might designate the wit that gives zest and liveliness to conversation. Here "hallowed pungency" may be its meaning. C.F.D. Moule writes that "loyal godliness" is not to be confused "with a dull, graceless insipidity" (p. 135).

The remainder of v.6 tells why we should cultivate this kind of speech: "so that you will know how to answer everyone." Conversation must be appropriate for each person we speak to.

VI. Conclusion (4:7–18)

The body of the letter, in which Paul has met head-on the false teachers threatening the church at Colosse, is complete. By a masterful exposition of the sovereign lordship and complete sufficiency of Jesus Christ, Paul has refuted their so-called "philosophy" with all its attendant errors (1:15-2:23); he has set forth the nature of the Christian life, calling attention to its springs of power, its heavenly aspirations, and its distinguishing characteristics (3:1-17); he has shown how the lofty principles of the gospel must affect relationships within Christian households (3:18-4:2); and he has earnestly exhorted his readers to pray (4:2-4) and given them practical advice for living in the pagan world (4:5, 6). Now all that remains is for him to mention some personal matters.

A. *Commendations*

4:7-9

> 7Tychicus will tell you all the news about me. He is a dear brother, a faithful minister and fellow servant in the Lord. 8I am sending him to you for the express purpose that you may know about our circumstances and that he may encourage your hearts. 9He is coming with Onesimus, our faithful and dear brother, who is one of you. They will tell you everything that is happening here.

7 These commendations, given to insure their welcome by the Colossian church, concern two men: Tychicus (vv.7, 8) and Onesimus (v.9). The former, who is described by Paul as "a dear brother" and "a faithful minister and fellow servant in the Lord," was probably the bearer of both this letter and the one we know as Ephesians (cf. Eph 6:21, 22). He was a native of the province of Asia and was earlier selected to be one of the two delegates of the churches who were to accompany Paul on his last visit to Jerusalem, probably as custodians of the offering that was given by the churches for the needy in Jerusalem (Acts 20:4; 24:17; Rom 15:25, 26; 1 Cor 16:1; 2 Cor 8; 9).

"Dear brother" (*agapētos adelphos*) shows that Tychicus was a much-loved fellow Christian. "Faithful minister" (*pistos diakonos*) may identify him as a loyal servant of Christ, but more likely the expression marks his relation to Paul. Wey. renders it "trusted assistant." Earlier Paul had used the same noun (*diakonos*) of Epaphras (1:7) and of himself (1:23). "Fellow servant" (which, like "minister," is qualified by "faithful") speaks of Tychicus as a bondslave of Christ with himself and others (*syndoulos*). The prefix *syn* ("fellow") before *doulos* ("bondslave") affirms Paul's sense of comradeship with him. In 1:7 Paul had called Epaphras his dear *syndoulos*.

8 Paul explains that he had a twofold purpose in sending (*epempsa*, an epistolary aorist, best translated into English by a present tense) Tychicus to the Colossians—viz., "that you may know about our circumstances and that he may encourage your hearts." Some think that the wording of this verse suggests that Paul had made a special point of including Colosse in the itinerary of Tychicus.

9 Accompanying Tychicus was Onesimus, the runaway slave who in the providence of God had met Paul in Rome and had apparently been led to Christ by him. (Cf. the commentary on Philemon in this volume.) Paul is now sending Onesimus back to Colosse —with no mention of his past, but with the heart-warming phrase that he is now "one of you."

B. *Greetings*

4:10–15

> [10]My fellow prisoner Aristarchus sends you his greetings, as does Mark, the cousin of Barnabas. (You have received instructions about him; if he comes to you, welcome him.) [11]Jesus, who is called Justus, also sends greetings. These are the only Jews among my fellow workers for the kingdom of God, and they have proved a comfort to me. [12]Epaphras, who is one of you and a servant of Christ Jesus, sends greetings. He is always wrestling in prayer for you, that you may stand firm in all the will of God, mature and fully assured. [13]I vouch for him that he is working hard for you and for those at Laodicea and Hierapolis. [14]Our dear friend Luke, the doctor, and Demas send greetings. [15]Give my greetings to the brothers at Laodicea, and to Nympha and the church in her house.

10,11 In vv.10–15 six persons join in sending greetings to the Colossian church. Three of them—Aristarchus, Mark, and Jesus Justus—were Jewish Christians. Aristarchus, a native of Thessalonica who had been arrested at the time of the riot in Ephesus (Acts 19:29), accompanied Paul to Jerusalem (Acts 20:4) and later on was with him on the journey from Caesarea to Rome (Acts 27:2). Here Paul calls him his "fellow prisoner" (*synaichmalōtos*). The term may be interpreted either literally or spiritually (i.e., one who, along with Paul, had been taken captive by Christ). Mark, called here "the cousin of Barnabas," wrote the gospel that bears his name. He appears in the NT with some frequency, and we know more about him than about any of the others mentioned in this passage (cf. Acts 12:12, 25; 13:13; 15:37–39; 1 Peter 5:13). Of Jesus Justus we know nothing beyond the mention of his name here.

There is a note of pathos in Paul's remark about these three: "These are the only Jews among my fellow workers for the kingdom of God." He felt keenly his alienation from his countrymen (cf. Rom 9:3; Phil 1:15–17). But these three, he adds, "have proved a comfort to me." "Proved" (*egenēthēsan*), an aorist tense, may point to a particular crisis when they stood by Paul. "Comfort" (*parēgoria*), used only here in the NT, is the word from which "paregoric" comes and denotes relief of pain.

12 Epaphras, mentioned in 1:7 as the founder of the Colossian church and as Paul's representative, is here described as "one of you" (cf. v.9) and as "a servant [bondslave] of Christ Jesus." Paul reminds the Colossians that Epaphras was continually wrestling (*agōnizomenos*; cf. 1:29 for the same word) for them in his prayers. He was concerned that they stand firm, mature, and fully convinced in relation to everything God wills. Undoubtedly he had in mind the danger of their wavering under the influence of the heretical teaching at Colosse.

13 Paul confirms Epaphras's anxiety for the Colossians and assures them that "he is working hard for [them] and for those at Laodicea and Hierapolis." "Working hard" is a free translation of *echei polyn ponon*, a phrase the key word of which (*ponon*) suggests heavy toil to the extent of pain. Here it may refer to the emotional distress Epaphras had experienced in reference to the people at Colosse.

Laodicea and Hierapolis were cities near Colosse. The former, which lay ten miles downstream to the west of Colosse, was situated on a plateau to the south of the River Lycus. On the other side of the river, six miles north of Laodicea, was Hierapolis. Laodicea was a city of great wealth and boasted a medical school. Names of its physicians appear on coins as early as Augustus. The church at Laodicea received the sternest denunciation of all the seven churches of Asia in the Book of Revelation. The name *Hierapolis* suggests the city owed its initial importance to religion. (The Greek word *hieros* means "holy," "sacred.") There were hot mineral springs in the area. After the death of Alexander the Great in 323 B.C., these cities, together with most of Asia Minor, came under the control of the Seleucid kings of Antioch. Antiochus III (233–187 B.C.) settled a large number of Jews in the area. In 190 B.C. this particular part of southwest Phrygia was ceded to the king of Pergamum; and Attalus III bequeathed his whole kingdom to Rome. Upon his death in 133 B.C., the whole district became the Roman province of Asia.

14 Luke and Demas are mentioned next; no descriptive phrase is used of Demas. (Cf. Philemon 24 and 2 Timothy 4:10 for the only other NT references to him.) Of Luke, Paul says very little. Interestingly enough, however, much of what we know about Luke is derived from this casual reference. It is here that we learn that Luke was a physician, and the context suggests that he was a Gentile (cf. v.11). The adjective *dear* confirms what is implied in Acts; namely, that Luke—assuming that he was author of Acts—was a trusted friend of Paul.

15 Greetings for the Christian "brothers" of Laodicea, for "Nympha," and for "the church in her house." A transliterated Greek name, "Nympha" may be either masculine or feminine, depending on the position of the accent mark. The versions differ. KJV and ASV interpret it as a man's name (Nymphas). NIV and NEB have "Nympha," a woman's name. The decision (i.e., whether to construe the name as masculine or as feminine) is made largely on the basis of the pronoun used with "house." At this point, however, the Greek MSS exhibit a variety of readings. Instead of "her" house (NIV, RSV, NEB), some texts have "his" house (cf. KJV); others, "their" house (cf. ASV). The femine pronoun represents perhaps the true reading. Numerically the MS evidence for it is slight, but the overall attestation is very strong.

The reference to the church in Nympha's "house" is significant. There were, of course, no church buildings in apostolic times, and in the NT, "church" always designates an assembly of believers, never the place where they met.

The location of Nympha's "house-church" is uncertain, though the context implies that it was in the vicinity of Laodicea. Some have suggested that it was in Hierapolis, a city near both Colosse and Laodicea (see Introduction, 1).

Notes

10 Ἀνεψιός (*anepsios*) was understood in the sense of "nephew" by the KJV translators, but the word did not take on this meaning till after the NT age.

C. *Instructions*

4:16,17

> ¹⁶After this letter has been read to you, see that it is also read in the church of the Laodiceans and that you in turn read the letter from Laodicea.
> ¹⁷Tell Archippus: "See to it that you complete the work you have received in the Lord."

These final instructions relate to three matters: the Colossian Epistle (v.16a), the epistle from Laodicea (v. 16b), and advice to Archippas (v.17).

16 After reading this letter, the Colossian Christians were to see to it that it was read also in the Laodicean church. Perhaps they first made a copy of it to keep for themselves and then sent the original to the Laodiceans. In return, the Colossians were to read "the letter from Laodicea." It has been conjectured that this is the epistle we know as Ephesians, but that seems highly unlikely. The most obvious conclusion is that Paul wrote to the Laodicean church an epistle that has not been preserved. A similar reference to a lost letter is in 1 Corinthians 5:9 (cf. Introduction, 1, and also the commentary on 1 Cor 5:9).

17 Archippus, to whom Paul sent a special message, appears again in Philemon 2. From the context there some think he was a member of Philemon's household. Indeed, many commentators think he was Philemon's son. The present verse implies that he had some ministerial responsibility in the Colossian church, though Paul gives no definite information about it. Perhaps he was serving as pastor in the absence of Epaphras.

Paul tells the Colossian church to instruct Archippus to "complete" the work assigned him. Some commentators, assuming that this charge implies a degree of failure on the part of Archippus, interpret Paul's words as a rebuke. But we cannot be sure that censure was what Paul meant. This could have been his way of letting the church know that Archippus had his full support.

D. *Benediction*

4:18

> ¹⁸I, Paul, write this greeting in my own hand. Remember my chains. Grace be with you.

18 When a stenographer's services were used to write a letter (as perhaps was Paul's custom; cf. Rom 16:22), it was normally the stenographer's task to compose the final greeting. Apparently, however, Paul regularly wrote the benediction in his own hand (cf. 2 Thess 3:17). So here at the end of this letter, he took the stylus and signed the letter in his own hand.

The letter ends as it began, with the simple but profound prayer: "Grace be with you."

PHILEMON

Arthur A. Rupprecht

PHILEMON

Introduction

1. Authorship
2. Date and Place of Origin
3. Destination
4. Occasion and Purpose
5. Literary Form
6. Theological Values
7. Bibliography
8. Outline

Philemon is a letter written by the apostle Paul to a Christian slave owner who lived in the Lycus Valley of Asia Minor. In it the apostle asks that the converted runaway slave, Onesimus, be received back into the household without punishment. There is also a hint that he should be loaned to Paul or granted his freedom so that he could help the apostle.

1. Authorship

Few, if any, dispute that Philemon is a letter written by the apostle Paul. It appeared early, in the Muratorian Fragment and in Marcion's canon. Only the Tübingen School of the nineteenth century questioned its authenticity. F.C. Baur claimed that the letter was written in the second century to instruct the church in handling the slavery question.

On the basis of the similarity of the final greetings in Philemon and Colossians, as well as on certain literary and theological considerations, some modern commentators have concluded that Colossians is "deutero-Pauline."[1] However, this is an unwarranted conclusion.

2. Date and Place of Origin

Those who hold that Colossians and Philemon were written at the same time, while Paul was in prison at Rome, date it c. A.D. 58–60. If it was written from Ephesus, as Duncan has suggested, a date c. A.D. 56 would be likely.[2] Duncan's argument that the appeal for lodging (v.22) demands an imprisonment in a place closer than Rome has real validity. Dodd answered him on the assumption that Onesimus would seek anonymity

---

[1]Eduard Lohse, *Colossians and Philemon*, p. 187.
[2]G.S. Duncan, *St. Paul's Ephesian Ministry* (London: Hodder and Staughton, 1929), pp. 72 ff.

at Rome.[3] The evidence suggests, however, that runaway slaves were apt to seek asylum almost anywhere. Until further evidence is found the question of the date will remain open to dispute.

3. Destination

The traditional view is that the letter was written to Philemon, a resident of the Lycus Valley in Asia Minor. As an alternative to this, Goodspeed suggested that Philemon is the lost letter to the Laodiceans (Col 4:16) on the ground that a letter referred to in this way would not have been lost. He identifies Onesimus with the bishop of Ephesus of the same name who put together the Pauline corpus. Goodspeed argued further that there is little likelihood that there would have been a third letter written at the same time as Colossians and Philemon.[4] To support his claim, however, it must be shown that Philemon was really a letter to the church and not to an individual. Knox follows Goodspeed, but claims that Archippus, who lived at Colosse, was the owner of the slave and the recipient of the letter.[5]

The letter is addressed to Philemon of Laodicea, who was to pass it along to Colosse and exert influence on Archippus to "complete the work" (Col 4:17), which may be Paul's request in behalf of Onesimus. The only questions have to do with which of the two cities in the Lycus Valley, Colosse or Laodicea, the letter was sent to and which of the two individuals Philemon or Archippus, the request was intended for. The evidence favors Philemon of Colosse as the recipient.

4. Occasion and Purpose

Paul wrote the letter to Philemon in typical epistolary form. He wanted to intercede in behalf of the latter's runaway slave, Onesimus. The apostle's suggestions for the handling of the matter are difficult to determine because of his obscure and deferential words. At a minimum he asked that Onesimus be reconciled to the household without harsh punishment. He also strongly hinted that the slave would be useful to him in the work of evangelism. Nowhere does Paul openly state that Philemon should set Onesimus free. Nor is it necessary to assume that Onesimus would be freed if he were to join Paul in his missionary work.

Brief and intensely personal, the letter is addressed to one person, Philemon,[6] but other interested parties are mentioned in the salutation. Apphia, his wife, would have had daily responsibility over the slaves of the household. Archippus, perhaps Philemon's son and possibly also a local pastor ("fellow soldier"), would look after the interests of the church, which is also mentioned in the salutation. No doubt the church at Colosse would find very significant the reconciliation of a runaway slave on the intercession of no less a person than the apostle Paul.

---

[3]C.H. Dodd, "The Mind of Paul: Change and Development," in *Bulletin of the John Rylands Library* 18 (1934); 69–80.

[4]E.J. Goodspeed, *The Key to Ephesians* (Chicago: University of Chicago Press, 1956), pp. xiv–xvi.

[5]John Knox, *Philemon among the Letters of Paul* (New York: Abingdon, 1959), pp. 91–108.

[6]In the phrase "the church that meets in your home" (v.2), "your" is singular and refers to Philemon as the recipient of the letter. C.F.D. Moule (*The Epistles to the Colossians and to Philemon* [Cambridge: Cambridge University Press, 1957], pp. 16, 17) argues that this reference has to be to Philemon whose name is first in the list. This fact is "fatal to the theory [Knox's] that Archippus is primarily the one addressed."

Some of the events that led to the writing of the letter can be stated without qualification. On the other hand, many of the tantalizing details are lost to us. Onesimus came in contact with Paul while the latter was in prison somewhere in the Roman world—most probably in Rome, though Caesarea and Ephesus are also possibilities (cf. Introduction to Colossians)—and was converted. Paul intimates that he had robbed his master in some way, but oddly he does not mention the details, possibly because of his sensitivity and tact. It is not likely that Paul did not know the details. Nor do we know whether or not Onesimus was a prisoner with Paul. It is most likely, however, that he was not, since the return of a fugitive slave was a complicated, technical procedure in Roman law by this time. Certainly a prisoner could not directly send back a runaway slave and fellow-prisoner. The best assumption is that the authorities were unaware of Onesimus's status and that Paul made unofficial arrangements for his return.

The traditional interpretation has been that Paul sent him back with Tychicus at the time of the writing of the Epistle to the Colossians. "If there is one thing certain, it is that Colossians and Philemon were written at the same time and place," said C.H. Dodd.[7]

A better explanation of the circumstances of the writing of Philemon may be that it was composed at a time prior to Colossians. The evidence for this is striking. According to Colossians 4, Tychicus and Onesimus were returning to Colosse together and would "tell all that is happening here" (v.9). It is usually assumed that this is the return of the runaway Onesimus. But if so, why is he described as a "faithful . . . brother" (v.9). Paul usually reserved the word *pistos* ("faithful") for fellow workers who showed great determination and endurance in the work of the gospel. It is a frequent word in inscriptions for a "trusted agent" or "commissioned one."[8]

Yet the description of one who had doubtless stolen from his master upon his illegal departure as a "faithful and dear brother" is not so serious as it seems. While in prison, Paul had undoubtedly led Onesimus to Christ, as the words "my son Onesimus, who became my son while I was in chains" (v.10) show. We do not know how long Onesimus, following his conversion, spent with Paul before going back to Colosse. Evidently it was long enough for him to become helpful to Paul (v.11) and to serve him in such a way as to lead to the affectionate expressions in vv.12, 13.

There are two other considerations that suggest that Colossians and Philemon were separated in time. Philemon 22 states clearly that Paul expects to be in Colosse soon. It is difficult to understand how "prepare a guest room for me, because I hope to be restored to you," can be interpreted as a figure of speech. On the other hand, in writing Colossians the apostle is greatly distressed at the direction in which the church has gone. Yet he only says, "Pray for us also, that God may open us a door for the word." If he had expected to be released from imprisonment soon, he would probably have mentioned this to the Colossians also.

As for the traditional view that Colossians and Philemon were written at the same time, two considerations support it—the geography and the final greetings. The geogra-

---

[7] *New Testament Studies* (Manchester: Manchester University Press, 1953), p. 90. Also, Moule, *Colossians and Philemon*, p. 22 *et passim*.

[8] See BAG, p. 670; TDNT, p. 204. Onesimus was a common slave name. Calvin could not bring himself to the conclusion that Onesimus of Colossians was the same as the runaway slave of Philemon. "For it is scarcely credible that this is the slave of Philemon, for the name of a thief and a fugitive would have been liable to reproach." (*Calvin's Commentaries: the Epistles to the Galatians, Ephesians, Philippians and Colossians*, trans. Parker [Edinburgh, 1965], p. 359.)

phy of both letters is the same. They are sent to a city or cities of the Lycus Valley. The names in the greetings at the end of both Epistles are very similar. Epaphras, Mark, Demas, and Luke appear in both. This coincidence has prompted a number of scholars to conclude that a Paulinist of the first century borrowed heavily from the setting of the Epistle to Philemon to give authenticity to his letter that we know as Colossians.

A final similarity in both Epistles is that Onesimus comes back. Note carefully, however, that he accompanies Tychicus in Colossians, but Tychicus is nowhere mentioned in Philemon. That Tychicus accompanied Onesimus when the latter returned as a runaway is only an assumption.

John Knox, following Goodspeed's suggestion that Philemon is the lost letter to the Laodiceans, interprets the events very differently. He sees Archippus as the intended recipient of the letter and Onesimus as his slave. Philemon is, therefore, the lost letter to the Laodiceans mentioned in Colossians 4:16, and the work Archippus was expected to complete (v.17) was the release of Onesimus for Paul's sake. Philemon, then, was a prominent member of the church at Laodicea who was expected to intercede with Archippus upon receipt of the letter. Knox based his hypothesis on Onesimus's becoming the bishop of Ephesus mentioned by Ignatius (*Eph* 1:3; 2:1; 6:2) and later being responsible for the collection of the Pauline Epistles. For this reason, Knox contends, Ephesians is at the beginning of the Pauline corpus and Philemon was uniquely preserved because of its importance to the bishop.[9] It must be said, however, that this theory can neither be proved nor disproved. There is no clear evidence that the bishop of Ephesus was, in fact, Onesimus, the runaway slave. Nor does the exegetical evidence actually support the contention that Archippus and not Philemon was the master of Onesimus.

5. Literary Form

The letter is unique in the Pauline corpus because it is a personal letter of commendation and recommendation. There are innumerable examples of similar letters, both pagan and Christian, from the Graeco-Roman world. Among these, Philemon belongs to the kind of letter written to intercede for a delinquent slave. A well-known parallel is the beautiful letter the younger Pliny wrote to Sabinianus on behalf of a slave of the latter (quoted by Lightfoot, *in loc.*). But even more beautiful is this page from Paul's personal correspondence—a true little masterpiece of tact and sensitivity.

It begins with a salutation, followed by expressions of thanks and petition, the principal subject matter, a conclusion, and greetings. Most of the Pauline Epistles follow this format, even when they are more in the nature of theological treatises.

6. Theological Values

Paul, Philemon, and Onesimus are *dramatis personae* in a real-life drama of profound social significance. Each has heard the claims of Christianity from totally different backgrounds. Paul was once a rigorous Jew of the Dispersion who advanced in Judaism beyond all his contemporaries. Philemon was a wealthy Asiatic Gentile. Onesimus was the most despicable of all creatures, a runaway slave. They find themselves united in the

---

9 *Philemon among the Letters of Paul.*

gospel of Christ. Here is a living example of Paul's statement that "there is neither Jew nor Greek, slave nor free, male nor female, for you are all one in Christ Jesus" (Gal 3:28). It was in this oneness that Paul sought a solution to the problem presented by the relationship of Onesimus to Philemon.

Neither Paul nor the other authors of the NT ever call for the abolition of slavery. For a new religion to do so would have been suicidal in the ancient world. Instead, he makes repeated appeals for Christian love. Philemon is not to act out of obligation to the apostle. He is to be motivated by the love of Christ within himself. Out of that, Paul suggests, should come more than mere reconciliation, "knowing that you will do even more than I ask" (v.21). Freedom of slaves, like all freedom, must come from the heart of Christ-inspired men. Under this compulsion, slavery must ultimately wilt and die. That it took so long for it to do so, that slavery was practiced by many Christians in America until the Civil War ended it, that it is still, in one form or another, in the world today—these humbling facts show the tenacity of socially entrenched sin and the failure of Christendom to deal with it. While all ethical behavior for Christians should arise out of love, rather than regulation or constraint, yet it takes fully committed disciples to put it into practice.

7. Bibliography

Calvin, John. *The Second Epistle of Paul the Apostle to the Corinthians and the Epistles to Timothy, Titus, and Philemon.* Translated by T.A. Smail. Edited by D.W. Torrance and T.F. Torrance. Grand Rapids: Eerdmans, 1964.

Harrison, P.N. "Onesimus and Philemon." In *Anglican Theological Review* 32 (1950): 268–294.

Knox, John. *Philemon Among the Letters of Paul.* New York: Abingdon, 1959.

Lightfoot, J.B. *St. Paul's Epistles to the Colossians and Philemon.* 1879. Reprint. Grand Rapids: Zondervan, 1957.

Lohse, Eduard. *Colossians and Philemon* in *Hermeneia.* Translated by Poehlmann and Karris. Philadelphia: Fortress Press, 1971.

Luther, Martin. "Preface to the Epistle of Saint Paul to Philemon, 1546 (1522)," in *Luther's Works,* American edition, vol. 35, ed. E. Theodore Bachmann. Philadelphia: Fortress, 1960.

Moule, C.F.D. *The Epistles of Paul the Apostle to the Colossians and to Philemon* in the Cambridge Greek Commentary. Cambridge: Cambridge University Press, 1957.

Müller, J.J. *The Epistles of Paul to the Philippians and to Philemon* in NIC. Grand Rapids: Eerdmans, 1955.

8. Outline

I. Salutation (1–3)

II. Thanksgiving and Prayer (4–7)

III. Plea for Onesimus (8–22)

IV. Greetings and Benediction (23–25)

Text and Exposition

I. Salutation

1–3

> [1]Paul, a prisoner of Christ Jesus, and Timothy our brother,
>
> To Philemon our dear friend and fellow worker, [2]to Apphia our sister, to Archippus our fellow soldier, and to the church that meets in your home:
>
> [3]Grace to you and peace from God our Father and the Lord Jesus Christ.

The salutation is significant for its departures from Paul's other salutations. The Epistle is in the form of an ancient letter of commendation, and Paul's opening words are calculated to suggest that his appeal for Onesimus should be favorably received.

Paul is a prisoner of Jesus Christ and therefore suffers for the sake of the gospel. His suffering is a mark of his apostleship, which in turn lends weight to any suggestion he might make. Furthermore, Timothy, a well-recognized young steward of the gospel, joins him in the appeal. Finally, Paul not only greets Philemon, the owner of Onesimus, but also his wife Apphia. She is as much a party to the decision as her husband, because according to the custom of the time, she had day-to-day responsibility for the slaves.

As for Archippus and the church, Paul includes them in the salutation with good reason. Archippus, one of the leading figures in the community (perhaps a pastor), and the church will bring appropriate pressure to bear on Philemon should he fail to fulfill the great apostle's request. Philemon would have had to have been a very strong-minded individual to resist the plea of Paul and his protege Timothy.

Notes

2 In the phrase κατ᾽ οἶκόν σου (*kat' oikon sou*, "in your home"), σου (*sou*, "your") is singular. A few have taken these words as a reference to Archippus's home, but the most logical understanding would be that this is a reference to the home of Philemon, since he is the first-mentioned in the greeting. This is not the only time Paul mentions a church in a private home; in Romans 16:5 he refers to the church in the house of Priscilla and Aquila and in Colossians 4:15 to the church in the house of Nympha. The early Christian Churches often met in homes. Not until about the third century do we have records of separate church buildings.

"Our fellow soldier" (τῷ συστρατιώτῃ ἡμῶν, *tō sustratiōtē hēmōn*) means nothing more than "fellow worker" in Pauline usage (cf. Phil 2:25).

Lohse (in loc.) cites examples of ancient letters in which additional names are listed alongside that of the recipient.

II. Thanksgiving and Prayer

4–7

> [4]I always thank my God as I remember you in my prayers, [5]because I hear about your love and faith in the Lord Jesus and your love for all the saints. [6]I pray that you may be active in sharing your faith, so that you will have a full understanding of every good thing we have in Christ. [7]Your love has given me great joy and encouragement, because you, brother, have refreshed the hearts of the saints.

4,5 In both pagan and Christian letters of the first centuries of the Christian era, the salutation was followed by an expression of thanksgiving and a prayer. Paul uses the fuller form of his thanksgiving. He tells when he gives thanks—"always ... in my prayers"—and also tells why he does so—"because I hear about your love and faith." Cf. Romans 1:8-10; 1 Thessalonians 1:2-5; Philippians 1:3-11; Colossians 1:3-8.

"I remember you" (v.4). The singular "you" (*sou*) here and again in v.6 supports the conclusion that the recipient of the letter is Philemon.

6 At this point, the prayer begins though the verb "I pray" is understood from the context. The prayer is in Greek that is unusually difficult to understand. With equal certainty one might suggest that 1) Paul prays that Philemon's participation in the faith will be made effective because of his full understanding of God's goodness to both of them; or, 2) he prays that Philemon will be active in the faith so that he will develop a full understanding of God's goodness to both of them. The former interpretation is more attractive than the latter one because of Paul's repeated suggestion that knowledge precedes good works (cf. Col 1:9, 10).

7 Paul has been repeatedly impressed by the expressions of Philemon's love. They have brought him much joy and comfort. Verse 7 is intended to justify Paul's expansive use of the phrases "full understanding" and "every good thing" in v.6. According to this interpretation, he is praying for great Christian maturity in his brother. The implication is that this maturity will find expression in Philemon's treatment of Onesimus.

Notes

---

4 "In my prayers." Ἐπί (*epi*, "in") with the genitive frequently had the meaning of "at the time of." It suggests that Paul still observed the formal times of prayer honored by Jews.

6 In other Epistles ὅπως (*hopōs*, "that") follows a verb of praying. Hence such a verb is understood here.

"We have" (NIV) is literally "in us" or "among us" (*en hēmin*) in Gr. "In you" (*en hymin*) has slightly better MS support than "in us," but the editors almost universally favor "in us." See B.M. Metzger, *A Textual Commentary on the Greek New Testament* (New York: United Bible Societies), p. 657, for the argument. Some MSS read παντός ἔργου ἀγαθοῦ (*pantos ergou agathou*, "of every good work"). The difficulty of the verse was felt early in the MS tradition.

7 Σπλάγχνα (*splanchna*, "hearts") literally means "bowels." To some Greeks, the emotions came from this part of the body. Paul's use of the word in v.12 and again in v.20 reveals the depths of his feelings in this situation. He does not argue rationally or theologically for Onesimus. He does so from the heart.

III. Plea for Onesimus

8-22

⁸Therefore, although in Christ I could be bold and order you to do what you ought to do, ⁹yet I appeal to you on the basis of love. I then, as Paul—an old man and now also a prisoner of Christ Jesus— ¹⁰I appeal to you for my son Onesimus, who

became my son while I was in chains. [11]Formerly he was useless to you, but now he has become useful both to you and to me.

[12]I am sending him—who is my very heart—back to you. [13]I would have liked to keep him with me so that he could take your place in helping me while I am in chains for the gospel. [14]But I did not want to do anything without your consent, so that any favor you do will be spontaneous and not forced. [15]Perhaps the reason he was separated from you for a little while was that you might have him back for good— [16]no longer as a slave, but better than a slave, as a dear brother. He is very dear to me but even dearer to you, both as a man and as a brother in the Lord.

[17]So if you consider me a partner, welcome him as you would welcome me. [18]If he has done you any wrong or owes you anything, charge it to me. [19]I, Paul, am writing this with my own hand. I will pay it back—not to mention that you owe me your very self. [20]I do wish, brother, that I may have some benefit from you in the Lord; refresh my heart in Christ. [21]Confident of your obedience, I write to you, knowing that you will do even more than I ask.

[22]And one thing more: Prepare a guest room for me, because I hope to be restored to you in answer to your prayers.

The situation of both Paul and Onesimus is all-important to the understanding of this section of the Epistle. Paul's circumstances are just as significant as those of Onesimus—a fact often overlooked by commentators. Because he is in prison, he cannot do the things a free man might do to help the slave. He can do little more than write a letter asking for clemency for his new-found brother and he can suggest that he hopes to visit the Lycus Valley soon to put additional pressure on Philemon. Under more usual circumstances, a free man could have assumed custody of a runaway slave after he had given guarantees of his return to the public officials, and he could have suggested that the slave be formally assigned to him for a time. This was not uncommon. A slave teacher of T. Pomponius Atticus attended M. Tullius Cicero and his family as much as he did his owner and patron. When he was manumitted, he received Cicero's praenomen (the first of the usual three names of a Roman) and Atticus's nomen (the second of the three names). He became M. Pomponius Dionysius (A.A. Rupprecht, *Slavery in the Late Roman Republic*. [diss. Ann Arbor: University of Michigan Press, 1960], pp. 91–94).

Onesimus's status was the lowest that one could reach in the ancient world. Because he was a runaway slave, he was protected by no laws and he was subject to all manner of abuse. Fugitive slaves usually went to large cities, remote parts of the Roman state, or into unsettled areas. At this time, their capture and return was largely an informal arrangement between the owner and a provincial administrator. They were frequently beaten unmercifully or put to tasks in which their life expectancy was very short.

Cicero mentions three runaway slaves in his works. He remarks of one, Licinius, a slave of the tragic actor Aesop, that he was being held in a public prison or in a *pistrinum*, a grain mill. Cicero was unsure. If the latter, Licinius would have been blindfolded and forced to walk in a circle all day long to turn the millstone—a task usually assigned to horses or mules. Cicero asks his brother, Quintus, to bring this slave back to Rome (*Q. Fr.* 1.2.14).

Paul must have put Philemon in a precarious position indeed. In pleading for forgiveness and restitution for Onesimus without a punishment that was obvious to all, he was confronting the social and economic order head on. While he does not ask for manumission, even his request for clemency for Onesimus and hint of his assignment to Paul defied Roman tradition. By this plea Paul is also giving new dignity to the slave class.

8 Paul first reminds Philemon of his apostolic authority. *Parrēsia* usually has the idea of

"freedom" or "boldness." Here it means "right" or "authority"—hence, "I could be bold and order you." The suggestion of authority was probably enough, coupled as it was with the appeals to love, old age, and imprisonment in v.9.

9 *Presbytēs* means "old age" but usually carries with it the connotation of authority. Thus, in ancient Sparta the ruling body was called a *gerousia* (from *gerōn* "old man"). Parallel to this was the Roman *senatus* (from *senex*). In antiquity, wisdom and authority were assumed to go with old age. Here, however, the stress is on the apostle's aged and feeble condition by the use of *toioutos hōs* ("such as I am").

10 "I plead with you for my son, Onesimus, who became my son while I was in chains." The imagery is very strong. The figure of the father and child was often used in Judaism and in the mystery religions as an illustration of the relationship of teacher and student or of leader and convert (see Lohse, p. 200).

"For my son." *Peri* usually means "concerning," but in this place, as elsewhere in his letters, Paul uses it in the sense of *hyper* ("in behalf of ").

11 There is a double play on words here. *Onesimus* was a common slave name. It meant "useful" or "profitable." This is also the meaning of *chrēstos,* which appears as *achrestos* ("useless") and *euchrēstos* ("useful") in this verse. *Chrēstos* in turn sounded so much like *Christos* that the Roman historian Suetonius (*Claud.* 25) takes this to be Jesus' name. An ancient reader would have thought this play on words much more clever and humorous than we would. That Paul uses it at the beginning of his plea for Onesimus shows us something of his exquisite sensitivity and tact. It is as if, realizing the radical nature (in view of the custom of the times) of what he was about to ask of Philemon, Paul deliberately introduces this bit of humor.

12 Again we see Onesimus as very dear to Paul. He is not simply the one "I am sending back." Paul adds, "him—who is my very heart."

13 The culmination of the appeal. Onesimus serves in place of (*hyper sou*) Philemon, already described as a man of great spiritual advancement (vv.6, 7).

14 The apostle has been speaking as an urbane, deferential, educated man of the classical world. But now, after he has cited a number of reasons for allowing Onesimus to remain with him, he goes further and urges Philemon to make his decision out of Christian love rather than obligation.

13,14 If Onesimus was so dear to Paul the prisoner that he wanted the comfort of his help, how could Philemon refuse Paul's plea for him? And observe Paul's sensitive regard for Philemon's personality (v.14).

15 The contrast between "for a time" and "forever" shows Paul's conviction that the hand of God was at work in the whole situation. It also shows his tact: instead of bluntly referring to Onesimus as a runaway, he speaks of his temporary separation from Philemon as a prelude to permanent reunion with him.

16 In similar fashion he contrasts "slave"—a temporal and demeaning condition—with "brother"—an eternal relationship in the Lord. The innate problem of the slavery of human beings always troubled the ancients. Onesimus was a slave, but in many of the ancient religions and in Greek and Roman law where religion was concerned, he would have been treated as an equal. Christianity was not unique in its claims of the enabling power of the love of Christ to break the economic and social barriers between people. In the ancient pagan religious experience men feared and appeased the gods. They did not, however, claim that they loved them or were loved by them as the motive for men to love one another. Paul loves Onesimus very much. Philemon will love him all the more because of long-standing human ties as well as their common faith.

Here, where Paul so sensitively suggests that Philemon take Onesimus back "no longer as a slave, but better than a slave," etc. (cf. also v.17), it almost seems as if emancipation is implied between the lines.

17 Now Paul uses a term from accountancy. "Partner" (*koinonos*), which is related to the common NT word *koinonia* ("fellowship"), here has the sense of "business partner" —a common meaning of the term in the papyri. No doubt Paul meant for the word to imply "fellowship" in the work of the risen Christ. Philemon is to receive Onesimus as he would receive Paul himself.

18 This wonderfully gracious offer to assume the financial obligation of Onesimus is an altogether astonishing statement. We can only speculate how Paul came to have such warm feelings toward him. Yet we cannot be certain the slave had robbed his master, though this was a common act of runaway slaves. It may be that Onesimus had confessed this to Paul. Or the loss may have been the result of the departure of a highly skilled slave from whose activities Philemon derived great income. In fact, slave prices in the Greco-Roman world were directly proportional to the skill and economic value of the slave. A common drudge brought only 500 *denarii* (a *denarius* was a laborer's ordinary daily wage), but skilled teachers, physicians, and actors were purchased for a hundred times as much.

Paul uses another accountant's word (*elloga,* "charge") to maintain the imagery. Observe Paul's tact in not saying that Onesimus had stolen, but he leaves that possibility open by his use of *adikeo* ("do wrong") and *opheilo* ("owe").

19 The subject is still the indebtedness of Onesimus. Now Paul says that he wrote these words himself. As in our own society, handwritten statements of obligation carried great weight and legal validity. So in v.19 Paul gives Philemon what amounts to a promissory note. Then in v.19b he shifts abruptly to another thought—viz., "not to mention that you owe me your very self." Preceding the "that" (*hina*) should be understood some phrase like "I am silent" (*sigo*), "so as not to mention," etc. In Paul's view, Philemon's spiritual indebtedness to him should easily cover all of Onesimus's wrongdoing. Again Paul's hint can hardly be missed: "I will repay it. Charge it to the bank of heaven."

What Paul did for Onesimus reflects the infinitely greater intercession and redemptive act of Christ for us, who because of our sin are all indebted to God in a way we cannot ouselves repay. As Luther said, "Here we see how Paul layeth himself out for poor Onesimus, and with all his means pleadeth his cause with his master, and so setteth himself as if he were Onesimus, and had himself done wrong to Philemon. Even as Christ did for us with God the Father, thus also doth Paul for Onesimus with Philemon. We are all his Onesimi, to my thinking" (*The New Century Bible*).

20 *Onaimēn* ("I do wish," "I would like") is the optative for expressing a wish and is the most common survival of the secondary mood of nonassertion. It was a regular element of ancient epistolary style. Its use here may be another play on words, since the name Onesimus comes from the same root.

Paul now returns to the vocabulary of v.7, where he told Philemon that he had refeshed the hearts of many. How, then, can he do less than that for the apostle to the Gentiles? In its relationship to v.7 this sentence is an excellent example of literary reenforcement.

21 Paul has avoided giving any commands to Philemon (cf. v.8), but he nonetheless expects "obedience." To what? The love of Christ? *Hyper ha legō*, ("beyond what I suggest") may be an intimation that Paul would like Onesimus set free from enslavement. He hints that Onesimus be loaned to him. Only emancipation could be beyond that. Paul never directly assaults the social and economic institutions of his day. Yet he clearly perceives in Christianity an ethic that reaches beyond human social institutions. Paul nowhere states that slaves should be set free, but he pleads for fair and gracious treatment of slaves on the basis of the love of Christ in the hearts of their owners.

22 Here the suggestion of an imminent visit lends more weight to Paul's hints and requests. The hope expressed in these words seems to imply that the apostle is nearby. He expects to be released soon and to see the outcome of his letter at first hand. Imprisonment at Ephesus, and perhaps, Caesarea, would best explain his circumstances. A trip from Rome would take weeks or even months in the best weather and would be all but impossible during periods of unsettled weather.

Notes

14 The meaning of "consent" for γνώμη (gnōmē) is frequently attested in the papyri. (See BAG, p. 162.)
16 Μάλιστα (malista, "especially") is an old superlative form. Here it intensifies ἀγαπητός (agapētos, "dear"). Πόσω μᾶλλον (posō mallon) is dative of degree of difference, lit., "more by much." "Very dear" and "even dearer" tr. well Paul's emphatic words.
17 Προσλαβοῦ (proslabou, "welcome") is the middle of προσλαμβάνω (proslambano, "receive kindly"). It always has a positive meaning: "to welcome into a circle of friends," or "take as a helper."
18 Cicero (Q. Rosc. 28) remarks that a talented slave purchased for 3,000 denarii had increased in value 35 times because of the training given him by the comedian Roscius. Seneca (Ep. 27.5) and Martial (1.58.1) both mention 50,000 d. as the price of an accomplished slave.
Ἐλλόγα (elloga) means "charge [to my account]." The form of the verb appears to be from ellogao instead of ellogeo (the actual root form); cf. Rom 5:13. Lohse (p. 204) gives parallel instances of this meaning from later Gr.
22 Ξενία (xenia) means "guest room." It also often means "hospitality," one of the highest of Classical and early Christian virtues. It would be wrong to try to separate the two meanings in this verse.

IV. Greetings and Benediction

23–25

> 23Epaphras, my fellow prisoner for Christ Jesus, sends you greetings. 24And so do Mark, Aristarchus, Demas and Luke, my fellow workers. 25The grace of the Lord Jesus Christ be with your spirit.

23,24 The five co-workers who send greetings to Philemon are also mentioned in Colossians 4:10–14. A sixth co-worker, Jesus Justus, is mentioned only in Colossians. Many conjecture that we should read here, "Epaphras my fellow prisoner in Christ, Jesus, Mark ... send greetings." The question remains as to why the same greetings were given in two letters that were sent at the same time. Some see the unity of the greetings as evidence that Colossians is not Pauline (see Lohse, p. 176–183). Others see it as evidence that the letters were written at the same time to the same place, while Paul was in the company of the same co-workers. One should not discount the possibility that Philemon preceded Colossians (see Introduction).

25 With his apostolic "grace," Paul ends this brief but unusually beautiful letter in which he reveals so much of himself.